PRINCIPLES OF HUMAN RIGHT

Principles of Human Rights Adjudication

By

CONOR GEARTY

OXFORD

UNIVERSITY PRESS

*This book has been printed digitally and produced in a standard specification
in order to ensure its continuing availability*

OXFORD
UNIVERSITY PRESS

Great Clarendon Street, Oxford OX2 6DP

Oxford University Press is a department of the University of Oxford.
It furthers the University's objective of excellence in research, scholarship,
and education by publishing worldwide in

Oxford New York

Auckland Cape Town Dar es Salaam Hong Kong Karachi
Kuala Lumpur Madrid Melbourne Mexico City Nairobi
New Delhi Shanghai Taipei Toronto
With offices in
Argentina Austria Brazil Chile Czech Republic France Greece
Guatemala Hungary Italy Japan South Korea Poland Portugal
Singapore Switzerland Thailand Turkey Ukraine Vietnam

Oxford is a registered trade mark of Oxford University Press
in the UK and in certain other countries

Published in the United States
by Oxford University Press Inc., New York

© C. Gearty, 2004

The moral rights of the author have been asserted

Database right Oxford University Press (maker)

Reprinted 2008

ISBN 978-0-19-928722-2

Preface

This book is an attempt to explain the Human Rights Act 1998, to show where it fits in the UK constitution, what the principles are that underpin it and why the cases have been decided under it in the way that they have. It is largely enthusiastic about the measure, the record of the courts in interpreting it, and the impact that the Act has had on British law. This may surprise those readers who are aware of my past record of opposition to proposals for a UK bill of rights. Unlike many of the earlier proposals for a change of this sort, the Human Rights Act does not subordinate the will of the representative branch to that of an unelected judiciary. The Act is more supportive than subversive of our parliamentary system of government. This makes it an easy measure for somebody with my kind of record to applaud and support. I like many of the elements of the Human Rights Act that other human rights lawyers deplore—its allowance for many exceptions to its rights; its respect for parliamentary sovereignty; and its deference to the executive where appropriate. So there are traces in what follows of my old antagonism both to unqualified rights' instruments and to unaccountable judicial power. The book is my effort to explain what it has been about this Act that has meant that it has fitted so well into the UK constitution and been, on the whole (so far), a great success.

One of the pleasures of finishing a book is to be able publicly to thank those who have (knowingly or unknowingly) helped so much with the writing of it. To the Leverhulme Trust I am very grateful for having provided me with a year off, during which time much of the basic reading for the book was done. My then university home, the School of Law at King's College London, was (as it remains) a highly congenial place in which to work, and I am very grateful to my many colleagues and friends at the School for their friendship and stimulating conversations. Keith Ewing in particular has been an important intellectual presence in my life, and a great colleague over many years. The LSE where I now work has been wonderfully supportive, particularly Martin Loughlin, who read and commented upon the book in draft form, and my colleagues at the Centre for the Study of Human Rights, Gerd Oberleitner, Joy Whyte, and Harriet Gallagher. I owe a great deal to my next door neighbour at the Centre, Francesca Klug, who is a research professor at the School, and who has been an immense scholarly and personal support to me for as long as I have been interested in the subject of human rights (which is a long time indeed). Colleagues at Matrix Chambers have taught me far more than they can ever appreciate about how legal principle applies in practice. John Louth, Gwen Booth, and Louise Kavanagh at OUP have been very supportive throughout, and the anonymous readers' comments on this book in draft form helped me to improve the text – I am grateful to them all. My last note of thanks must be for my family, Eliza and Owen and my wife Diane. The children have through their good humour and joy with life helped me more than they will ever know. Diane's love and friendship has been instrumental in making me the adult I am. It is to her, in inadequate recognition of what she has given me, that I dedicate this book.

Contents

Table of Cases

UK CASES

EUROPEAN COMMISSION/COURT OF HUMAN RIGHTS

OTHER JURISDICTIONS

Table of Statutes and Statutory Instruments

STATUTES

STATUTORY INSTRUMENTS

Table of Conventions, Constitutional Documents, and International Instruments

PART ONE

INTRODUCTION

1

Making Sense of the Human Rights Act

This book sets out an argument for a particular interpretation of the United Kingdom's Human Rights Act. The reading of the Act proposed here is rooted in principle while being at the same time constitutionally coherent, respectful of the traditions of the common law and sensitive to the limitations as well as the strengths of the adjudicative process. The argument in the book also fits well with the spirit and with much of the language both of the Human Rights Act and of the European Convention on Human Rights that lies embedded in that measure. This is not, therefore, the volume to turn to in order to find all the Human Rights Act cases decided on every point, or to have answered a particular query about practice or procedure. The authorities are dealt with non-exhaustively and always from the perspective of principle. It will be argued that the leading decisions under the Act are largely supportive of the book's thesis. Indeed where they are not, it is suggested that they are wrong; one of the great advantages of having a thesis of the sort developed here is that it facilitates critical evaluation of the case law. Having read this book, it should be possible to say how any particular case should (from the perspective of principle) be decided, and to make an informed guess (on the basis of the judicial record) as to how it will be decided.

The Human Rights Act deserves the fuss that surrounds it, the huge array of books that it has inspired and the many puzzled questions that it has begged. The measure burst fully into British law only as recently as 2 October 2000 and is short by legislative standards, just 22 sections and four schedules. Speaking before the measure had taken full effect, in the first big case on it to reach the House of Lords, Lord Hope of Craighead remarked that it was 'now plain that the incorporation of the European Convention on Human Rights into our domestic law will subject the entire legal system to a fundamental process of review and, where necessary, reform by the judiciary'.[1] Since these remarks were made, some issues have been resolved but many new ones have emerged, and cases clarificatory of this or that aspect of the measure have been matched by decisions that have raised futher questions. In the breadth of its ambition and in the potential reach of its terms, British law has never before seen anything like this piece of legislation. The remit of the Human Rights Act cannot be discerned

---

[1] R *(Kebilene) v Director of Public Prosecutions* [2000] 2 AC 326, 374–375.

from mere scrutiny of its provisions: these are wide enough to incorporate an array of arguments, and to render at least linguistically credible the full range of advocacy, from the straightforward to the manifestly absurd. Thus the Act's most famous requirement, that so 'far as it is possible to do so', legislation must be 'read and given effect in a way which is compatible with Convention rights'[2] says nothing more explicitly about what the limits of the possible might be, leaving distinguished judges such as the Lord Chief Justice Lord Woolf to ruminate vaguely, in another early leading case, about the 'most difficult task which courts face' under the Human Rights Act being 'distinguishing between legislation and interpretation'.[3] There are similar such hostages to exactitude scattered across the whole statute.

When is it right for courts to flex their interpretive muscles under the Human Rights Act and (to use Lord Hope's word) 'reform' the law? When is it wrong? How are we to tell the difference between interpretation (which is, it would seem, an acceptable judicial task) and legislation (which is most certainly not)? We know what judges can do under the Human Rights Act (practically anything), but what *should* they do? To answer these questions, we need to go further than the words of the Act and more deeply into the philosophy behind the measure than the judges have (so far) been prepared (and perhaps even able) to go. Locating the Act in its constitutional, institutional, and political context makes it possible to develop a set of organizing principles with which to make sense of the measure, and through which to discipline and manage its impact on UK law. In this book, three such organizing principles are suggested. These are the principle of respect for civil liberties; the principle of legality; and the principle of respect for human dignity. Clear evidence can be marshalled, from the terms of the Human Rights Act itself, and from the parliamentary proceedings that accompanied its enactment, that these principles or versions of them make up the basic building blocks of our domestic rights measure. As we shall see when we explore their meaning further, not only are these three core ideas part of Britain's legal heritage but they are also entrenched within the texts of the founding statute of the Council of Europe, and the European Convention on Human Rights to which that Council gave birth. They are also to be found in the case law of the European Court of Human Rights which was set up by the European Convention to adjudicate on disputes about its remit.

The entire corpus of case law under the Convention, and the Convention itself, can be read as an attempt, sometimes successful, sometimes misguided, sometimes disastrously counter-productive, to put one or other or all of these three principles into effect. For their part, the British courts that have striven to make sensible rulings on the Human Rights Act since its implementation have intuitively found the task easier when they have connected the measure to established

---

[2] See s 3(1).
[3] *Poplar Housing and Regeneration Community Association Ltd v Donoghue* [2001] EWCA Civ 595, [2002] QB 48, para [76].

norms and traditional legal perspectives. Manifestly, respect for civil liberties, the rule of law and human dignity have been three such immediately recognizable values. This is not to say that such principles have always been adhered to in UK law, or that the Human Rights Act is merely duplicatory of the status quo. It is also clearly not the case that the priorities accorded these various principles in particular situations have been identical as between the domestic and the European legal order; there are marked divergences in the realization of these principles as between the two legal systems. But nor is it true to assert that the Act is an alien growth, marooned on a body with a quite different and antagonistic genetic code; the Convention upon which the Act is based is, after all, largely a creation of British statecraft.[4] Whatever differences might appear in practice, it is clear that at an abstract level of principle the Act and the pre-existing legal culture have been pushing in the same direction. The two are, broadly speaking, 'singing from the same hymn sheet'. Having sent its scholarly missionaries to continental Europe to assist in its recovery from a dark age of lawlessness, the common law must now learn to accommodate the descendents of those missionaries, newly confident and proud of their success, back in the home cathedral.

Approaching the Human Rights Act in a way which locates it in its political and legal context and explains it as reflective of three basic principles which are common to European and British legal culture is the goal of this work. But the book also seeks to go further in its analysis of what is entailed in the proper application of the Human Rights Act in domestic law. For it is clear that the three principles that underpin the Human Rights Act can never be realized in the abstract: they require case law to render them real. Naturally many cases involve situations in which principle is not involved at all or only very remotely engaged, and in these circumstances the argument of this book is that the Human Rights Act should not be permitted to have a large impact. But adjudicative situations also often involve a collision between principle, properly defined, and the complex, often messy fact situation to which the principle in question is required to be applied. It will be argued that the Human Rights Act does not necessitate an imposition of principle whatever the circumstances: the ideology of human rights as evidenced by the Act and the Convention upon which it is based is not so decontextualised and absolutist as that. Precisely because so much interpretation is 'possible' under the Human Rights Act, and because so many of the rights set out in the Convention are qualified either expressly or by the inevitably open-textured nature of language, it has been and remains necessary for the judges also to develop mechanisms of self-restraint, habits of mind which inculcate judicial forbearance where this is judged the appropriate stance to adopt. Knowing when self-control is called for, when it is more prudent not to act than to act, makes new demands of our senior judiciary. The three principles of activism discussed above have the virtue of being recognizably legal in character

---

[4] AWB Simpson, *Human Rights and the End of Empire. Britain and the Genesis of the European Convention* (Oxford: Oxford University Press, 2001).

and moral in their call for a response. Refusing to swoop to the rescue of a claimant when the language of the law suggests that you can if you choose requires new depths of judicial courage and an awareness of the needs of the public interest and of public administration with which past generations of judges, protected by parliamentary sovereignty and schooled in the virtues of judicial restraint, have not needed to be familiar.

In this book, therefore, to accompany the three principles of judicial activism discussed above, and to add depth to their meaning, I shall discuss three aspirations, the proper realization of which will promote the long term success of the Human Rights Act and thereby entrench further our three principles within UK law. These are the aspirations of institutional competence, of proportionate intrusion, and of analytical coherence. As regards the first of these it is clear that there are certain things that, in a properly functioning representative democracy, judges simply should not do. This takes us into a discussion of the frequently debated topic of judicial deference. In relation to the second, what is brought to mind are situations where, correct though the judge's intervention might appear to be, it will nevertheless be right to hang back because the good that the ruling might do will in all likelihood be overwhelmed by the difficulties it is likely to cause, and that therefore insistence upon it would represent a disproportionate intrusion in a pre-existing legal scheme. Our third aspiration concerns those occasions when judges dive into an area with enthusiasm only to become enmeshed in case law of such complexity and aridity that the point of the original engagement quickly becomes lost while new and unexpected problems of incoherence are created. This is a problem that has always been present in the precedent-based common law but which the Human Rights Act now threatens greatly to exacerbate. What these three aspirations combine to say is that sometimes it will be right for the judge to hesitate, to say—against his or her own moral intuitions—that bad though the case is it does not call for his or her intervention, or (even worse) that though it does cry out for a *Deus ex machina*, it is not the judge's role to play God.

This book is primarily concerned with applying principles of human rights adjudication in a specific legal context, that of the United Kingdom. Right though it is to rely on comparative case law for guidance on the interpretation of the Human Rights Act, it would be wrong to succumb to the temptation to view such jurisprudence as authoritative. The United Kingdom has neither a written constitution such as in the United States, the Republic of Ireland and the Republic of South Africa, nor has its legislature explicitly empowered the courts to overturn legislation in breach of human rights as is the case in Canada. The courts in this jurisdiction can be relied upon not to smuggle a power of legislative review into the law, as happened in the US some 200 years ago[5] and has been attempted in Australia more recently.[6] Parliament has transferred a limited

---

[5] *Marbury v Madison* 5 US (1 Cranch) 136 (1803).
[6] *Australian Capital Television Pty Ltd v Commonwealth of Australia* (1992) 117 CLR 106.

power to the courts to exercise in certain defined circumstances in a way that promotes the concept of human rights whilst protecting the untrammelled power to act that is still viewed in Britain as an essential aspect of representative democracy. Properly understood, the Act is a brilliant reconciliation of two apparent opposites, a particularly British solution to a contemporary dilemma which, if it can be proved to work, could be as successfully exported to other jurisdictions as the common law and civil liberties were during previous golden ages. The object of this book is not to reopen arguments about the rights and wrongs of legislating for human rights but to make a contribution to the task of making proper sense of the Act, and thereby to help it to realize its potential.

2

The Impossible Demand: Human Rights and Representative Democracy

A. The legal conception of 'human rights'

In chapter one I have made the ambitious claim that it is possible to identify three principles that underpin the Human Rights Act, determining its remit and guiding judges as to the right decisions to make in individual cases. This assertion is so important to the integrity of the argument laid out in this book that it needs a chapter devoted to its justification. I begin this discussion by looking first both at the content of the rights set out in the Act, and at the way in which the measure goes about protecting those rights. Familiar ground though this might seem to many of us, it is necessary to look afresh at the range of rights in the Convention so as to be able to capture (or recapture) a lively appreciation of just how particular the approach taken in that document is to the whole issue of rights. The same is true too of the Human Rights Act: we need to remind ourselves of quite how particular is the means of rights' protection adopted by that measure. Having done this preliminary, ground-clearing work, I explore how the Convention and the Act are creatures of their time and place, with the former having had to survive in a philosophical climate that has been hostile to absolute or natural rights (and indeed remains so), and the latter having had to be delivered out of a local constitutional and legal culture that has been equally antagonistic to such basic entitlements. The prevalence of rights talk is such that these assertions might seem counter-intuitive, but they provide vital clues to why legal rights have developed in the way that they have. I argue that it is in the making of alliances with the many enemies of rights talk that both the Convention and the Human Rights Act have forged their identities. This process has generated the framework of rights' adjudication to be found in both documents, with the prioritization of the three principles of respect for civil liberties, legality and human dignity that I argue is inherent in each.

   It is not at all eccentric to introduce our discussion by asserting that the key to understanding the Human Rights Act is to appreciate that it is not entirely about human rights. Indeed it is not about them at all, if that phrase is meant to convey the existence of certain inalienable and fundamental entitlements that inhere in us all as human beings. Even the rights in the Convention that appear absolute in this way are uncertain around the edges. The guarantee of the right to life in Article 2 of the Convention, for example, might or might not include the unborn child/embryo, or might do so only in particular circumstances.[1] The same article also imposes, though how far is not clear, certain duties on the state to act to protect life.[2] The declaration in Article 3 that '[n]o one shall be subjected to torture or to inhuman or degrading treatment or punishment' is shown by the jurisprudence of the European Court of Human Rights to have plenty of grey areas around its fringes in which disputes have been able to thrive.[3] The rights also jostle between themselves for our attention: does the right to respect for privacy (in Article 8) allow two of us to degrade each other in private if we both desire it (thereby apparently breaching Article 3)? Can a woman point to the absolute right to 'security of person' in Article 5 and to her entitlement to privacy when taxed over her decision to terminate a pregnancy and therefore, allegedly, end a 'life'? Can a seriously ill person choose to have his or her life ended by another? In a case involving an apparent invasion of privacy by the press, does one start with the privacy right or with the guarantee of freedom of expression (Article 10)?

The answer to none of these questions is to be found clearly laid out in the text of the European Convention or of the Human Rights Act. Even where a case contains neither definitional uncertainties nor any conflict of rights, it is still by no means guaranteed that the law will give priority to the particular right in issue in untrammelled terms. The Human Rights Act provides three ways in which the Convention rights there set out can be trumped by non rights-based considerations. First, there are the explicit and implied restrictions on many of the rights themselves. The majority of articles contain limitations and exceptions to the freedoms which they purport to guarantee. Articles 8 (on privacy), 9 (on thought, conscience and religion), 10 (on freedom of expression), and 11 (on freedom of assembly and association) are of this sort. Each of these provisions characteristically outlines a large number of purposes in pursuit of which the right in question can be limited. These 'legitimate aims' (to use the parlance of the Strasbourg court) include such matters as the 'interests of national security', 'public safety', 'the economic well-being of the country', 'the prevention of disorder or crime', 'the protection of health or morals' and so on: we need not recite the whole range of them here; it is enough to appreciate that they are open-ended categories into which it is possible to fit almost any kind of governmental restriction of the right in question. Because this is the case, the really important

---

[1] *Paton v United Kingdom* (1980) 3 EHRR 408; *Brüggemann and Scheuten v Federal Republic of Germany* (1977) 3 EHRR 244; *Open Door Counselling and Dublin Well Woman v Ireland* (1992) 15 EHRR 244. Note that throughout this book I cite the year of the Strasbourg decision together with the volume number of EHRR. This makes it easier to trace the development of the Strasbourg Law.

[2] *McCann v United Kingdom* (1996) 21 EHRR 97; *Osman v United Kingdom* (1998) 29 EHRR 245.

[3] *Campbell and Cosans v United Kingdom* (1982) 4 EHRR 293; *Tyrer v United Kingdom* (1978) 2 EHRR 1. Cf the different views on the meaning of torture taken by the European Commission and the European Court in *Ireland v United Kingdom* (1978) 2 EHRR 25.

point about the limitation of these rights is that each restriction is itself restricted, by reference to what is 'prescribed by' or 'in accordance with' law and what is 'necessary in a democratic society'.[4] Thus as we shall see, many of the decisions on these articles, both in Strasbourg and in the British courts, turn on the judges' opinion as to what is 'necessary' in this sense, an ironical task in such cases as it is (by definition) the unelected and unrepresentative judiciary that is being required to make these findings of democratic necessity, often in the process contradicting the evaluations of a democratic assembly (if a law were not necessary why was it enacted?).

Other rights set out in the Convention are also qualified, though in different ways. The right to liberty in Article 5 has many exceptions explicitly attached to it. Article 1 of the first protocol on the protection of property, subjugates the right it asserts to the counter-entitlement of the state 'to enforce such laws as it deems necessary to control the use of property in accordance with the general interest or to secure the payment of taxes or other contributions or penalties'. Even the deprivation of one's possessions is permitted 'in the public interest and subject to the conditions provided for by law and by the general principles of international law'. Convention rights which appear unequivocal on their face have been interpreted by the European Court of Human Rights in a way which has undermined their apparent absolutism. Article 14 is of this sort. Baldly stating that '[t]he enjoyment of the rights and freedoms set forth in this Convention shall be secured without discrimination on any ground such as sex, race, colour, language, religion, political or other opinion, national or social origin, association with a national minority, property, birth or other status', the provision has in fact been read as permitting exactly such discrimination so long as it is, in the eyes of the court, serving a legitimate aim and is proportionate in all the circumstances.[5] The guarantee encapsulated in the head note to Article 6 as the 'right to a fair trial' has led to similar balancing of rights and the public interest, albeit in the context of what are the ingredients that make up this still absolute right to fairness. Though all of this is inevitable, since as we shall see presently even the most enthusiastic of philosophical proponents of rights nowadays accepts that there must be exceptions,[6] the European Court of Human Rights has sometimes seemed to carry the process to extraordinary lengths. This has resulted in really quite remarkable infringements of freedom managing from time to time to emerge from Strasbourg scrutiny seemingly entirely human rights-compliant.

The second way in which the Convention rights in the Human Rights Act provide an internal mechanism for their own supersession is composed of three

---

[4] And see also, more generally, Art 18: 'The restrictions permitted under this Convention to the said rights and freedoms shall not be applied for any purpose other than those for which they have been prescribed'.

[5] See eg *Abdulaziz, Cabales and Balkandali v United Kingdom* (1985) 7 EHRR 471.

[6] And see for a good illustration of the point M J Perry, *The Idea of Human Rights, Four Inquiries* (New York: Oxford University Press, 1998), 106.

override clauses which have the capacity to trump rights even where the exceptions and limitations examined above have failed to do so. These provisions are
also to be found in the Human Rights Act. Under Article 16, '[n]othing in
Articles 10, 11 and 14 shall be regarded as preventing the High Contracting
Parties from imposing restrictions on the political activity of aliens.' This curious
clause has not as yet attracted much attention, jurisprudential or otherwise,
though it is clear that it could be highly relevant to any discussion of the
compatibility with the Convention of laws passed designed to curb the political
speech of inflammatory non-Europeans living in or seeking to come to Britain.[7]
Article 17 is of broader application. It states that '[n]othing in this Convention
may be interpreted as implying for any state, group or person any right to engage
in any activity or perform any act aimed at the destruction of any of the rights
and freedoms set forth herein or at their limitation to a greater extent than is
provided for in the Convention.' The European Court has been slow to deploy
Article 17 in the cases before it and has generally speaking not felt required to do
so.[8] In the Human Rights Act, the 'Convention rights' set out in Sch 1 are
required to be 'read with' Articles 16 and 17, so these articles have a potential
for engagement with British law which is as yet unclear.

The most important of these override clauses is the power of derogation.[9]
Article 15(1) provides that '[i]n time of war or other public emergency
threatening the life of the nation, any High Contracting Party may take measures
derogating from its obligations under this Convention to the extent strictly
required by the exigencies of the situation, provided that such measures are not
inconsistent with its other obligations under international law.' Article 15(2) goes
on however to render this power of derogation impossible in the cases of firstly,
the right to life in Article 2 ('except in respect of deaths resulting from lawful acts
of war'); secondly, the prohibitions on torture and slavery in Articles 3 and 4(1)
respectively; and thirdly, the guarantee against retrospective punishment in Article 7. In the Human Rights Act, these derogation provisions are to be found in
the text of the Act (s 14 and Sch 3, Pt 1), and indeed when the Act first came into
force a derogation (arising out of the political and security crisis in Northern
Ireland) was in place.[10] A subsequent derogation has been entered in relation to
the detention provisions of the anti-terrorism legislation enacted at the end of
2001.[11] The state has the power to determine when to derogate, with the duty in
relation to the Council of Europe being one of report and explanation only.[12]

---

[7] See *R (Farrakhan) v Secretary of State for the Home Department* [2002] EWCA Civ 606, [2002]
QB 1391, esp at para [70] *per* Lord Phillips of Matravers giving the judgment of the court: 'this article
appears something of an anachronism half a century after the agreement of the Convention'.

[8] See *German Communist Party v Federal Republic of Germany* app 250/57 (1957) 1 *Yearbook of
the European Convention on Human Rights* 222.

[9] For reservations, see Human Rights Act, ss 15 and 17.

[10] Now removed following entry into force of the Terrorism Act 2000.

[11] The Human Rights Act 1998 (Designated Derogation) Order 2001 (SI 2001/3644).

[12] European Convention on Human Rights, Art 15(3).

In such cases the European Court does continue to assert its supervisory jurisdiction, albeit with a self-denyingly light touch.[13]

The third and final mechanism for the limitation of rights to be mentioned here is inherent in the construction of the Human Rights Act itself. Under the Convention system as applied to UK law prior to the implementation of the Human Rights Act, decisions of the European Court of Human Rights did not take effect automatically in domestic law. In this way, they differed from the decisions of their sister court, the European Court of Justice in Luxembourg. Instead, the Convention itself set down a mechanism which entrusted the implementation of such decisions to member states, supervised by the Committee of Ministers of the Council of Europe.[14] The Human Rights Act has made no difference to this arrangement. Section 2 of the Act specifically requires only that European Court decisions be taken into account so far as they are relevant to the proceedings in which a question relating to a Convention right has arisen. This provision makes no distinction between UK-originating and other Strasbourg cases and requires in neither case that such rulings be automatically given any domestic effect. So it remains the responsibility of government to decide how to translate such Strasbourg decisions into domestic law. As a matter of procedure, ministers can however now avail of a 'fast-track' method of implementation set out in the Human Rights Act where an adverse European Court ruling has implications for pre-existing domestic legislation,[15] but this is only a new mechanism for the discharge of an international law duty rather than the imposition of a totally fresh obligation.

The relevance of all this to our current discussion about the qualified nature of the implementation of the Convention rights in domestic law is that the Human Rights Act has mimicked the Strasbourg scheme in relation to the consequences that flow from a domestic case in which an adverse finding on human rights is made. True there have not been and are not likely to be many such decisions. As I noted in chapter one, the Human Rights Act contains a powerful interpretive mandate to the courts to construe Acts of Parliament '[s]o far as it is possible to do so' in a way which is compatible with Convention rights,[16] and as things have turned out most statutes have so far been found to be capable of yielding up a Convention-compatible meaning if examined closely enough. But if this proves to be impossible (and in this book I will argue that these declarations should be made far more frequently),[17] the Human Rights Act expressly prohibits the judges from taking the next (and from the human rights perspective, logical) step of striking down the legislation. Under s 3(2)(b), the interpretive power

---

[13] See *Brannigan and McBride v United Kingdom* (1993) 17 EHRR 539. But see Opinion 1/2002 of the Commissioner for Human Rights, Mr Alvaro Gil-Robles on certain aspects of the United Kingdom 2001 derogation from European Convention on Human Rights, Art 5(1) (Comm DH (2002) 7. Strasbourg, 28 August 2002).

[14] European Convention on Human Rights, Art 46.

[15] s 10(1)(b) and (2); Sch 2.

[16] Human Rights Act, s 3(1).

[17] See below pp 47–54.

referred to above is specifically declared not to 'affect the validity, continuing operation or enforcement of any incompatible primary legislation'. Instead in such circumstances, a higher court may issue a declaration of incompatibility.[18] Such a declaration is specifically stated not to 'affect the validity, continuing operation or enforcement of the provision in respect of which it is given'.[19] Instead, just as with the Strasbourg rulings, the executive branch must decide what to do.[20] The responsible minister might decide to do nothing, and as regards domestic rulings of incompatibility there is no international law duty to act and no committee of ministerial colleagues to push him or her along. However if he or she 'considers that there are compelling reasons' for so acting, the minister 'may by order make such amendments to the legislation as he considers necessary to remove the incompatibility'.[21] Otherwise the matter falls to be resolved, if it is to be resolved at all, as part of the ordinary political process, with an amendment to the incompatible legislation perhaps securing the approval of both Houses of Parliament, perhaps not.

B. The paradox of human rights law

These then are the various provisions in the Human Rights Act that put the legal flesh on the bare bones of 'human rights'. They take us a long way from any simplistic version of what the demands of human rights law might be expected to entail: once fleshed out, the full corpus of the law is very different from the skeletal moral position from which we started. There is a world of a difference between 'natural' rights, however defined, and the 'human rights' concretized in the European Convention that I have been discussing here.[22] It will be apparent

---

[18] Human Rights Act, s 4(4). For the definition of a higher court for these purposes, see s 4(5).

[19] Human Rights Act, s 4(6).

[20] At the time of writing there have been seven such declarations of incompatibility that have been made and not subsequently overturned on appeal: *R (H) v Mental Health Review Tribunal, North and East London Region and another* [2001] EWCA Civ 415, [2001] QB 1; *International Transport Roth GmbH v Secretary of State for the Home Department* [2002] EWCA Civ 158, [2002] 3 WLR 344; *R (Wilkinson) v Commissioner of Inland Revenue* [2002] EWHC 182 (Admin), upheld [2003] EWCA Civ 814, [2003] 1 WLR 2683; *R (Anderson) v Secretary of State for the Home Department* [2002] UKHL 46, [2003] 1 AC 837; *R (D) v Secretary of State for the Home Department* [2002] EWHC 2805 *R (M) v Secretary of State for Health* [2003] EWHC 1094 (Admin); and *Bellinger v Bellinger* [2003] UKHL 21, [2003] 2 AC 467. Four further declarations have been overturned on appeal, either because no Convention right had been infringed or because the public authority involved was required to act: *R (Alconbury Developments Ltd) v Secretary of State for the Environment, Transport and the Regions* [2001] UKHL 23, [2003] 2 AC 295; *Matthews v Ministry of Defence* [2002] EWCA Civ 773, [2002] 1 WLR 2621, (upheld in the Lords: [2002] UKHL 4, [2003] 1 AC 116); *Wilson v Secretary of State for Trade and Industry* [2003] UKHL 40; *Wilson v Secretary of State for Trade and Industry* [2003] UKHL 40, [2003] 3 WLR 568 and *R (Hooper, Withey, Naylor and Martin) v Secretary of State for Work and Pensions* [2003] EWCA Civ 813 *R (Hooper, Withey, etc.)* is now: [2003] EWCA Civ 813, [2003] 1 WLR 2623.

[21] Human Rights Act, s 10(2): see Joint Committee on Human Rights, Making of Remedial Orders (7th report, HL 58, HC 473 of Session 2001–2, 17 December 2001).

[22] For an excellent analysis, see D Feldman, *Civil liberties and Human Rights in England and Wales* 2nd edn (Oxford: Oxford University Press), ch 1.

by now that 'human rights law' is a complex legal field in which it is by no means obvious that a human right as such—even where such a thing can be successfully identified—is bound to succeed. Many human rights proponents are disappointed by this, and criticize the Human Rights Act for its incompleteness. They pine for an absolutist, more natural rights-oriented approach. Instead of joining in the regrets, however, we should celebrate such limitations as evidence of the Act's potentially redeeming coherence. If the Human Rights Act does ultimately succeed, it will be because—not in spite of—the weak version of 'rights', riddled with exceptions, that it seeks to guarantee. To justify these remarks, of which many human rights advocates might not intuitively approve, we need now to turn to the contemporary context of human rights as a philosophical idea. As indicated at the start of this chapter, it is this intellectual context that has created our modern perception of what is understood by human rights, and it is in turn this understanding (grafted in its European Convention mode onto an unsympathetic British constitutional system, as we shall see shortly) that has produced the Human Rights Act in its current shape, with the prioritization of principle that in turn supplies the central argument of this book.

To make this distinction clearer between human rights *simpliciter* and human rights *law*, I need now to trace the way in which the philosophical content of our subject has evolved over the years. The point of this discussion is to demonstrate that while many of the criticisms of the idea of human rights that have been perennially made and are still being articulated have validity, they do not apply to the concept as it has been realized in the UK Human Rights Act. Though the child of rationalism, human rights discourse (as it would be called today) has always been particularly vulnerable to scholarly attack. The idea was first paraded on the streets of post-Enlightenment Europe in the course of the French Revolution, with its Declaration of the Rights of Man and the Citizen, issued in 1789. Though perhaps more rhetorical than philosophical in intention, it was as the latter that the great nineteenth century thinker Jeremy Bentham tore it apart, in his justly celebrated *Anarchical Fallacies; being an Examination of the Declaration of Rights Issued during the French Revolution*.[23] In an early era of 'glib generalities', it is worth recalling what Bentham had to say about the deployment of the kind of language that he believed was epitomized in talk of human rights:

The more *abstract*—that is, the more *extensive* the proposition is, the more liable is it to involve a fallacy. ... Hasty generalization, the great stumbling-block of intellectual vanity!—hasty generalization, the rock that even genius itself is so apt to split upon!— hasty generalization, the bane of prudence and of science![24]

Bentham's criticism of the Declaration flowed from this sceptical starting position and depended for its effect entirely on the unqualified claims that the

---

[23] See J Waldron (ed), *'Nonsense upon Stilts.' Bentham, Burke and Marx on the Rights of Man* (London: Methuen, 1987), at p 46. For what follows I have drawn upon my 'Reflections on Human Rights and Civil Liberties in Light of the United Kingdom's Human Rights Act 1998' (2001) 35 *University of Richmond Law Review* 1.

[24] Ibid 47–48 (emphasis in original).

French document contained. Article I of the Declaration, that '[m]en (all men) are born and remain free' drew from him the following withering response:

No, not a single man: not a single man that ever was, or is, or will be. All men, on the contrary, are born in subjection, and the most absolute subjection—the subjection of a helpless child to the parents on whom he depends every moment for his existence.[25]

Article II's assertion of the 'natural and imprescriptible rights of ... liberty, property, security and resistance to oppression' inspired Bentham to make his famous assault on human rights:

In proportion to the want of happiness resulting from the want of rights, a reason exists for wishing that there were such things as rights. But reasons for wishing there were such things as rights, are not rights; – a reason for wishing that a certain right were established, is not that right—want is not supply—hunger is not bread.

That which has no existence cannot be destroyed—that which cannot be destroyed cannot require anything to preserve it from destruction. *Natural rights* is simple nonsense; natural and imprescriptible rights, rhetorical nonsense, – nonsense upon stilts.[26]

Bentham thought the whole idea of a written document like the Declaration was misplaced:

What should it have done, then? To this question an answer is scarcely within the province of this paper: the proposition with which I set out is, not that the Declaration of Rights should have been worded differently, but that nothing under any such name, or with any such design, should have been attempted.[27]

The alternative and better approach from Bentham's perspective was to enact laws which were focused, targeted at particular ends and which would have a far more effective (because realizable) enforcement mechanism than could ever accompany declarations of human rights.

As though Bentham's strictures had not been enough, human rights French-style also received severe intellectual punishment from that other towering figure in nineteenth century political philosophy, Karl Marx. The attack did not in this case depend on the formula of words chosen by the French revolutionaries. In his essay, *On the Jewish Question*, Marx excoriated the individualism and the selfishness of human rights. The right to liberty was the 'freedom ... of a man treated as an isolated monad and withdrawn into himself'.[28] The right of a man to property was 'the right to enjoy his possessions and dispose of the same arbitrarily, without regard for other men, independently from society, the right of selfishness'.[29] The right to equality merely guaranteed that 'each man shall without discrimination be treated as a self-sufficient monad'.[30] None of these 'so-called rights of man [went] beyond egoistic man, man as he is in civil society, namely an individual withdrawn behind his private interests and whims and separated from the community'.[31]

---

[25] Ibid 49.   [26] Ibid 53 (emphasis in original).   [27] Ibid 62.
[28] Ibid 146.   [29] Ibid.   [30] Ibid.
[31] Ibid 147.

Despite their withering assaults on human rights, it is certainly the case that neither Bentham nor Marx can be accused of being indifferent to the importance of human dignity. What they deplored was the shoddiness of the short cuts taken by the (absolutist) language of rights and the deployment of that language to prevent political debate. Bentham's ideas were well-tuned to the movement for representative democracy that was emerging in the early nineteenth century. Marx did not dismiss out of hand the possibility that some kind of rights approach might be helpful: I shall return to these ideas in the next chapter when I elaborate further on the first key organizing principle for the Human Rights Act, that of respect for civil liberties.[32]

The Benthamite and Marxist critique of rights held sway for over 100 years while the push for the universal franchise preoccupied the energies of those intent on making the world a better place. The precision of democratically based legislation, specifically designed to achieve social change, appealed more to progressive forces than the vague rights talk that had been so badly mauled by key figures on the Left. The unexpected political renaissance of human rights in the second half of the twentieth century, which produced the Convention which is (via the Human Rights Act) the subject of this book, was made possible by enormous tragedy. After 1945, it seemed impossibly pedantic to argue that human rights could have no place in the new world that was being constructed out of the ashes of the old. Whatever the logic of the argument, confidence in the virtues of Benthamite positivism could not survive a realization of the crimes against humanity that had been committed by elected leaders unrestrained by law. And in the immediate post-war period, Marx's legacy seemed to have been appropriated by an all-powerful ruler in the Soviet Union who gave every impression of viewing citizens' rights as, if anything, even more subversive than the human rights that Marx had so despised. So western Europe turned back to human rights, as a means of defending itself from both the democratic centralism to its east and the fascism that would lurk forever in its past. The West German and Italian constitutions were reconstructed with strong rights components.[33] It was at this time that the European Convention on Human Rights was agreed,[34] as were the Universal Declaration of Human Rights,[35] and the Genocide Convention.[36] Human rights charters and agreements on many diverse subjects were achieved in the decades that followed.[37]

The movement was, however, more a politico-moral and legal crusade than a true change in the intellectual climate. The world of ideas in post-war Europe in

---

[32] See pp 33–37 below.

[33] See generally M Mandel, 'A Brief History of the New Constitutionalism, or "How We Changed Everything so that Everything would Remain the Same"' (1998) 32 *Israel Law Review* 250.

[34] On the origins of which see AWB Simpson, *Human Rights and the End of Empire. Britain and the Genesis of the European Convention* (Oxford: Oxford University Press, 2001).

[35] GAOR 3rd session, res 217A (10 December 1948).

[36] UNTS, vol 78, p 277.

[37] There is a good survey, though now slightly dated, in P Sieghart, *The Lawful Rights of Mankind* (Oxford: Oxford University Press, 1986).

which these human rights instruments were to become so firmly rooted remained perhaps even more inimical to the notion of untouchable moral universals, and therefore of imprescriptible human rights, than had been the culture that had produced Bentham and Marx. Picking up where these earlier critics had left off, a new generation of energetic thinkers, many still active today, turned its critical powers on the very concept of human rights.[38] Writers like Michael Sandel,[39] Charles Taylor[40] and other 'communitarian' thinkers have launched a series of well-known intellectual assaults on the very basis of rights. That doyen of contemporary legal philosophers, Joseph Raz, has written of right-based moralities that they are 'impoverished moral theories' which are 'unlikely to provide adequate foundation for an acceptable humanistic morality'.[41] The critique goes far beyond the utilitarianism of Bentham and the communism of Marx. In a public lecture, Richard Rorty demonstrated how much of contemporary critical thinking on human rights is bound up with new ways of looking at the person. Speaking in 1993, Rorty described how we 'are coming to think of ourselves as the flexible, protean, self-shaping, animal rather than as the rational animal or the cruel animal'.[42] The problem with human rights lay not with its existence as a social fact but with the claims that it seemed to make to universal absolutes:

One of the shapes we have recently assumed is that of a human rights culture ... In an article called 'Human Rights Naturalized', [the Argentinian jurist and philosopher Eduardo] Rabossi argues that philosophers should think of this culture as a new, welcome fact of the post-Holocaust world. They should stop trying to get behind or beneath this fact, stop trying to detect and defend its so-called 'philosophical pre-suppositions.' On Rabossi's view, philosophers ... are wrong to argue that human rights cannot depend on historical facts.[43]

Rorty regards 'Rabossi's claim that human rights foundationalism is *outmoded*' to be 'both true and important'.[44] The continued commitment shown by so many to the search for universality cannot be finally dispensed with 'as long as we think that there is an ahistorical power which makes for righteousness—a power called truth, or rationality' somewhere out there waiting to be discovered by the clever use of our minds:

---

[38] All that can be done here is merely to scratch the surface of contemporary thinking on truth and human rights. For an excellent general survey see R Plant, *Politics, Theology and History* (Cambridge: Cambridge University Press, 2001).

[39] MJ Sandel, *Liberalism and the Limits of Justice* 2nd edn (Cambridge: Cambridge University Press, 1998).

[40] C Taylor, *Sources of the Self: The Making of the Modern Identity* (Cambridge, Mass: Harvard University Press, 1989).

[41] J Raz, 'Right-Based Moralities' in J Waldron (ed), *Theories of Rights* (Oxford: Oxford University Press, 1984), 183. See further J Raz, *Ethics in the Public Domain. Essays in the Morality of Law and Politics* (Oxford: Clarendon Press, 1994), ch 11.

[42] R Rorty, 'Human Rights, Rationality and Sentimentality' in S Shute and S Hurley (eds), *On Human Rights* (New York: Basic Books, 1993) 111, 115.

[43] Ibid 115–116.

[44] Ibid 116 (emphasis in the original).

The question 'What is Man?' in the sense of 'What is the deep ahistorical nature of human beings?' owed its popularity to the standard answer to that question: We are the *rational animal*, the one which can know as well as merely feel. The residual popularity of this answer accounts for the residual popularity of Kant's astonishing claim that sentimentality has nothing to do with morality, that there is something distinctively and transculturally human called 'the sense of moral obligation' which has nothing to do with love, friendship, trust, or social solidarity. As long as we believe *that*, people like Rabossi are going to have a tough time convincing us that human rights foundationalism is an outmoded project.[45]

Rorty's answer to the dilemma this poses for human rights advocacy is to avoid altogether the issue of moral obligation, it being 'a mark of intellectual immaturity' even to raise the point.[46] There are no absolutes out there to be fathomed on the world's behalf by the very brightest of its human creatures. Instead we should recognize that our improvement over the past 200 years, such as it is, is more 'easily understood not as a period of deepening understanding of the nature of rationality or of morality, but rather as [a time] in which there [has] occurred an astonishingly rapid progress of sentiments in which it has become easier for us to be moved to action by sad and sentimental stories.'[47] The idea of human rights certainly exists today – but does so as a set of social facts rather than as a collection of revealed truths.

Of course there are exceptions to the trend I have been seeking to identify. Carlos Santiago Nino has written a well-received book which seeks to construct a rational foundation for human rights.[48] The explorations of Alan Gewirth in the same field, though complex, have been highly influential.[49] Ronald Dworkin continues to argue valiantly and with great skill for his idea of 'rights as trumps'.[50] In the realm of positive law, there is still admiration for the precision of Wesley Hohfield's analysis of rights,[51] but even there the commitment to rights is not unqualified; in fact rather the reverse. In a recent book, three distinguished philosophers who acknowledge that they 'all worship at the temple of Hohfield' recognize that what this 'signifies ... is simply a belief that the idea of a "right" has a meaning with sufficiently definite logical properties, and sufficient independence of the endlessly varying contents of rights, to deny the label of "rights" to many social relations—prevailing and proposed—that are currently so described.'[52] Even that most unequivocal of rights enthusiasts, John Finnis, is

---

[45] R Rorty, 'Human Rights, Rationality and Sentimentality' in S Shute and S Hurley (eds), *On Human Rights* (New York: Basic Books, 1993), 122 (emphasis in the original).

[46] Ibid 134.   [47] Ibid.

[48] *The Ethics of Human Rights* (Oxford: Clarendon Press, 1991). Also of interest are N Bobbio, *The Age of Rights* (Cambridge: Polity Press, 1996), chs 1 and 3; A Halpin, *Rights and Law. Analysis and Theory* (Oxford: Hart Publishing, 1997); C Adjei, 'Human Rights Theory and the Bill of Rights Debate' (1995) 58 MLR 17. A valuable general study is J Feinberg, *Rights, Justice, and the Bounds of Liberty. Essays in Social Philosophy* (New Jersey: Princeton University Press, 1980).

[49] On whom see Plant, n 38 above, ch 9.

[50] 'Rights as Trumps' in *Theories of Rights*, n 41 above, ch 7.

[51] WN Hohfield, *Fundamental Legal Conceptions as Applied in Judicial Reasoning* (WW Cook (ed)) (New Haven: Yale University Press, 1923).

[52] H Steiner, 'Working Rights' in MH Kramer, NE Simmonds and H Steiner, *A Debate over Rights. Philosophical Inquiries* (Oxford: Clarendon Press, 1998) 233, 234.

defensive in his claims: 'So we too need not hesitate to say that, notwithstanding the substantial consensus to the contrary, there are absolute human rights.'[53] It is difficult to resist the answer-begging power of the question posed by another leading critic of rights, Costas Douzinas, in relation to 'the greatest political and ethical problem of our era': 'if the critique of reason has destroyed the belief in the inexorable march of progress, if the critique of ideology has swept away most remnants of metaphysical credulity, does the necessary survival of transcendence depend on the non-convincing absolutisation of the liberal concept of rights through its immunisation from history?'[54] Why keep transcendence on such unconvincing terms?

The important point for this book, and in particular this chapter, is to assess how these criticisms of the idea of human rights impact on the human rights law project, epitomized in the European Convention on Human Rights and the Human Rights Act. Echoing Richard Rorty, Rabinder Singh's pragmatic professionalism is directly in point here: 'Since World War Two, in particular, the age-old problem of whether there are human rights and where they come from—whether from pure reason, natural law, divine origin or universal custom—has been largely avoided, if not resolved, by the social fact that the international community has come to accept a set of principles as being of global application.'[55] In an important sense the human rights agreements of today are not the powerful instruments that their titles might have led the observer to assume. We have already seen this in relation to the European Convention. These documents are modest in their goals even if they are noisy in their rhetoric, diminishing their grandiloquence with unenforceability and (where they are enforceable) their claimed universality with self-contradictory attenuations. The criticisms of the philosophers (old and modern) have been met, implicitly if not explicitly, and a large gap has opened up between the *idea* of human rights and the *fact* of human rights *law*. The Universal Declaration of Human Rights is just that—a declaration, rather than a piece of legislation in the traditional sense, or even in the international law sense. Its pronouncement changed nothing in any kind of tangible way. It is a reaffirmation of human dignity intended to inform rather than predetermine political debate. Had some post-war Benthamite disciple attacked its 'anarchical fallacies', its drafters would have been entitled to respond that he or she had entirely missed the point: the declaration is a mission statement for humanity, not a legal charter guaranteeing an impossible Nirvana.

The same point can be made, albeit to a lesser extent, about the other international and national human rights instruments which have been promulgated since the second world war. Though they do contain enforcement mechanisms, these are not of powerful design or intended for instant deployment.

---

[53] *Natural Law and Natural Rights* (Oxford: Clarendon Press, 1980), 225.

[54] C Douzinas, 'Human Rights and Postmodern Utopia' (2000) 11 *Law and Critique* 219, 221. See generally his *The End of Human Rights* (Oxford: Hart Publishing, 2000) for an excellent analysis, both scholarly and stimulating.

[55] *The Future of Human Rights in the United Kingdom: Essays on Law and Practice* (Oxford: Hart Publishing, 1997), 38.

Committees of experts meet and report to other committees which review national records and perhaps cross-examine local officials.[56] When the international community has embraced the language of human rights it has been careful to ensure that it has not thereby agreed to bring such rights about; the rod that it has made for its back has been rhetorical rather than legally real. At the domestic level, recent constitutional instruments—echoing the European Convention – have been explicit about the concessions that the language of human rights must make to political reality. The Canadian charter of rights and the New Zealand Bill of Rights both make the rights that they guarantee subject to override where particular kinds of necessity demand.[57] This is the tradition into which the Human Rights Act inserts the European Convention on Human Rights: rights not so much as trumps but rather as a suit expressing certain assumptions about the person, themselves heavily qualified, which can even so be 'trumped' by the dictates of representative democracy.

We can confidently say therefore that, far from being eccentrically diluting, the qualifications inserted into the European Convention on Human Rights and the Human Rights Act make these documents very much part of the human rights *law* mainstream. There is enough of a commitment to the old idea of rights for us to say of the Convention and the Human Rights Act that both instruments are concerned with individual human dignity; our recalling of the content of the Convention at the start of this chapter will have effectively demonstrated the point. But that there is more going on is evident both from the importance attached to civil liberties such as expression, assembly and association, and from the qualifications and controls that are placed on many of the assertions of human dignity and civil liberties that are to be found in each measure, limitations that in each case flow out of a commitment to representative democracy that antedates the new rights talk and has not been obliterated by it. Where the subversion of human dignity and/or civil liberties is tolerated by either measure as necessitated by a democratically expressed public interest, then this is required to be achieved through an open process of law-making, a demand that serves to reinforce the democratic system by inculcating a culture of legality while also protecting rights by making their removal in particular situations harder to achieve. It is out of this nexus of a devotion to human dignity which is on the one hand qualified by a realistic sensitivity to the democratic status quo and on the other fortified by a commitment to legality that the idea of human rights law as we understand the concept today has sprung. The subject flows out of a

---

[56] See eg Arts 16–22 of the Covenant on Economic, Social and Cultural Rights; Arts 8–14 of the Convention on the Elimination of All Forms of Racial Discrimination. Cf the provisions in the Covenant on Civil and Political Rights, Arts 28–45.

[57] The Canadian Charter of Fundamental Rights and Freedoms (1982) permits interferences with rights only insofar as these can be said to be within 'such reasonable limits ... as can be demonstrably justified in a free and democratic society' (s 1). The rights set out in the New Zealand Bill of Rights Act 1990 may also (subject to the overriding supremacy of the legislature) be qualified only by reference to 'such reasonable limits prescribed by law as can be demonstrably justified in a free and democratic society' (s 5).

triangular set of relations, between human dignity, democracy/civil liberties and legality.

C. The British constitutional tradition and the challenge of the Human Rights Act

We need now to turn to the second challenge the Human Rights Act has faced, fitting itself into a domestic culture that has long been antipathetic to any kind of supra-parliamentary system of rights. We have already said enough to demonstrate that the promulgation of human rights instruments in practice amounts to an invitation to the judicial branch to resolve the conflicts that inevitably arise when the rhetoric of rights collides either with itself or with the democratic public interest. Like all similar modern rights' instruments, the Human Rights Act leaves to the courts the job of resolving the ambiguities within, the breadth of the exceptions to, and the clash of priorities as between the various rights drawn from the European Convention that it sets out in its first schedule. This is why the constitutionalisation of rights always entails an increase in judicial power, why Lord Hope was perfectly right to speak of the Human Rights Act (as we saw he did in chapter one, in *Ex p Kebilene*) having ushered in a 'fundamental process of review and, where necessary, reform *by the judiciary*'.[58] While it is true that, as we have noted earlier in this chapter, legislation cannot be struck down by the courts for non-compliance with Convention rights (with the declaration of incompatibility being all that is available in such circumstances), s 3(1) contains a compensatory principle of interpretation so robust as to make the absence of such a judicial override power less noticeable than would normally be the case. Set out in full it states as follows:

So far as it is possible to do so, primary legislation and subordinate legislation must be read and given effect in a way which is compatible with the Convention rights.

This provision is to apply to 'primary legislation and subordinate legislation whenever enacted'[59] and is supplemented by the equally wide-ranging duty on public authorities to be found in s 6(1):

It is unlawful for a public authority to act in a way which is incompatible with a Convention right.

The Human Rights Act appears on its face to mark a radical breach with British constitutional tradition, a point that I made briefly in chapter one but which I now need to develop more fully. The first point of comparison with the past lies in the vagueness of the Convention rights. As we have already seen, there is no precision in the drafting, no effort to address particular situations, no anticipation of future problems. Instead, as we have also seen, there is a series of rather

---

[58] *R (Kebilene) v Director of Public Prosecutions* [2000] 2 AC 326, 375. Emphasis added.
[59] s 3(2)(a).

grand claims, with various qualifications of an equally general nature. United Kingdom statute law has never seen the like of this before: ordinarily, legislation on both general and rights-related matters is lengthy, complex, and precisely targeted at particular mischiefs. This is true of laws passed both before and after the Act, such as the equality and race relations legislation of the 1960s and 1970s and (more recently) the Freedom of Information Act 2000. This unique aspect of the Human Rights Act—its generality—is matched by a second, remarkable feature: its imperialism. The technical Interpretation Acts aside, no other piece of legislation has ever so baldly claimed the kind of pervasive priority that s 3(1) asserts on behalf of the Human Rights Act. Not even the European Communities Act 1972 had the temerity to express itself so boldly (though of course that might have been because it was playing an even bigger game with Parliament's sovereignty).[60] The breadth of s 3(1), with its talk of what it 'is possible to do' so as to ensure that 'primary legislation and subordinate legislation [are] read and given effect in a way which is compatible with the Convention rights', sets out to brush aside the traditional remit ascribed to past laws, to ignore the purpose of such measures, to reject their literal, even their plain, meanings just so long as any or all of this is required to produce compatibility with its terms. Laws not yet passed are to be subjected to the same test of orthodoxy.[61] Thus does faith in the Convention's version of human rights become the new dogma for our sceptical age[62], with litigation in place of Inquisition and judges in the role of the Dominicans – ever vigilant in the pursuit of orthodoxy even if it means putting words on the wrack to force new meanings from them.

The British constitution used to be very different. Its overriding feature was its neutrality. This was what made it *par excellence* a 'political constitution'.[63] Writing in 1930, Harold Laski noted that 'an individual abstracted from society and regarded as entitled to freedom outside its environment [was] devoid of meaning'.[64] Though supportive of the idea of a bill of rights, Laski saw that its effectiveness depended on the judiciary, whose 'members, after all, are human beings, likely, as the rest of us, to be swept off their feet by gusts of popular passion.'[65] Nearly 50 years later, in a famous lecture, Professor John Griffith from the LSE attacked rights theory as 'another attempt to hide in a mist of words the conflict which is the characteristic of our society'.[66] Thus, Article 10 of the Convention, purporting to guarantee freedom of expression, was a 'statement of a political conflict pretending to be a resolution of it'.[67] To Griffith,

---

[60] European Communities Act 1972, s 2. See *R (Factortame) v Secretary of State for Transport (no 2)* [1991] 1 AC 603.

[61] Human Rights Act 1998, s 3(2)(a).

[62] F Klug, *Values for a Godless Age* (London: Penguin, 2000).

[63] JAG Griffith, 'The Political Constitution' (1979) 42 *MLR* 1. In Professor KD Ewing's words, 'constitutional law does not stand above politics: they are two sides of one coin': 'The Politics of the British Constitution' [2000] *PL* 405, 436.

[64] *Liberty in the Modern State* (London: Faber and Faber, 1930), 20.

[65] Ibid 53.

[66] 'The Political Constitution', n 63 above, 11.

[67] Ibid 14.

'conflict [was] at the heart of modern society'[68] and law was not, and could not ever be, 'a substitute for politics':[69]

In this political, social sense there are no over-riding human rights. No right to freedom, to trial before conviction, to representation before taxation. No right not to be tortured, not to be summarily executed. Instead there are political claims by individuals and by groups.[70]

Until the enactment of the Human Rights Act, and much to the dismay of advocates of human rights, Professor Griffith's analysis of the British constitution was an accurate one. In the traditional model, parliamentary sovereignty functioned as a kind of empty vessel into which the (temporary) victors in the endless political fray could pour their ever-contingent versions of right and wrong. Even the process of determining who won the electoral game could be changed, but then changed back again if subsequent elected representatives had the chance and the desire. Echoing Bentham, 'rights' emerged from this political process in the form of legal entitlements backed by an appropriate enforcement mechanism. Frequently they were not described as rights at all, with it not being necessary or desirable to present the gains achieved by such legislation in such dramatic, rhetorical terms. In controversial areas of ethical and moral dispute, the non-use of the language of rights avoided the consequence of one side feeling it had won its right while the other felt that it had been taken away.

The outstanding, comparative example in this regard relates to the law on abortion. In the United States, there can be little doubt that the effective award, by the Supreme Court in *Roe v Wade*,[71] of a qualified right to terminate a pregnancy under the general rubric of an (implied) constitutional right to privacy inflamed those whose campaigning zeal for the protection of the unborn had been presented in rights terms, in their case the need to protect the 'right to life'. In the United Kingdom in contrast, the reformation of the abortion law took place in Parliament, on a free vote on a private member's bill, and, rather than award a right to any group, merely removed from the criminal law certain terminations under certain circumstances.[72] The energies of reformers ever since have been concentrated on this piece of legislation, with victories being won and lost in the usual ebb and flow of politics.[73] The issue has never been as divisive as in the United States, or indeed in other countries where the conflict has been constitutionalized.[74] The establishment of gay rights, the decision to abolish capital punishment, and the exemption from the full rigours of the law for those who commit or attempt to commit suicide have been resolved in a similar way. The provision of a 'free vote' is crucial here, with parliamentary representatives being freed of their obligations to their respective political parties and being able therefore to vote in accordance with their consciences. Nor is this jurisdiction merely of historical interest; as new ethical and social challenges have been increasingly thrown up by scientific progress, members of Parliament

[68] Ibid 2.   [69] Ibid 16.   [70] Ibid 17.   [71] 410 US 113 (1973).
[72] See Abortion Act 1967.   [73] See Human Fertilisation and Embryology Act 1990, s 37.
[74] Eg Ireland: see CA Gearty, 'The Politics of Abortion' (1992) 19 *JLS* 441.

have in recent years frequently been asked to vote on where they judge the public interest truly to lie. Recent legislation such as the Disability Discrimination Act 1995, the Public Interest Disclosure Act 1998 and the Disability Rights Commission Act 1999 reflect the ongoing engagement of the legislative branch in matters that in other more rights-based systems have become the primary responsibility of the courts.[75] The litany of recent legislation just cited shows that it would be an exaggeration to say that the Human Rights Act has supplanted the old constitutional order. But there can be little doubt that the Act increases the temptation to the legislature to dodge difficult issues, thereby leaving them to the judges to resolve. To an extent this has always been possible under the traditional framework[76] but viewed overall one of the more noticeable features of the pre-Human Rights Act British constitution has been the relatively minimal role that it has accorded the judiciary.

There are convincing historical reasons for this marginalization of the adjudicative branch. To some extent, the judges were being permanently punished (at least until 1998) for having been on the wrong side in England's seventeenth century civil wars.[77] Even their one zone of autonomy, the common law, has always been susceptible of being overridden by the legislature. Content to play second fiddle, the courts have traditionally interpreted Acts of Parliament in a narrow fashion, rarely seeking to destabilize or embellish the ordinary meaning of the statutes that have come before them for adjudication. During much of the twentieth century, the courts chose to adopt a similarly restrained approach to the control of executive power, giving ministers a wide latitude in the interpretation of their statutory powers and being very reluctant to say of any act or omission of such a person that it transgressed the powers allowed them by Act of Parliament. Until as late as the mid 1980s, the royal prerogative, exercisable though it largely was by the government of the day, was not even theoretically susceptible of judicial review.[78] This inactivity of the judicial branch has facilitated a dynamic political culture but it has made for a dull legal one, with political parties fighting savagely for control of the parliamentary process through which each could, if successful, impose its preferred vision of right and just conduct on the community as a whole. The subsidiary role of the judges, who were after all unelected, unrepresentative and unexposed to public accountability, was perceived to be an essential element in Britain's representative democracy. Indeed, hard though it

---

[75] Of course the courts remain important under these pieces of legislation but their role is as the interpreters of sections specifically targeted at particular issues; it is right therefore to think of their task as secondary in the way that it is not where Parliament has entrusted them with the concretization of very general legislative statements in a wide range of (unforeseen and unforeseeable) circumstances.

[76] As eg with regard to the question of when a person in a permanent vegetative state should be allowed to die: see *Airedale NHS Trust v Bland* [1993] AC 789.

[77] See P Craig, 'Ultra Vires and the Foundations of Judicial Review' (1998) 57 *CLJ* 63 for some historical data. Also valuable is R Stevens, *The English Judges. Their Role in the Changing Constitution* (Oxford: Hart Publishing, 2002).

[78] *Council of Civil Service Unions v Minister for the Civil Service* [1985] AC 374. Other than on this point of the reviewability of the prerogative, the case adopts a very cautious approach to judicial power, and a deferential attitude to executive decision-making in the field of national security.

might now be to believe, there were serious debates and arguments about whether even the small amount of judicial power wielded by British judges in the old dispensation was already too much and in need of even further curtailment.[79]

The Human Rights Act certainly appears to represent a large breach with the constitutional tradition that we have just been describing. True, it is a positivist measure in the narrow sense of being rooted in statute law and (like all such law) being capable of being repealed. But its implanting of general (albeit qualified) rights within the UK legal system makes it a piece of positive law with very strong natural law edges. As noted above, moreover, and in a further positivist twist, the Act does not entirely transcend the pre-existing constitutional system, with respect for parliamentary sovereignty having survived intact. The judges are being sent two apparently contradictory messages: on the one hand, apply these broadly based and generalized human rights whose meaning is not at all self-evident in a wide-ranging way, if necessary by distorting Parliament's intention in specific instances; on the other hand, always respect parliamentary sovereignty. How are the judges to pull off the trick of being positive law servants and natural law masters at one and the same time? As indicated in chapter one, this book is largely concerned with answering this question.

We have already seen earlier in this chapter that a close examination of the text and the broader context of the European Convention points us in the direction of principle as a way of concretizing how far the open-textured words in the document should extend. The Human Rights Act incorporates these principles not only in the schedule giving effect to the Convention rights but also in its own structure. The respect for parliamentary sovereignty shown by the Act, for example, is not foreign to the framework of rights adopted in the European Convention, with its derogations and public interest opt-outs but is, as I shall argue in greater detail in chapter three, integral to it. The same can be said of legality, the respect for which is inherent in the measure viewed as a whole. But the value of the three principles I have identified as being central to the Convention—respect for civil liberties, legality, and human dignity—goes further than this. They also serve to fit the Human Rights Act and the European Convention much more comfortably within the British constitutional tradition than the bald words and large claims in these instruments, viewed in isolation, would suggest. I shall develop this point in greater detail in the three chapters that follow this one, when I explore each idea in turn, and show how much part of the British tradition as well as of contemporary human rights law are the principles of respect for civil liberties, legality, and human dignity. But I can make here the general point that these principles help not only to make sense of what the Convention is all about, a point I developed in the last section, but they also act as a bridge between the new order introduced by the Human Rights Act and the longstanding concerns of the British constitutional system. So the breach with the past suggested by the wording of the Human Rights Act turns on

---

[79] Famously JAG Griffith, *The Politics of the Judiciary* 5th edn (London: Fontana Press, 1977).

closer examination to be far less dramatic than at first appeared, with the measure more often echoing than drowning out what went before.

D. Human rights and judicial power

It remains for us finally to address a virulent strain of intellectual opposition which has not yet been directly tackled in the course of this chapter, and which we can view as part both of the general and the particular British critique of rights that we have been discussing up to now. This is an attack on rights which is less rooted in philosophical assaults on the concept's intelligibility, of the type launched by writers like Richard Rorty and the communitarians whom we have already discussed, than it is focused on the political consequences of the alleged philosophical vacuity of rights talk. These critics share the recently expressed view of four leading political scientists, that rights are merely 'claims, and claims are contested, bolstered, qualified, expanded, withdrawn and redrawn'[80] in every political community. The critique flows directly from the insight which I developed in the last section, namely the realization that rights talk inevitably involves increased judicial power and that it is no answer to this objection to stress the qualified nature of rights; on the contrary the argument of the critics *depends* on rights being circumscribed in this way since it is the consequent need for balancing rights and exceptions that opens the door to judicial power. And it is upon the judicial branch that the energy of these critics is focused. Professor M A Glendon's hugely influential book, which appeared in 1991, concentrated on what the title to the work called the 'impoverishment of political discourse' that flowed from 'rights talk'.[81] In a similar vein has been the work of Tom Campbell from the Australian National University, a critic of the philosophical underpinnings of the rights discourse as well as of its political consequences.[82] Other scholars who have been similarly scathing from across different areas of legal scholarship and across continents have been the American-based Mark Tushnet,[83] and the Canadian, Michael Mandel.[84] The writer has himself been an enthusiastic member of this camp in the past.[85] Do the concessions that

---

[80] PM Sniderman, JF Fletcher, PH Russell and PE Tetlock, *The Clash of Rights. Liberty, Equality, and Legitimacy in Pluralist Democracy* (New Haven: Yale University Press, 1996), 78.

[81] *Rights Talk. The Impoverishment of Political Discourse* (New York: The Free Press, 1991).

[82] See eg his 'Human Rights: A Culture of Controversy' (1999) 26 *JLS* 6. Also very important in this field has been Martin Loughlin: see most recently his 'Rights, Democracy, and Law' in T Campbell, KD Ewing and A Tomkins (eds), *Sceptical Essays on Human Rights* (Oxford: Oxford University Press, 2001), ch 3.

[83] See his 'Living with a Bill of Rights' in C Gearty and A Tomkins (eds), *Understanding Human Rights* (London: Mansell Publishing Ltd, 1996), ch 1.

[84] M Mandel, *The Charter of Rights and the Legalisation of Politics in Canada* 2nd edn (Toronto: Thompson Educational Press, 1994). For an Australian contribution, see T Ison, 'The Sovereignty of the Judiciary' (1985) 10 *Adelaide Law Rev* 3.

[85] See KD Ewing and CA Gearty, *Democracy or a Bill of Rights* (London: Society of Labour Lawyers, 1991).

the Human Rights Act has made to parliamentary sovereignty disarm these critics?

One of the most articulate of the critics is the writer's former colleague and frequent co-author KD Ewing, from King's College London. In a contribution to the debate that preceded incorporation which was published in 1994 under the explosive title, 'The Bill of Rights Debate: Democracy or Juristocracy in Britain?',[86] Ewing asked the key question underlying this whole position, namely whether it was possible to 'reconcile with the first principles of democratic self-government the transfer of sovereign power from an elected legislature to an unelected judiciary'.[87] According to Ewing, those principles were three in number, the first being that 'of equal participation; that is to say, the right of us all to participate as equals in the policy-making institutions of government'.[88] The second of Ewing's principles flowed 'naturally from the first and relates to the fact that because of the sheer size of contemporary society it is not possible for us all to participate in the making of decisions'.[89] Given that because of this not everybody can join in decision-making, principle required that 'in a system of representative government, the representatives must be selected by the community they claim to represent'.[90] The third of Ewing's principles then went on to require 'that those who hold representative positions must in some sense be accountable to the people they represent for the decisions they purport to take on their behalf'.[91]

We should recall that the proposed bills of rights that were being bandied about for the UK during the mid 1990s were very much more robust than the one that finally emerged in the Human Rights Act, and in particular involved a greatly entrenched judicial power with a correspondingly diminished parliamentary remit. So what Ewing had in his sights (together with the rest of us who shared his views on this issue in the 1980s and 1990s) was a much more absolutist document than the one that was finally to emerge. Nevertheless his criticisms have a timelessness to them which makes them still relevant today. As regards the principle of equal participation, it was 'clear that this is not something that can be met by a process of adjudication. Judicial office is closed to all but a very few members of the community, above all by the conditions of appointment laid down in legislation.[92] The system from which the United Kingdom draws its senior judiciary comes close 'to creating the over-representation of people who have particular intellectual qualities'.[93] At the present time it 'is socially exclusive and in practice denies access to people

---

[86] KD Ewing, CA Gearty and BA Hepple (eds), *Human Rights and Labour Law. Essays for Paul O'Higgins* (London: Mansell, 1994), ch 7.
[87] Ibid 147–148.
[88] Ibid 149.
[89] Ibid.
[90] Ibid 150.
[91] Ibid.
[92] Ibid 151.
[93] Ibid 152.

from disadvantaged backgrounds'.[94] In a country with decision-making under a bill of rights, 'the people who make these decisions—the people with ultimate authority to make political decisions for a community—are not in any sense representative of the community they serve'.[95] Because of all of this, the third principle, that of accountability 'perhaps assumes even more importance'.[96] But while judges do usually give reasons for their decisions in public, they 'never allow themselves to be questioned publicly about a decision and will only rarely give public insights into the personal political values that inform their decisions'.[97] Ewing concludes that the 'effect of a Bill of Rights or an incorporated European Convention is to empower the judges to unsettle decisions made in the political arena by the people's representatives and thereby frustrate the democratic process'.[98] He views this as wrong in principle, and therefore not as redeemable even by a robust reform of the judicial branch: 'while [such] initiatives and proposals are important and potentially very valuable, they do not begin to address the three very fundamental concerns' that he has raised.[99]

These are strong criticisms of the whole bill of rights project, and they have to be addressed by all those who care deeply enough about their democratic credentials to want to square their commitment to human rights with their (surely more than merely ostensible) respect for this particular form of government. After all that we have said in this chapter, it must be clear that one familiar bolt-hole is no longer credibly present on the field of battle: the idea of human rights as a set of absolute universals hovering above the political fray like some rational Guardian Angel, ready to swoop at the first hint of unacceptable belligerence below, is dubious metaphysics and, whenever it touches the earth of real situations, immediately begs more questions than it can meaningfully answer. Another possible response is to refer back to the attempt the Human Rights Act makes to achieve a balance between parliamentary and judicial power and to draw from this the conclusion that because the judges do not have (to use Professor Ewing's words quoted above) 'ultimate authority', there is nothing to get too excited about in relation to this particular measure (as opposed to others elsewhere, for example, where judicial power is more firmly entrenched). But while recognizing this is indeed the case, Ewing's comment on the Act after its enactment was that it was 'unquestionably the most significant formal redistribution of political power in this country since 1911, and perhaps since 1688'.[100] We should also recall Lord Hope's view that its enactment precipitates a 'fundamental ... review' of the 'entire legal system'.[101] So something is definitely going on here which makes Ewing's three principles of democratic government as relevant in relation to the Human Rights Act as they would be to another kind of, more firmly entrenched, rights' measure.

---

[94] KD Ewing, CA Gearty and BA Hepple (eds), *Human Rights and Labour Law. Essays for Paul O'Higgins* (London: Mansell, 1994), ch 7.
[95] Ibid.   [96] Ibid 153.   [97] Ibid 154.
[98] Ibid 156.   [99] Ibid 172.
[100] KD Ewing, 'The Human Rights Act and Parliamentary Democracy' (1999) 62 *MLR* 79, 79 (footnote omitted).
[101] See n 58 above.

The truth is that the Human Rights Act does not yet know clearly where it is going. We return to the underlying paradox of the measure: Parliament has thrown down two routes—respect for parliamentary sovereignty and for judicially-enforceable human rights—and forbidden the courts from going down either too enthusiastically. The professor of international law at the University of Helsinki, Marti Koskenniemi, is a critic of rights language whose work bridges the gap between the philosophical generalities of Rorty and the political awareness of Ewing. In his contribution to *The EU and Human Rights*, entitled 'The Effect of Rights on Political Culture'[102] Koskenniemi makes two central points which he usefully summarizes at the start of his essay:

> First, while the rhetoric of human rights has historically had a positive and liberating effect on societies, once rights become institutionalised as a central part of political and administrative culture, they lose their transformative effect and are petrified into a legalistic paradigm that marginalizes values or interests that resist translation into rights-language. In this way, the liberal principle [drawn from John Rawls] of the 'priority of the right over the good' results in a colonization of political culture by a technocratic language that leaves no room for the articulation or realisation of conceptions of the good.
>
> Secondly ... rights-rhetoric is not as powerful as it claims to be. It does not hold a coherent set of normative demands that could be resorted to in the administration of society. To the contrary, despite its claim for value-neutrality, rights-rhetoric is constantly reduced to conflicting and contested arguments about the political good. The identification, meaning, and applicability of rights are dependant on contextual assessments of 'proportionality' or administrative 'balancing' through which priorities are set among conflicting conceptions of political value and scarce resources are distributed between contending social groups. Inasmuch as such decision-making procedures define what 'rights' are, they cannot themselves be controlled by rights. To this extent, the 'priority of the right over the good' proves an impossible demand, and insisting upon it will leave political discretion unchecked.[103]

In this chapter we have already begun the work of suggesting ways in which the judiciary can, by meeting the 'impossible demand' made by the Human Rights Act, preserve the idea of representative democracy while acting to protect human rights in a coherent and principled way. This book is an argument for adopting a certain approach to the Human Rights Act which makes a success of it and which therefore defends it from the criticisms, both domestic and profound, that we have encountered here. The key is to identify the underlying principles of the protection of civil liberties, legality, and respect for human dignity as the triad of ideas upon which human rights in its legal incarnation in the United Kingdom depends, and then sensibly to connect these foundational principles to the prevailing democratic culture in a way which recognizes that they have to connect to other societal interests. In chapters three to five I consider these three principles in greater detail, justifying the claim I have

---

[102] P Alston (ed), *The EU and Human Rights* (Oxford: Oxford University Press, 1999), ch 3.

[103] Ibid 99 (footnote omitted). For a most thoughtful analysis of many of the issues discussed in this chapter, and indeed in this book, see S Sedley, *Freedom, Law and Justice* (London: Sweet and Maxwell, 1999).

made in broad terms here that they are rooted in the Convention, in the Human Rights Act and in the case law generated by both documents. In chapters six to eight I appraise the operation of these three principles in practice, identifying three aspirations which those striving sensibly to interpret the Human Rights Act should always have in mind. It is in this balance between principle and pragmatism, between a concentration on human rights broadly defined on the one hand and the democratically defined public interest on the other, that we find an answer to the myriad of questions raised by this unique piece of British legislation.

PART TWO
THE CORE PRINCIPLES

3

The Principle of Respect for Civil Liberties

A. The legal conception of civil liberties

It may at first glance seem odd that I should start my intensive inquiry into the principles underpinning the Human Rights Act at so traditional a point. More books on human rights have been published in the past three years than civil liberties scholarship has been able to muster in a succession of generations of study. The subject may be about to revive, however, precisely because of the enormous breadth, depth, and range of the Human Rights Act. David Feldman's magisterial study of the whole field remains, in its second edition published in 2002, resolutely entitled *Civil Liberties and Human Rights in England and Wales*.[1] Helen Fenwick's excellent study, *Civil Rights: New Labour, Freedom and the Human Rights Act*[2] is concerned primarily with classic civil liberties issues such as the law on freedom of police powers, counter-terrorism and surveillance, and the regulation of public protest. The authors of a recent textbook, entitled *Civil Liberties Law: the Human Rights Era*[3] confess to it being 'both an exciting and a confusing time to be a civil liberties lawyer.'[4] In explaining their choice of title, at which some 'readers may be surprised',[5] they expressed the hope 'that such an emphasis may assist in deflating the unhelpfully swollen status of "human rights" in some accounts'.[6]

The language of human rights is certainly too broad to be able in itself to provide any kind of coherent guide to the principles that should underpin the relationship between the individual and the state in a representative democracy. It is too vulnerable to the kind of criticisms that we saw being made in chapter one. On the other hand, some kind of theory is needed if human rights is not to collapse into incoherence. Despite its narrow conception in some legal circles, civil liberties can be presented as a coherent set of ideas, rooted in an underlying political philosophy which in turn reflects a particular way of looking at the world. So it is natural rather than strange that consideration of civil liberties should flow directly

---

[1] Oxford: Oxford University Press.
[2] Harlow: Longman, 2000.
[3] N Whitty, T Murphy and S Livingstone, *Civil Liberties Law: The Human Rights Act Era* (London: Butterworths, 2001).
[4] Ibid v.
[5] Ibid 5.
[6] Ibid 6.

from our discussion in chapter two of the political and philosophical context of the Human Rights Act, particularly since (as we shall see) a persuasive argument can be constructed that the version of human rights articulated in the European Convention and the Human Rights Act is strongly civil libertarian in content. Of course there are grey areas at the definitional edges of civil liberties, just as there are in every legal subject; it is perfectly true, for example, that since the 'dominant civil liberties paradigm has been sovereign state versus the individual, with the former presented as an enemy (or, at least prone towards knowing neglect) of civil liberties',[7] the subject has never been so clear as to 'the circumstances in which state intervention or regulation is appropriate in public and private spheres'.[8] How far civil liberties law strays into criminal justice and prison law is another open question. That there are these (and other) uncertainties about the boundaries of the discipline need not preoccupy us in this chapter.

Our interest here lies not in laying out a thorough theoretical framework for civil liberties law but rather in capturing the essence of the subject insofar as it contains a set of ideas that inform the content of the European Convention on Human Rights and, in so doing, provides the first of our three principal guides to the meaning of the Human Rights Act. The subject of civil liberties is best viewed as being concerned with those freedoms which are essential to the maintenance and fostering of our representative system of government.[9] With the memory of which rights are in the Convention clear in our minds from chapter two, it will be apparent that there is potential for a large overlap between the Convention and civil liberties. I shall deal with the former later in this chapter but it is useful first to consider the idea of civil liberties in the abstract, and to build on the preparatory political thinking in which I engaged in chapter two. Once civil liberties is seen as intimately connected with representative government, it will be immediately understood that the freedom at its core, the entitlement upon which the utility of the remaining liberties depend, giving them added zest and meaning, is the right to vote. Here we have an example of a civil liberty, indeed on this account the key liberty, which is realizable only through positive state action: our right to vote cannot exist in the abstract; it requires a large state machinery to make it work. To be effective it also needs to be by way of a secret ballot and to be a right capable of being exercised at regular intervals and, in combination with the use of the right by others, to have the capacity to produce a legislature to make laws on behalf of the community over which it presides which body is broadly speaking representative of that community. It must follow, therefore, that the right to vote is closely associated with an equally core entitlement, the right to stand for Parliament, and if successful to sit and vote in that assembly. A properly functioning representative democracy will also insist that each vote carries a broadly equal weight, and will not permit certain affluent electors to buy the power to be heard at the expense of other interests; the electoral playing field should be an equal one.

---

[7] N Whitty, T Murphy and S Livingstone, *Civil Liberties Law: The Human Rights Act Era* (London: Butterworths, 2001), 11.

[8] Ibid 12.   [9] See Feldman, n 1 above, Parts II and IV.

Other civil liberties are valuable because they make meaningful the exercise of this core right to vote, but they are reliant more on state inaction than action. At this point, the roots of the subject in the concept of negative liberty become apparent. The freedom to think for oneself, to believe what one wishes and to say what one wants are essential if a democratic assembly is going to be truly and properly representative. The right to associate with others and to assemble together are essential for the same reason. The access by voters to relevant information can also be seen to be an important civil liberty, since the uninformed vote is also a less effective one. It surely also goes without saying that a state which arbitrarily kills, imprisons, or tortures its citizens so chills the political atmosphere that it cannot be described as democratic, regardless of how free speech formally is or how regularly secret votes are polled: freedom cannot be constructed on such authoritarian foundations. Adherence to these core civil liberties produces an assembly that is both representative and accountable (through the ballot box and through the political energy that the prospect of the vote inspires) for the power that it exercises. Civil liberties also requires as a matter of basic principle that the relationship between the individual and the state be regulated by law, but since the second of my major principles in this book is the principle of legality there is no need to emphasize that strand to the subject at this juncture: I deal with it extensively in the next chapter.

A consequence of thinking about liberty, expression, assembly and so on, and also the entitlement to vote, as civil *liberties* rather than human *rights* is to focus attention away from the possibility of these being absolute entitlements vested in human beings as such and to divert the analytical spotlight instead onto their utility as part of the essential fabric that goes into the making of our democratic tapestry. This absence of any assertion of absolutism is the most powerful (non) claim that civil liberties make on our attention. Civil liberties are defined by reference to an underlying political philosophy rooted in representative democracy, which definition at the same time permits, also by reference to that same underlying ideological premise, exceptions to be made to them. With this singular intellectual swoop, civil liberties law rises above the endless debates provoked by rights talk, about when this kind of reckless speech should be allowed and when not, about why this assembly should be restricted and this other not: human rights law has no coherent way of answering these questions without drawing on some deeper set of principles. Civil liberties law, in contrast, has the benchmark of democratic necessity readily to hand.

It is true that this is a very democratic reading of civil liberties and the origins of the subject could also be credibly explained away as a product of bourgeois liberalism, the creation of a zone of autonomy for the individual. It is also the case that the problem of the tyrannical inclinations of the majority cannot help but come into view on this reading of the subject, and I address this issue directly in my concluding chapter. It should be clear by now, however, why whatever its origins and its faults the principle of civil liberties fits so snugly into the British constitutional tradition that I have described in chapter two. As I there noted, the English common law tradition has long understood the organizing utility of the principle of civil liberties, even if, as we shall see shortly, it has not always applied it consistently in moments of adversarial crisis. The individual has generally been free to assert his or her civil liberties unless constrained by law from doing so. While there has never been a civil liberty to incite to kill, it has always been possible to campaign for the restoration (or extension) of the death penalty, even for a community style lynch law. The civil liberty to assemble has never extended to a freedom to riot. (This is not to say that a riot is always wrong, merely that rioters can never claim to be exercising a civil liberty, whatever other claims they might validly or invalidly make.) There is a civil liberty to vote, but no right to insist on a particular system, this being a matter for Parliament to determine. Laws are readily permitted which control expression, assembly, association and other civil liberties where the effect of such laws is to serve some large public interest while not harming or diminishing the political capacities of those subject to them. The impartiality of these laws—their universal application—helps copper-fasten their legitimacy. None of us object to noise control laws if it means that all political activists have to curb their vocal enthusiasms at certain times, just as we are glad that the laws against litter and the obstruction of the highway contain no loopholes allowing campaigners to inundate the high street with leaflets or protestors to bring Oxford Street to a halt in rush hour. It is because it is often the case that ostensibly neutral laws are deployed partisanly to penalize particular groups that the law on police discretion (especially in relation to breaches of the peace) is so closely related to civil liberties, and this also explains why such straightforward matters as binding over orders, bail applications and the routine deployment of mainstream public order legislation are often also to be found straying into the subject.

As we saw in chapter two, Marx grasped but did not greatly develop the distinction I am making here between the rights of the citizen (civil liberties) and the rights of man (human rights). His criticisms of the latter were so swingeing that the former could not help but be neglected, contaminated by linguistic association with its then (and for long after) derided partner. Rejecting democratic centralism with its disregard of civil liberties, certain writers in the Marxist tradition developed a more positive view of civil liberties than Marx had had of human rights. This was rooted in the characteristically optimistic socialist belief that, given the chance and a level political playing field, the mass of voters would indeed choose socialism. On this view, therefore, the vote was nothing to be frightened of; there was no need defensively to condemn it as a bourgeois sleight-of-hand. The most influential of these writers was Eduard Bernstein, whose *The Preconditions of Socialism* was first published in German in 1899, with an English translation following 10 years later. Bernstein defined democracy as 'the absence of class government. This indicates a state of society in which no class has a political privilege which is opposed to the community as a whole.'[10] Bernstein considered 'the idea of the oppression of the individual by the majority' to be 'absolutely repugnant to the modern mind'[11], not least because democracy and justice were to him integrally related concepts:

As we understand it today, the concept of democracy includes an idea of justice, that is, equality of rights for all members of the community, and this sets limits to the rule of the majority—which is what government by the people amounts to, in any concrete case. The more democracy prevails and determines public opinion, the more it will come to mean the greatest possible degree of freedom for all.[12]

The vote was essential to the realization of this attractive—and socialist— scenario:

The right to vote in a democracy makes its members virtual partners in the community, and this virtual partnership must in the end lead to real partnership. With a working class undeveloped in numbers and culture, universal suffrage may for a long while seem no more than the right to choose 'the butcher'. However, as the workers grow in numbers and awareness, it becomes an instrument for transforming the people's representatives from being the masters into being the real servants of the people. Although the English workers vote for members of the old parties in parliamentary elections and thus superficially appear to be the 'tail' of the bourgeois parties, in industrial constituencies it is nonetheless this 'tail' that wags the dog rather than the other way round—not to mention the fact that the extension of the suffrage in 1884, together with the reform of local government, has given Social Democracy full rights as a political party in England.[13]

To Bernstein, 'the victory of democracy, the creation of democratic social and political organisations, [was] the indispensable precondition for the realisation of socialism'.[14] This did not of course mean that democracy mandated socialism. From Disraeli's One Nation policies, through Chamberlain's imperialism, to the Cold War of the past and the counter-terrorist state of the present, what Bernstein would have called the bourgeois have found many ways of fighting back and of accommodating democracy to their needs.

B. Civil liberties in Britain

Before making the case for a close fit between civil liberties and the rights set out in the European Convention and the Human Rights Act, it is important to add an historical dimension to the inquiry. It is one thing to talk about theory, quite another to ask about practice. It needs to be asked how Britain has fared in the protection it has accorded civil liberties, as I have understood that term in the opening section of this chapter. Without addressing this question, I will be

---

[10] *The Preconditions of Socialism* (H Tudor (ed and trans)) (Cambridge: Cambridge University Press, 1993), 140.
[11] Ibid 141.
[12] Ibid.
[13] Ibid 144.
[14] Ibid 157.

ill-equipped to assess the likely or actual impact of the Human Rights Act in the
civil libertarian field, in bad times as well as good. The issue involves analysis of
all three branches of government. Starting on the very largest of historical scales,
the genius of the UK constitution since the middle of the seventeenth century has
lain in its capacity for self-democratization, with the fear of revolution (rather
than its completed fact) being a sufficient spur to action. The key to this has been
the principle of legislative supremacy.[15] The final taming of royal power in
favour of parliamentary sovereignty that occurred in the 20 years that followed
the 'glorious revolution' of 1688 involved important new statutes, such as the
Bill of Rights Act 1688, the Act of Settlement 1700, and the Act of Union with
Scotland 1707, but no new way of transacting constitutional business, of the
type that had been tried briefly by Cromwell a generation before and was to
be adopted by the founders of the United States a century—and an Enlightenment—later. The representative idea had been inherent in the House of Commons since its emergence in medieval times, and during the nineteenth and
twentieth centuries, in a succession of statutes passed as a result of intense
popular pressure, Parliament managed to transform its lower house into a
representative assembly which both ushered in and was suited to the new democratic era. By 1928 it was right to categorize Britain's constitution as being based
on universal mass suffrage (though some plural voting did survive until 1948).

    The pre-democratic anachronism of the House of Lords lingered on in an
unreconstructed fashion long into the democratic era, albeit with its powers
pruned by the Parliament Acts passed in 1911 and 1949, and with a series of
non-legal conventions greatly diminishing its influence in practice. Its composition was further transformed in 1999, in a way that made it less undemocratic
than it had been but without challenging the lower house's claim to a superior
democratic legitimacy. The new Labour administration that was elected in 1997
tackled many constitutional and civil liberties issues in its first term, the reform
of the House of Lords among them, but it did so via the traditional route of
parliamentary enactment rather than through the establishment of a new constitution. Thus the Scotland, Northern Ireland, and Government of Wales Acts,
arranging for devolved government in these parts of the United Kingdom, the
Representation of the People Act 2000 (on, among other issues, the control of
election campaign financing) and the Freedom of Information Act 2000 may
indeed be seen as combining together to produce a basic UK constitution which
is more a 'written constitution' than it was before, and certainly more democratic. None of this alters the fact, however, that the nation's constitutional
process has not changed: it is as dynamic, fluid, and vigorous as ever, and
untrammelled by any requirement other than for the approval of the Parliament
of the day for any measures that might be proposed.[16]

---

[15] J Goldsworthy, *The Sovereignty of Parliament* (Oxford: Clarendon Press, 1999) is a very good
study.
[16] Subject of course to the constraints of international and EU law.

In such a system, it would be surprising if civil liberties were not at least occasionally the victims of parliamentary antagonism from time to time. The right to vote has been suspended in war-time, but it has always, so far, been restored as soon as circumstances have been judged to allow. The right of prisoners sentenced to more than a year in jail to sit in the Commons was hurriedly removed in 1981 when just such a person—the Irish Nationalist Bobby Sands—was returned by the constituents of two Northern Ireland counties while he was on hunger strike in the Maze prison (a protest from which he was subsequently to die).[17] The system of local taxation introduced in 1988—and immediately labelled a poll tax by its opponents—was perceived by some to be an indirect attack on the right to vote by appearing to identify those exposed to local taxation primarily by reference to the electoral register.[18] It has however been in the context of the protection of the civil liberties of expression, assembly and association that Parliament has, historically, been at its most cavalier. The political freedoms of particular persons and groups have been effectively suspended, particularly during war-time but also during periods of great internal conflict, such as occurred during the general strike in 1926 and in the depression years of the early 1930s.[19] The cold war of the post-war decades produced its own litany of illiberal parliamentary actions, as did the counter-terrorism crisis which overlapped with the end of the Cold War and which is still ongoing.[20] Laws like the Emergency Powers Act 1920 and the anti-terrorism legislation passed with disconcerting frequency since 1974 rather undermine Bernstein's assumption that democracy and justice are inextricably linked, particularly when the secondary legislation promulgated by reference to such measures and the exercise of official discretion under them is also taken into account.

This story of parliamentary excess, which is well known, has tempted many to turn to the judicial branch in search of civil libertarian consolation. Certainly the rhetoric of this part of state power has been supportive of civil liberties, with the Victorian father of contemporary English constitutional law erecting a large part of his theory of government around the principled excellence of the judiciary in this regard.[21] The empirical narrative tells a rather different story, however. The judiciary's hostility to Parliament in the seventeenth century, and its enthusiastic avowal of royal power, was one of the key factors underlying Parliament's assertion of its omnipotence in the aftermath of the 'glorious revolution'. When the courts finally reconciled themselves to the reality of parliamentary

---

[17] Representation of the People Act 1981.

[18] Local Government Finance Act 1988. The tax did not survive for long: see Local Government Finance Act 1992.

[19] See generally KD Ewing and CA Gearty, *The Struggle for Civil Liberties. Political Freedom and the Rule of Law in Britain, 1914–45* (Oxford: Oxford University Press, 2000).

[20] See generally KD Ewing and CA Gearty, *Freedom under Thatcher. Civil Liberties in Modern Britain* (Oxford: Clarendon Press, 1990).

[21] See AV Dicey, *Lectures Introductory to a Study of the Law of the Constitution* 2nd edn (London: Macmillan, 1885).

sovereignty, during the first half of the nineteenth century,[22] they found that they were wholly unprepared for the next phase in Parliament's development, namely democratization. Their hostility to a constitution rooted in the exercise of power by other than those who owned property was still capable of being spotted in the law reports as late as 1910,[23] and their antipathy to the entitlement of women to vote was manifest in their rejection of a series of sometimes quite cleverly constructed legal challenges that were launched in the late Victorian and Edwardian periods: it was apparently 'a principle of the unwritten constitutional law of the country that men only were entitled to take part in the election of representatives to Parliament'.[24]

Nor have the courts excelled at the protection of the liberties of expression, assembly and association in the face of the kind of legislative hostility to which I have already briefly referred. The story is a depressing one, altogether too long to recount here, with there being only a few dissents and not much more to show by way of a response to the endless cases legitimizing the exercise of state power in ways that were inimical (at times grievously so) to individual liberty.[25] Indeed the courts went even further, on many occasions plundering the common law for novel forms of state repression that not even the more reactionary of cabinet members had dared put before Parliament.[26] The process continued with depressing consistency throughout the democratic era, beginning with the first world war and working its way through the various crises of the twentieth century. Eventually the end of the Cold War in 1989 and the great alleviation in the level of subversive violence that occurred with the IRA ceasefire in 1994 provided some space for a realignment of judicial practice in line with the still frequently deployed language of civil liberties. For the first time, decisions such as in *Director of Public Prosecutions v Jones*[27] and *Redmond-Bate v DPP*[28] showed a judicial branch sensitive to the underlying importance of the exercise of civil liberties, in the context of association and assembly in the first case and assembly and expression in the second. The 1990s may come in retrospect to be seen as an Edwardian-style golden age, when freedom thrived in the gap between the end of the Cold War and the start of the new counter-terrorist world order that was inaugurated with the attack on the World Trade Centre and the Pentagon that occurred on 11 September 2001. It was in this liberal atmosphere,

---

[22] See eg *Edinburgh & Dalkeith Railway v Wauchope* (1842) 8 Cl and F 710, 8 ER 279. Goldsworthy, n 15 above, is the classic account.

[23] *Amalgamated Society of Railway Servants v Osborne* [1910] AC 87, esp the speech of Lord Shaw of Dunfermline.

[24] *Nairn v The University Court of the University of St Andrew*, 1907, 15 SLT 471, 473 *per* Lord McLaren. See subsequently *Nairn v The University Court of the University of St Andrews* [1909] AC 147. Earlier cases include *Chorlton v Lings* (1868) LR 4 CP 374 and *Chorlton v Kessler* (1868) LR 4 CP 397.

[25] See generally *The Struggle for Civil Liberties*, n 19 above.

[26] The classic examples are *Elias v Pasmore* [1934] 2 KB 164; *Thomas v Sawkins* [1935] 2 KB 249; and *Duncan v Jones* [1936] 1 KB 218.

[27] [1999] 2 AC 240.

[28] *The Times*, 28 July 1999.

and perhaps marking its highest point, that the Human Rights Act took full effect, on 2 October 2000.

C. Civil liberties and the European Convention on Human Rights[29]

I have already mentioned (in chapter two) the rights that are set out in the European Convention and it will now be apparent that there are clear overlaps between those rights and civil liberties as I have developed the term in this chapter. There is no doubt that respect for civil liberties is embedded in the European Convention, which we should not forget declares itself to be concerned with 'fundamental freedoms' as well as with 'human rights'. In the recitals to the document, which was agreed in Rome on 4 November 1950,[30] the signatories reaffirmed 'their profound belief in those fundamental freedoms which are the foundation of justice and peace in the world and are best maintained on the one hand by an effective political democracy and on the other by a common understanding and observance of the human rights upon which they depend'. Many of the substantive provisions of the Convention (and subsequent protocols) aimed at securing this 'effective political democracy' mirror the core civil liberties that we have been discussing. Under Article 3 of the first protocol to the Convention, agreed in Paris on 20 March 1952, the 'High Contracting Parties undertake to hold free elections at reasonable intervals by secret ballot, under conditions which will ensure the free expression of the opinion of the people in the choice of the legislature'. The basic essentials for a properly functioning democratic society are established in the body of the Convention itself, with Article 2 declaring that '[e]veryone's right to life shall be protected by law', Article 3 prohibiting in absolute terms 'torture' and 'inhuman or degrading treatment or punishment', and Article 4 forbidding 'slavery', 'servitude', and the performance of 'forced or compulsory labour'. The 'right to liberty and security' in Article 5 is necessarily more complex and qualified than the prohibitions that appear in Articles 2–4, but a clear consequence flowing from it is that persons cannot consistently with the Convention be held without trial, or with no expectation of a trial, on the basis of their political beliefs. Any trial that does occur must satisfy the procedural requirements of Article 6, which among other safeguards, guarantees defendants a 'fair and public hearing . . . by an independent and impartial tribunal established by law'.

Having ensured that there should be no drastic punishment lurking in the shadows of a seemingly free society, the Convention then goes on to consolidate its vision of an 'effective political democracy' with a series of guarantees dealing with the civil liberties of thought, conscience, and religion (Article 9), expression

[29] See generally A Mowbray, 'The Role of the European Court of Human Rights in the Protection of Democracy' [1999] *PL* 703; CA Gearty, 'Democracy and Human Rights in the European Court of Human Rights: A Critical Reappraisal' (2000) 51 *NILQ* 381.

[30] European Treaty Series, no 5.

(Article 10), and assembly and association (Article 11). These provisions are widely drawn and intended to complete the spectrum of rights which underpins the democratic state from the moment an idea is first hatched, through its articulation, translation into a political platform and thence, via the right to vote, into a legislative assembly where, if sufficient support is achieved, it can be translated into law. The closeness to our theoretical model of civil liberties, discussed earlier in this chapter, is marked, and it gets closer still. For, just as we saw in theory that the freedoms underpinned by civil liberties can be qualified by reference to democratic necessity, so we see that the Convention contemplates exactly such a possibility. The exceptions to and derogations from rights that I mentioned at the start of chapter two can now be seen in their proper context. Naturally, an 'effective political democracy' is not required to prove its worth by committing suicide, so '[i]n time of war or other public emergency threatening the life of the nation any High Contracting Party may take measures derogating from its obligations under this Convention to the extent strictly required by the exigencies of the situation, provided that such measures are not inconsistent with its other obligations under international law'[31] and provided also that torture, slavery, servitude, or retrospective punishments are not deployed.[32] The taking of life is also not permitted in any circumstances other than, significantly and again rightly from the point of view of principle, 'in respect of deaths resulting from lawful acts of war'.[33]

In the same vein is Article 17, prohibiting 'any State, group or person any right to engage in any activity or perform any act aimed at the destruction of any of the rights and freedoms set forth herein or at their limitation to a greater extent than is provided for in the Convention'. We also saw in chapter two that each of the freedoms of thought, conscience, religion, expression, assembly, and association set out in Articles 9–11 is subject to a variety of widely drawn exceptions which we should now especially note must all be 'in accordance with' or 'prescribed by' law and be 'necessary in a democratic society' for the realisation of the aim in question. The principle of legality is as I earlier mentioned a key part of civil liberties and one which I specifically address in the next chapter. The idea that a right, which is itself necessary in a democratic society (if it were not it would not be in the Convention in the first place) being restricted on the basis of an overriding and somehow deeper democratic necessity is contradictory only if the question is addressed solely as one of human rights. If we see these fundamental freedoms as civil liberties, we are guided to look at them not as individual rights standing alone but rather as the building blocks of a democratic society; on this basis we can recognize them as political freedoms rather than personal entitlements. Once understood like this, it becomes clear that they may on occasion have to yield to the greater good of the political community as a whole. Of course this focuses attention on the tricky questions of when such qualifications should be made and who should make them, but these are practical difficulties

---

[31] Art 15(1).   [32] Art 15(2).   [33] Ibid.

rather than principled objections. The problem of the partisan exercise of discretion is however explicitly addressed in Article 14, under which the 'enjoyment of the rights and freedoms set forth in this Convention' is guaranteed against 'discrimination on any ground such as sex, race, colour, language, religion, political or other opinion, national or social origin, association with a national minority, property, birth or other status'.

When I turn to the case law of the European Court of Human Rights I find a body of judges that has generally been profoundly alive to the deep civil libertarian roots in the charter that it is their responsibility to interpret. In its first judgment on the guarantee of free elections, the court described the Article as one which 'enshrines a characteristic principle of democracy' and therefore as 'of prime importance in the Convention system'.[34] Dismissing an argument that because the Article began with a reference to the obligations of the high contracting parties it could not therefore empower ordinary people in the way that other Convention rights did, the court described the construction of the article as derived from 'the desire to give greater solemnity to the commitment undertaken' and to 'the fact that the primary obligation in the field concerned is not one of abstention or non-interference, as with the majority of the civil and political rights, but one of adoption by the State of positive measures to "hold" democratic elections'.[35] The court noted that Article 3 'applies only to the election of the "legislature", or at least of one of its chambers if it has two or more' but remarked that the 'word "legislature" does not necessarily mean only the national parliament; it has to be interpreted in the light of the constitutional structure of the State in question'.[36] These words were to prove particularly prescient in light of the court's later holding, by 15 votes to two, that the inability of a British citizen resident in Gibraltar to vote in elections to the European Parliament involved a violation of Article 3 of the first protocol by the UK government.[37]

The court has been equally principled and robust in its defence of freedom of expression in the political sphere, an area in which it has had many more cases through which to develop its views. The leading case remains the 1986 decision in *Lingens v Austria*.[38] The applicant was the publisher of a magazine in Vienna which printed a couple of pieces critical of the then Austrian Chancellor and accusing him of protecting former members of the Nazi SS for political reasons and of aiding their participation in Austrian politics. At the private suit of the Chancellor, the publisher was convicted of criminal defamation, fined, and issues of his magazine were confiscated. The relevant law under the Austrian Criminal Code was extremely broad, covering '[a]nyone who in such a way that it may be perceived by a third person accuses another of possessing a contemptible

---

[34] *Mathieu-Mohin and Clerfayt v Belgium* (1987) 10 EHRR 1, para [47].
[35] Ibid para [50].
[36] Ibid para [53].
[37] *Matthews v United Kingdom* (1999) 28 EHRR 361.
[38] (1986) 8 EHRR 407.

character or attitude or of behaviour contrary to honour or morality and of such a nature as to make him contemptible or otherwise lower him in public esteem.'[39] There were more severe punishments if the defamation was printed or broadcast and, though there was a defence where truth could be proved, the nature of the crime made this very difficult in most circumstances. In unanimously condemning as a breach of Article 10 of the Convention the intimidatory action launched by the Chancellor, the court laid down some important general principles which have acted as its key benchmarks in subsequent cases:

[t]he Court has to recall that freedom of expression, as secured in paragraph 1 of Article 10, constitutes one of the essential foundations of a democratic society and one of the basic conditions for its progress and for each individual's self-fulfilment. Subject to paragraph 2, it is applicable not only to 'information' or 'ideas' that are favourably received or regarded as inoffensive or as a matter of indifference, but also to those that offend, shock or disturb. Such are the demands of that pluralism, tolerance and broadmindedness without which there is no 'democratic society.' These principles are of particular importance as far as the press is concerned. Whilst the press must not overstep the bounds set, *inter alia*, for the 'protection of the reputation of others', it is nevertheless incumbent on it to impart information and ideas on political issues just as on those in other areas of public interest. Not only does the press have the task of imparting such information and ideas: the public also has a right to receive them. ...

Freedom of the press furthermore affords the public one of the best means of discovering and forming an opinion of the ideas and attitudes of political leaders. More generally, freedom of political debate is at the very core of the concept of a democratic society which prevails throughout the Convention.

The limits of acceptable criticism are accordingly wider as regards a politician as such than as regards a private individual. Unlike the latter, the former inevitably and knowingly lays himself open to close scrutiny of his every word and deed by both journalists and the public at large, and he must consequently display a greater degree of tolerance.[40]

This is the European Court of Human Rights at its most principled, and therefore most fearless. The case law which has followed in the years since the *Lingens* case bears testimony to the robustness of the court's conception of political liberty.[41] One case, *Jersild v Denmark*,[42] is of particular interest from a theoretical perspective. The applicant was a journalist working for the Danish Broadcasting Corporation. He made a programme which featured a group of self-avowedly racist youths, who were living in the Copenhagen area. During the interview with them that was broadcast, the youths made several derogatory and racist remarks about black people in general and immigrant workers in particular. Under the Danish Penal Code, racially insulting remarks were prohibited by law, and the public prosecutor subsequently instituted proceedings against both the three youths and the applicant, together with his head of department, for having aided and abetted the making of the remarks. All five were convicted

---

[39] See the Austrian Criminal Code, Art 111.   [40] n 38 above, paras [41]–[42].
[41] See esp *Castells v Spain* (1992) 14 EHRR 445.   [42] (1994) 19 EHRR 1.

before the local courts. The applicant and his boss appealed to the Danish Supreme Court where however their convictions were upheld. The applicant then took his case to Strasbourg.

The European Court of Human Rights held by 12 votes to seven that the applicant had been a victim of the violation of his article 10 rights. While recognizing 'the vital importance of combating racial discrimination in all its forms and manifestations'[43] the majority nevertheless saw the case as one primarily concerned with press freedom. 'Although formulated primarily with regard to the print media,' the principles the court had developed in earlier cases 'doubtless appl[ied] also to the audio-visual media.'[44] Having regard therefore to the particular nature of the medium before it, and taken as a whole, 'the feature could not objectively have appeared to have as its purpose the propagation of racist views and ideas'.[45] The item 'was broadcast as a part of a serious Danish news programme and was intended for a well-informed audience' and did not require a counter-balancing point of view to that of the youths within the programme itself, particularly when 'the natural limitations on spelling out such elements in a short item within a longer programme' were taken into account.[46] The *Jersild* decision is rightly celebrated for the depth and maturity of its commitment to media freedom. Its civil libertarian roots are evident not only in its ringing endorsement of the role of the broadcasting media in our political culture, but also in its recognition that speech of this nature has limits. The court had 'no doubt that the remarks in respect of which the [youths] were convicted were more than insulting to members of the targeted groups and did not enjoy the protection of Article 10'.[47] The freedom of expression protected by Article 10 was qualified by its underlying role in a liberal democratic state, and the unfocused apolitical stirring up of hatred could not hide under its tolerant umbrella.

The civil liberties guaranteed in Article 11 of the Convention have tended to be overshadowed by the breadth the court has accorded to Article 10. Thus in *Steel and others v United Kingdom*,[48] a case involving a number of persons who were involved in political 'direct action' of various sorts, the issues before the court were analysed as raising a series of Article 10 freedom of expression points rather than the right to assembly under Article 11. Of the three kinds of action before the court, however, the conduct that came closest to the peaceful communication of political views was the type that secured the court's sympathy and ultimately a favourable ruling. These were the three applicants who had been arrested for handing out leaflets outside a conference devoted to the sale of fighter helicopters. The protest had been 'entirely peaceful' with there having been no significant obstruction or attempt to obstruct those attending the conference or to take any other kind of

---

[43] Ibid para [30].   [44] Ibid para [31].   [45] Ibid para [33].   [46] Ibid para [34].

[47] Ibid para [35], citing earlier Commission decisions in *Glimmerveen and Hagenbeek v The Netherlands* (1979) 18 DR 187 and *Künen v Germany* (reported as *X v Federal Republic of Germany*) (1982) 29 DR 194.

[48] (1998) 28 EHRR 603.

action that might have provoked the attendees to violence.[49] The court was unanimous that their arrest had infringed their Article 10 rights.[50] The remaining two applicants were not so lucky; their noisy and intrusive protests (obstructing a grouse shoot and breaking into motorway construction sites) had not been without any risk of disorder and had interfered markedly with the rights of others, and the court accordingly found against them. The Strasbourg judges seem to have got the civil libertarian balance right; the more the communication of political ideas is achieved through conduct rather than words, then the greater the interest of the state in controlling that expression is bound to be. Where the action is not peaceful, the chances are that it is not protected by Article 10 (or 11). The court is not saying that there is no (moral) right to engage in disruptive direct action, merely that there is no civil liberty to do so if the price a democracy must pay for such tolerance is legal anarchy.

Where Article 11 undoubtedly comes into its own as a discrete civil libertarian protection is in relation to its guarantee of freedom of association. This is a civil liberty that analytically is more clearly distinct from freedom of expression than is freedom of assembly. Its importance lies in its protection of one of the key attributes of a healthy democratic culture, the political party. The point has become important recently in relation to Turkey, where the attempt to ban domestic political organizations opposed to the government brought the country before the European Court of Human Rights twice in 1998. The first and most important of these cases was *United Communist Party of Turkey and others v Turkey*.[51] The Turkish Constitutional Court had by order dissolved the Communist Party and transferred its assets to the Treasury, with the founders and managers of the party being banned from holding like offices in any other political body. In Strasbourg, the government argued that it was faced with 'a challenge to the fundamental interests of the national community, such as national security and territorial integrity'[52] and that this justified the action it had taken, which it admitted was draconian.

The court was unanimous in its disagreement. The safeguards set out in Articles 10 and 11 applied 'all the more in relation to political parties in view of their essential role in ensuring pluralism and the proper functioning of democracy'.[53] Furthermore, '[t]he fact that their activities form part of a collective exercise of freedom of expression in itself entitles political parties to seek the protection of Articles 10 and 11 of the Convention.'[54] The free expression of opinion implicit in the guarantee of the right to vote in Article 3 of the first protocol would be 'inconceivable without the participation of a plurality of political parties representing the different shades of opinion to be found within a country's population'.[55] It followed that 'only convincing and compelling reasons'[56] could justify restrictions on a party's freedom of association, none

---

[49] (1998) 28 EHRR 603, para [64].   [50] Ibid para [110]. Art 5 was also infringed: see para [64].
[51] (1998) 26 EHRR 121. See also *Socialist Party and others v Turkey* (1998) 27 EHRR 51. See generally M Koçak and E Örücü, 'Dissolution of Political Parties in the Name of Democracy: Cases from Turkey and the European Court of Human Rights' (2003) 9 *European Public Law* 399.
[52] *United Communist Party v Turkey* ibid para [49].   [53] Ibid para [43].   [54] Ibid.
[55] Ibid para [44].   [56] Ibid para [46].

of which could be found in this case. This did not mean that 'the authorities of a State in which an association, through its activities, jeopardises that State's institutions' were not entitled to fight back: 'some compromise between the requirements of defending democratic society and individual rights is inherent in the system of the Convention'.[57] But in this case the ban on the party had been so immediate that no pattern of subversive action could be pointed to.[58]

The European Court of Human Rights has not always got the application of its principles right in these political speech and association cases. During the Cold War period, for example, the European Commission had not found objectionable under the Convention a ban on the German Communist Party. Relying on Article 17, which as we have seen prohibits the abuse of rights, the Commission concluded that the aim of the party was to establish a socialist-communist system by means of a proletarian revolution and the dictatorship of the proletariat and that even if the party could now be shown to be trying to seize power only through constitutional methods, it did not follow from this that it had denounced its basic revolutionary principles.[59] A couple of cases in the 1980s upheld Germany's controversial prohibition on the employment of extremists in the civil service.[60] Britain's and Ireland's media restrictions on members of a lawful political party, Sinn Féin, were likewise found to pass muster at around the same time.[61] In vain did the Turkish lawyers seek to catch the court's eye with some of these embarrassing skeletons from the Convention's past. A narrow reading of Article 10 led the court to its conservative decision in *Appleby v United Kingdom*,[62] restricting speech rights in a shopping mall owned by a private company. A different kind of error from the perspective of principle can be seen in *Bowman v United Kingdom*,[63] where restrictions on the funding of political campaigns designed to prevent the well-resourced securing an undue advantage at election time were analysed in very narrow terms by the court, in a way which seemed not to appreciate the importance of the principle of political equality.[64] Viewed overall however the record of the court in the sphere of political freedom is not a bad one. The court appreciates that civil liberties are at the core of the Convention and has sought to assert them in a principled and coherent manner.

D. Civil Liberties and the Human Rights Act

The largest claim that the Human Rights Act can make for the attention of civil libertarians is in its determined protection of the principle of parliamentary

---

[57] Ibid para [32].   [58] Ibid para [58].

[59] *German Communist Party v Federal Republic of Germany*, app 250/57 (1957) 1 *Yearbook of the European Convention on Human Rights* 222.

[60] *Glasenapp v Germany* (1986) 9 EHRR 25; *Kosiek v Germany* (1986) 9 EHRR 328. See now *Vogt v Germany* (1995) 21 EHRR 205.

[61] *Brind v United Kingdom* (1994) 18 EHRR CD 76; *Purcell v Ireland* (1991) 70 DR 262.

[62] (2003) 37 EHRR 783.

[63] (1998) 26 EHRR 1.   [64] See Gearty, n 29 above.

supremacy.[65] It may be that here the emphasis of the civil libertarian differs from that of the human rights enthusiast. Whether or not this is in fact the case, from the point of view of theory, and in particular from the perspective of the kind of political philosophy that I outlined in chapter two, it is surely clear that there would be little point in the protection of the right to vote, and of such freedoms as those of assembly, association, and expression, if the political community in which these entitlements were exercised was one in which the ultimate decisions were not taken by the representatives of the people but by an elite guardianship of unelected officers: there is more to the exercise of civil liberties than the right to make irrelevant political noise. Here we should recall the critique of writers like Ewing and Tushnet whom we discussed in chapter two, and remind ourselves of the need I then identified to meet their objections to untrammelled judicial supremacy. The Human Rights Act does rise to this challenge, in a unique and a sophisticated manner. I have already mentioned in general terms in chapter two the way in which the Human Rights Act preserves parliamentary sovereignty. It is now necessary to explore this point further and to show how this protection of parliamentary sovereignty represents an assertion of civil libertarian principle in its highest form.

The key interpretive power is, as we have seen, set out in s 3(1), to the effect that '[s]o far as it is possible to do so, primary legislation and subordinate legislation must be read and given effect in a way which is compatible with the Convention rights.' This is subject to further exposition in the three paragraphs to be found in s 3(2). The first of these, subsection 2(a), is expansionist in that it declares the section to apply 'to primary legislation and subordinate legislation whenever enacted'. But paragraphs (b) and (c) are quite different in style:

This section—

(b) does not affect the validity, continuing operation or enforcement of any incompatible primary legislation; and

(c) does not affect the validity, continuing operation or enforcement of any incompatible subordinate legislation if (disregarding any possibility of revocation) primary legislation prevents removal of the incompatibility.

The other key provision in the Act, s 6, is qualified in the same way. While subsection (1) declares it to be 'unlawful for a public authority to act in a way which is incompatible with a Convention right', subsection (2) goes on to disapply this subsection if:

(a) as a result of one or more provisions of primary legislation, the authority could not have acted differently; or

(b) in the case of one or more provisions of, or made under, primary legislation which cannot be read or given effect in a way which is compatible with the Convention rights, the authority was acting so as to give effect to or enforce those provisions.

---

[65] For an interesting analysis of the inter-relationship between the legislative process and human rights, see D Feldman, 'Parliamentary Scrutiny of Legislation and Human Rights' [2002] *PL* 323.

In the same vein is subsection (6) which expands the notion of an 'act' in subsection (1) to include a failure to act while at the same time specifically excluding 'a failure to—(a) introduce in, or lay before, Parliament a proposal for legislation; or (b) make any primary legislation or remedial order'. Where a high level court[66] finds 'that a provision is incompatible with a Convention right, it may make a declaration of that incompatibility'[67] but such a ruling 'does not affect the validity, continuing operation or enforcement of the provision in respect of which it is given'[68] and furthermore is specifically stated not to be 'binding on the parties to the proceedings in which it is made'.[69]

The construction of the Human Rights Act in relation to its effect on statutory provisions is both complex and at the same time fundamental to the Act's underlying intention to respect civil liberties and thereby to reconcile legislative sovereignty with the language of human rights. The parliamentary debates show a legislature that was very much alive to the need to preserve its sovereign power and they also reveal an executive that was keen to provide the necessary assurances. At the outset of the Bill's passage through the Lords, where it began its journey into law, the person primarily identified with the measure, the then Lord Chancellor Lord Irving of Lairg, assured peers that its purpose was to maximize 'the protection of human rights' but only insofar as this could be done 'without trespassing on parliamentary sovereignty'.[70] The then Home Secretary Jack Straw was even more emphatic in the Commons, promising the House that the Act contained no explicit or implicit assault on its sovereign power.[71] One of the main areas of debate in Parliament concerned what should happen where a declaration of incompatibility was issued by a court. Initially the Bill had provided the executive with a wide discretion as to how to respond but in its final version the Act permits a Minister 'by order [to] make such amendments to the legislation as he considers necessary to remove the incompatibility' only where he or she 'considers that there are compelling reasons for proceeding' in this way.[72] Even then Parliament was alive to the possibility of abuse and insisted on a fairly elaborate procedure for the involvement of both Houses in the promulgation of such orders.[73] But clearly Parliament wanted the routine response to declarations of incompatibility (if there was to be a response) to be by way of primary enactment rather than executive rule-making.

---

[66] The courts that fall within this description are set out in s 4(5) and include the House of Lords, the Court of Appeal and the High Court. This does not include the EAT: *Whittaker v P and D Watson and M Watson*, Employment Appeal Tribunal, 7 February 2002.

[67] s 4(2). The same sort of declaration can also be made in relation to incompatible subordinate legislation the content of which is required by its parent Act: see s 4(4).

[68] s 4(6)(a).

[69] s 4(6)(b). For the minister's power where it is subordinate legislation that has attracted the declaration of incompatibility, see s 10(3).

[70] H L Debs, 3 November 1997, col 1229.

[71] See eg H C Debs, 16 February 1998, cols 771–772.

[72] s 10(2).

[73] See generally Sch 2.

None of this is the conduct of a legislature that has given up the sovereign ghost. Nor is it the action of a body that does not expect declarations of incompatibility to be issued. The frequency of such declarations depends on the ambit of s 3. The more Convention-compatible interpretations of legislation that are deemed to be 'possible' under subsection (1), the less recourse there needs to be to s 4. On the other hand, the less such interpretations are found to be 'possible', the more reliance needs to be placed on the incompatibility procedure. The wider the range of the possible, the more the judges control the process; the narrower the magic the word can work, the more there will be left for Parliament and the executive to do. This is the outer frontier of the Human Rights Act at which the legislative and judicial powers jostle for supremacy. Unfortunately Parliament did not provide in its proceedings any very exact guidance as to what 'possible' should mean, and the Act is also lacking in this regard. The most important input was that of the Lord Chancellor who was clear that the term was wider than both 'probable' and 'reasonably possible'.[74] In the leading cases since the Act came into force, the judges have been feeling their way to some kind of principled position, where traditional statutory interpretation is permitted under s 3(1) but 'judicial legislation' is not.

A very helpful early exploration of how best to approach s 3 is to be found in Lord Woolf CJ's judgment for the Court of Appeal in *Poplar Housing and Regeneration Community Association Ltd v Donoghue*.[75] The substantive ruling in the case is highly controversial and we will need to return to it in a later chapter but it does not concern us now. As far as s 3 is concerned, Lord Woolf observes that 'unless the legislation would otherwise be in breach of the Convention section 3 can be ignored (so courts should always first ascertain whether, absent section 3, there would be any breach of the convention)'.[76] Then, '[i]f the court has to rely on section 3 it should limit the extent of the modified meaning to that which is necessary to achieve compatibility.'[77] This is the context in which it is not question-begging to say that 'section 3 does not entitle the court to *legislate* (its task is still one of *interpretation*, but interpretation in accordance with the direction contained in section 3)'.[78] Then, finally for present purposes, '[t]he views of the parties and of the Crown as to whether a "constructive" interpretation should be adopted cannot modify the task of the court (if section 3 applies the court is required to adopt the section 3 approach to interpretation).'[79] Lord Woolf modestly regards these points as 'probably self-evident'[80] but the obvious often needs to be spelt out, and the great virtue of his analysis is that it makes the starting point clear. A judge (and indeed for that

---

[74] H L Debs, 18 November 1997, col 535.
[75] *Poplar Housing and Regeneration Community Association Ltd v Donoghue* [2001] EWCA Civ 595, [2002] QB 48.
[76] Ibid para [75(a)].
[77] Ibid para [75(b)].
[78] Ibid para [75(c)]. Emphasis in the original.
[79] Ibid para [75(d)].
[80] Ibid para [75].

matter any legal adviser) needs to form a preliminary view as to the compatibility with the Convention of the provision under scrutiny *before* s 3 is brought into play. This is not a compatibility/incompatibility of the type referred to in s 3(1) since the section is concerned with a compatibility/incompatibility that is subsequent to its operation on the provision in question. Lord Woolf must therefore be referring to some kind of presumptive or provisional incompatibility: only where the measure throws up such an apparent incompatibility is s 3 brought in to work its interpretive tricks.

Under Lord Woolf's scheme, the judge must first identify a provisional incompatibility in a statutory provision. He or she should then ask whether it is 'possible' for the provision to 'read and given effect' in a way which is compatible with the Convention rights. One approach to what is 'possible' would be to adopt a very broad, human rights oriented perspective, to the point of requiring an explicit statement from Parliament to the opposite effect before the possibility of some Convention-compatible position is discountenanced in favour of an incompatible meaning.[81] The influence of European Union law, with its externally guaranteed supremacy, is evident in the views of those who take this position: Parliament is subjugated to one European legal order (subject to express repeal); why should it not be subjugated to another on the same terms? The distinguished law lord Lord Steyn came close to this position in a couple of important cases during the summer of 2001.[82] His view is best expressed in the following extract from the first of those cases, *R v A*:

[T]he interpretative obligation under section 3 of the 1998 Act is a strong one. It applies even if there is no ambiguity in the language in the sense of the language being capable of two different meanings... Parliament specifically rejected the legislative model of requiring a reasonable interpretation. Section 3 places a duty on the court to strive to find a possible interpretation compatible with Convention rights.... Section 3 .... requires a court to find an interpretation compatible with Convention rights if it is possible to do so.... In accordance with the will of Parliament as reflected in section 3 it will sometimes be necessary to adopt an interpretation which linguistically may appear strained. The techniques to be used will not only involve the reading down of express language in a statute but also the implication of provisions. A declaration of incompatibility is a measure of last resort. It must be avoided unless it is plainly impossible to do so. If a *clear* limitation on Convention rights is stated *in terms*, such an impossibility will arise.[83]

---

[81] What follows is roughly based on CA Gearty, 'Reconciling Parliamentary Democracy and Human Rights' (2002) 118 *LQR* 248. For an energetic critique based on the opinion that I have fundamentally contradicted myself in that article, see G Phillipson '(Mis)-reading Section 3 of the Human Rights Act' (2003) 119 *LQR* 183, and for my reply see, 'Revisiting Section 3(1) of the Human Rights Act' (2003) 119 *LQR* 551. For a different view altogether, see G Marshall, 'The Lynchpin of Parliamentary Intention: Lost, Stolen or Strained' [2003] *PL* 236. Compare R Clayton, 'The Links of What's "Possible": Statutory Construction under the Human Rights Act' [2002] *EHRLR* 559.

[82] *R v A (No 2)* [2001] UKHL 25, [2002] 1 AC 45; *R v Lambert* [2002] UKHL 37, [2002] 2 AC 545.

[83] *R v A* ibid para [44] citing remarks of Lord Hoffmann in *R (Simms) v Secretary of State for the Home Department* [2000] 2 AC 115 (emphasis in the original). To similar effect is *R v Lambert* ibid para [42]. Given the importance of his dicta in this area, also of interest is Lord Steyn, 'Democracy through Law', the 2002 Robin Cooke Lecture, 18 September 2002. (Copy with author.)

Lord Steyn seems to be suggesting in the last sentence quoted here that only where such an express disclaimer is to be found would s 3(1) fail in its interpretive task and a declaration of incompatibility therefore become necessary. The difficulty with this approach, however, is that it is not what Parliament intended when it passed the Human Rights Act; nor is it what the wording of the Act suggests. Had it been, there would have been no need for the elaborate incompatibility process; everything would have been vulnerable to judicial override unless it were expressly said to be immune from review. There are plenty of constitutional and statutory models available which would, suitably adapted, have captured the essence of such an approach—the Canadian, the South Africa, even the Scotland and Northern Ireland Acts in relation to their legislatures' (admittedly) subordinate legislation—but Parliament chose to rely on none of them. The European Communities Act 1972 lay on the shelf waiting to be used as a precedent but it too was ignored.

Instead the legislature chose the model that it did, precisely because it wanted to protect the actions of the representative assembly from judicial condemnation not only in situations where Parliament consciously chose to 'flout' the Human Rights Act but also where there was no possible way in which Parliament's legislative actions could be rendered compatible with that Act. The second limb of this just-stated qualification on judicial power is in many ways more important to the integrity of the measure than the first; without it, the balance of the Act would have been tipped altogether too much in the direction of human rights/judicial power. It would be quite wrong for the judges now to rewrite the measure to achieve a degree of power which Parliament consciously and quite deliberately withheld from them. Even at the time that he was tentatively outlining his robust approach, Lord Steyn was not in an obviously mainstream position so far as his colleagues on the appellate committee were concerned, with Lord Hope of Craighead in particular asserting that legislation would be unimpugnable even in the absence of an express disclaimer of human rights if the process of s 3 reconciliation involved 'by necessary implication' a contradiction of the meaning of the words under scrutiny, at least insofar as that meaning reflected 'the plain intention of parliament'.[84] In subsequent cases in the House of Lords, Lord Hope's perspective on the appropriate interpretive approach has predominated.[85] In *Re S*, Lord Nicholls of Birkenhead commented, in a speech with which all his colleagues agreed,[86] that Lord Steyn's observations in *R v A (No 2)* were 'not to be read as meaning that a clear limitation on Convention rights in terms is the only circumstance in which an interpretation incompatible with Convention rights may arise'.[87] It is not wholly surprising, therefore, that in

---

[84] *R v A (No 2)*, n 82 above, para [108]. None of the other of their lordships in this case made their position on the point as clear as either Lord Hope or Lord Steyn.

[85] *Re S (Minors) (Care Order: Implementation of Care Plan); Re W (Minors) (Care Order: Adequacy of Care Plan)* [2002] UKHL 10, [2002] 2 AC 291; *R (Anderson) v Secretary of State for the Home Department* [2002] UKHL 46, [2003] 1 AC 837.

[86] Lords Mackay of Clashfern, Browne-Wilkinson, Mustill, and Hutton.

[87] n 85 above, para [40].

the most recent House of Lords decision on the breadth of s 3, Lord Steyn has fallen back into line with his colleagues on the point.[88]

This still leaves open the question of how far to push the boundaries of the possible under s 3(1). A possible answer might be to weave s 3(2) into Lord Woolf's step-by-step approach. Let us say that a judge has spotted an apparent incompatibility with the Convention in a statutory provision before him or her. In assessing the limits of the possible, the judge would then look not at s 3(1) in isolation but together with s 3(2)(b)'s prohibition on that subsection affecting 'the validity, continuing operation or enforcement of any incompatible primary legislation'. Subsection 3(2)(b) would then function as a guide, but not a conclusive guide, to how far the possible in s 3(1) would be permitted to go. On this basis one could say that s 3(1) should be able to operate creatively upon a provision, but only until such a time as a proposed reading would have the effect of so impairing the operation and/or effectiveness of the clause under scrutiny as to render it for all practical purposes a dead letter, or close to a dead letter. The impact on a provision's 'continuing operation' or 'enforcement' of a s 3(1) reinterpretation would need to be much more than merely slight to engage the saving clause in subsection 2(b) but it should in principle take much less than a total stifling of an Act's purpose under the weight of s 3(1) before the proviso in s 3(2)(b) is permitted to come riding to the rescue. The section is not well drafted on this key point: better from the perspective of this approach would have been something along the lines of the following: 'An interpretation of a provision (whether of primary or subordinate legislation) which substantially impairs its continuing operation or enforcement is not a possible interpretation for the purposes of s 3(1).'

This approach surely has much to commend it. The issue ultimately resolves itself into a matter of balance: s 3(1) is given some life, but its sibling opposite in subsection 3(2)(b) then ensures that the limits of possibility envisaged in s 3(1) are properly delimited. The plain words of the provision under scrutiny, the mischief at which it is aimed, the necessity of particular forms of interpretation to the achievement of its statutory goals, and Parliament's intent in acting as it did will all be quite proper considerations for the court to take into account when balancing their power of interpretation in s 3(1) against the limits on that power imposed by s 3(2)(b). If we turn to the case law we find some recent support for an approach among the senior judiciary which if it does not expressly root itself in s 3(2) nevertheless echoes the underlying rationale for reliance on it. Lord Hoffman has referred generally to the need to reconcile human rights and democracy.[89] Lord Bingham likewise has expressed the view that '[j]udicial recognition and assertion of the human rights defined in the Convention is not a substitute for the processes of democratic government but a complement to

---

[88] *R (Anderson) v Secretary of State for the Home Department*, n 85 above, para [59]. See also Lord Bingham at para [30] and Lord Hutton at para [81].
[89] See in particular his remarks in *R (Alconbury Developments Ltd) v Secretary of State for the Environment, Transport and the Regions* [2001] UKHL 23, [2003] 2 AC 295, paras [69]–[70].

them'.[90] The most sophisticated attempt at clear exposition attempted so far has been by Lord Nicholls of Birkenhead in *Re S*[91] where he observed that:

a meaning which departs substantially from a fundamental feature of an Act of Parliament is likely to have crossed the boundary between interpretation and amendment. This is especially so where the departure has important practical repercussions which the court is not equipped to evaluate. In such a case the overall contextual setting may leave no scope for rendering the statutory provision Convention compliant by legitimate use of the process of interpretation.[92]

This is not that far from the second position outlined here. That approach has the merit of concretizing these general judicial statements in the actual words to be found in the Human Rights Act, surely an essential project for anyone seriously concerned with mapping the boundaries between the legislative and judicial branches in a system which still explicitly upholds the primacy of Parliament. The integrity of the Human Rights Act depends on s 3 being properly interpreted by the senior judges. And far from being frightened by the principle of parliamentary sovereignty, the judges should see it as an important complement to that of civil liberties and the two concepts together as vital pieces in the legalistic jigsaw that is the Human Rights Act.

E. Applying the principle of civil liberties under the Human Rights Act

Thus far we have been concerned with the large and important question of the extent to which the Human Rights Act is itself constructed so as to guarantee the ongoing primacy of the most important civil liberty of all, the right fully to participate in a properly functioning democracy. As we noted at the conclusion of the last section, rather than abuse the concept of legislative supremacy, as many lawyers are wont to do, it should be celebrated as the realization of civil liberties in its highest form. In saying this however we have to recognize that Parliament does not itself necessarily protect civil liberties, and that it can deploy the concept of legislative supremacy in a way which diminishes rather than supports the civil liberties of the whole community. We have already discussed the extensive historical evidence supportive of this dismal observation. It is clear from our perspective a century on that Bernstein was being ridiculously idealistic when he said that 'the idea of the oppression of the individual by the majority'

---

[90] *Brown v Stott* [2001] 2 WLR 817, 834–835.

[91] n 85 above. Also very illuminating are two judgments by Moses J: *R (Hooper and others) v Secretary of State for Works and Pensions* [2002] EWHC 191 (Admin), paras [157]–[161] and (on s 6(2)(b)) paras [169]–[185]; *R (Wilkinson) v Commissioners of Inland Revenue* [2002] EWHC 182 (Admin), paras [34]–[49]. For the somewhat different approach of the Court of Appeal in each case see *R (Hooper, Withey, Naylor and Martin) v Secretary of State for Works and Pensions* [2003] EWCA Civ 813, [2003] 1 WLR 2623 and *R (Wilkinson) v Commissioners of Inland Revenue* [2003] EWCA Civ 814, [2003] 1 WLR 2683.

[92] Ibid para [40]. To similar effect is *R (Anderson) v Secretary of State for the Home Department*, n 85 above.

was 'absolutely repugnant to the modern mind' and that the 'more democracy prevails and determines public opinion, the more it will come to mean the greatest possible degree of freedom for all'.[93] As we noted earlier in this chapter, there is manifestly a potential problem of abuse in equipping a representative assembly with full power both to determine how its membership should be composed and how extensively civil liberties such as expression, assembly, and association should be permitted to be truncated. This is such a large issue that as I earlier indicated it will be necessary to return to it, which I will do in the concluding chapter. This chapter has shown that the European Court of Human Rights has been alive to the problem and has intervened where it has thought it appropriate in relation to legislative, executive, and sometimes judicial acts of member states. Clearly there is a similar role for the domestic courts in relation to legislative and executive acts under the Human Rights Act.

As far as the substance of the measure itself is concerned, Parliament felt sufficiently exercised about the importance of freedom of expression to an effective representative democracy to decide to devote a specific section of the Human Rights Act to its protection. Under s 12(3) a court considering the granting of relief which might affect the exercise of the freedom of expression of a person who is neither present nor represented shall not grant the remedy sought 'unless the court is satisfied that the applicant is likely to establish that publication should not be allowed'.[94] In *Attorney General v Punch Limited*[95], Article 10 and s 12(3) of the Act formed the background to a decision which considered the operation of the common law of contempt in light of the case law that had grown up during the litigious frenzy generated by the *Spycatcher* book during the late 1980s.[96] A later Court of Appeal decision has many interesting observations on the operation of the section in the context of the prior restraint of publications.[97] However on the key question of principle, the case law on Articles 10 and 11 has not so far revealed a sea-change in judicial attitudes to civil liberties. In *Percy v Director of Public Prosecutions*,[98] a conviction under public order law for defacing the US flag was set aside because it amounted to an inappropriate interference with political speech. In *Westminster City Council v Haw*,[99] a long-time protestor against British government policy towards Iraq was able to use Article 10 successfully to resist an injunction based on obstruction of the highway, in this case Parliament Square. But set against these early

---

[93] Bernstein, n 10 above, 141. See further CA Gearty, 'Civil Liberties and Human Rights' in P Leyland and N Bamforth, (eds), *Public Law in a Multi-Layer Constitution* (Oxford: Hart Publishing, 2003), ch 14 .

[94] On which see *Douglas v Hello! Ltd* [2001] QB 967.

[95] [2002] UKHL 50, [2003] 1 AC 1046. See further *Jockey Club v Buffham* [2002] EWHC 1866 (QB), [2003] QB 462.

[96] See particularly *Attorney General v Newspaper Publishing plc* [1988] Ch 33.

[97] *Cream Holdings Ltd v Banerjee* [2003] EWCA Civ 103, [2003] 3 WLR 999.

[98] [2001] EWHC 1125 (Admin). Cf *Norwood v Director of Public Prosecutions* [2003] EWHC 1564 (Admin) in which the display of a racially offensive poster was found to be unprotected by Art 10.

[99] [2002] All ER (D) 59, 4 October 2002, Gray J.

decisions of a couple of lower courts must now be placed the disappointing House of Lords decision in *R (ProLife Alliance) v BBC*.[100]

The claimant desired to transmit a party political broadcast comprising a video containing graphic footage of an actual abortion, including clear images of aborted foetuses. The organization taking the case was a registered political party opposed to abortion and was fielding a sufficiently large number of candidates in the forthcoming general election to be entitled to a party political broadcast. Despite this, and acting on behalf of all terrestrial broadcasters, the BBC refused transmission of the video on the grounds of taste and decency.[101] Overturning an earlier decision by Scott Baker J, the Court of Appeal insisted that the video should have been broadcast. Extensive reliance was placed on the Article 10 jurisprudence of the Strasbourg court, with the new atmosphere ushered in by the Human Rights Act being well captured in the first sentence of the leading judgment, by Lord Justice Laws: 'This case is about the censorship of political speech.'[102] To his lordship, it was 'difficult to think of a context in which the claims of free speech [were] more pressing'.[103] Disappointingly, when the case came before it, the House of Lords took a much narrower line. In overturning the court below, their lordships stressed the presumptive competence of the broadcasting authorities and in doing so paid much less attention than had the Court of Appeal to the underlying issues of principle involved. Decided on a narrow basis after a concession by the claimants that the statutory framework itself was not under attack, the Lords' ruling was a missed opportunity, at least as far as developing and deepening the Human Rights Act's concern for civil liberties was concerned.

As in other fields of law, the courts have been anxious to connect the new legislation with the common law culture into which it has been inserted. In *Ashworth Hospital Authority v MGN*,[104] a spirited attempt to use Article 10 greatly to expand the protection for journalistic sources provided by the Contempt of Court Act 1981, s 10 was firmly rebuffed, with the Master of the Rolls Lord Phillips asserting that the Convention 'should not, in practice, result in [the] court applying a different approach to that which' was applied under the pre-1998 Act law.[105] This kind of thinking lies behind another of the leading

---

[100] [2002] EWCA Civ 297, [2002] 3 WLR 1080; and in the Lords [2003] UKHL 23, [2003] 2 WLR 1403 (Lord Scott dissenting). See A Scott, '"A Monstrous and Unjustifiable Infringement?" Political Expression and the Broadcasting Ban on Advocacy Advertising' (2003) 66 *MLR* 224.

[101] Relying on the Broadcasting Act 1990, s 6(1).

[102] n 100 above, para [1].

[103] Ibid. See A Geddis, 'What Future for Political Advertising on the United Kingdom's Television Screens?' [2002] *PL* 615. For a less enthusiastic Court of Appeal decision, albeit in the immigration field, see *R (Farrakhan) v Secretary of State for the Home Department* [2002] EWCA Civ 606, [2002] 2 QB 1391. Another disappointing decision, albeit with a national security dimension that may explain it, is *R (O'Driscoll) v Secretary for State for the Home Department and the Metropolitan Police Commissioner* [2002] EWHC 2477 (Admin).

[104] [2001] 1 WLR 515 (CA), [2002] UKHL 29, [2002] 1 WLR 2033 (HL).

[105] Ibid para [71]. The House of Lords took a similar approach: see in particular Lord Woolf CJ at paras [38] and [49].

cases on Article 10 and civil liberties post implementation of the Human Rights Act, *R v Shayler*.[106] The defendant was a former member of the Security Service (MI5) who facilitated the publication in the press of a number of articles about the Service and who was as a result charged with various offences under the Official Secrets Act 1989. In preliminary proceedings he sought to argue that his conduct had been intended to expose serious and pervasive illegality or iniquity in the Service and that as such it was a defensible manifestation of his right to freedom of expression under the Human Rights Act. In the Court of Appeal, the Lord Chief Justice Lord Woolf, sitting with Wright and Leveson JJ, denied that the Official Secrets Act had been this radically altered by the European Convention.

The court acknowledged that it was 'well established in the jurisprudence of the European Court of Human Rights that the dangers inherent in prior restraint are such that it calls for the most careful scrutiny'.[107] Nevertheless 'it has always been accepted that members of the security and intelligence services are in a special situation and article 10(2) of the Convention recognises the need to treat national security issues differently when it provides that the exercise of the right to freedom of expression may be subject to such conditions and restrictions as are "prescribed by law and are necessary in a democratic society, in the interests of national security ... "'.[108] The issue was to 'an extent . . . one of proportionality'[109] and when the whole statutory framework was taken into account, including in particular the alternative paths the defendant could have taken to draw attention to his concerns, it was not clear to the court that his action had been justified by reference to his guaranteed—but qualified—right to freedom of expression. The House of Lords took broadly the same line on this part of the appeal when the case came before it, drawing attention in particular to the fact that any refusal to authorize disclosure could be subjected to rigorous judicial scrutiny.[110] Moreover, as the Court of Appeal had remarked '[i]n an area as sensitive as this it does appear to us appropriate to show a degree of deference to the legislators' decision.'[111] This last remark is of interest and I shall return to it when we consider the tricky issue of justiciability, in other words, when it is inappropriate for a court to intervene with an executive act even where principle might suggest that it should. Here the principle of civil liberties was required to bow both before this counter-value, born out of respect for separation of powers and also before a second of our legitimate aspirations for the Human Rights Act (also to be discussed later), that human rights legislation should not disproportionately intrude upon pre-existing law, especially statute law. Parliament had in the Official Secrets Act and in related legislative

---

[106] [2001] EWCA Crim 1977, [2001] 1 WLR 2206 (CA), [2002] UKHL 11, [2003] 1 AC 247.
[107] Ibid para [74].
[108] Ibid para [73].
[109] Ibid para [80].
[110] n 106 above, paras [31]–[33] *per* Lord Bingham; para [72] *per* Lord Hope of Craighead; and paras [111]–[115] *per* Lord Hutton.
[111] n 106 above, para [82].

and administrative measures designed a system precisely to reflect its view of the right balance between the various interests that were to the fore in the *Shayler* case, and it was not appropriate for the judges now to dive in with the Human Rights Act, disrupting delicately balanced relations.

Similar reasoning underpinned the Divisional Court decision in *R (Pearson and Martinez) v Home Secretary*,[112] albeit it might be thought with less easily defensible results. The case concerned the civil liberty which as we have seen is of primary importance both in theory and in the case law of the Strasbourg court, the right to vote. Legislation passed in 1983 declared that '[a] convicted person during the time that he is detained in a penal institution in pursuance of his sentence is legally incapable of voting at any parliamentary or local government election.'[113] Despite the statement in *Mathieu-Mohin and Clerfayt v Belgium* that this was an area in which states enjoyed 'a wide margin of appreciation',[114] it might be thought that principle pointed very strongly in the direction of a declaration of incompatibility when Pearson and Martinez mounted their challenge to this disenfranchisement. The denial of the right to vote was a punishment which was additional to the sentence formally meted out to imprisoned convicted persons. Prisoners belonged to a category of persons that was already powerless—a classic case of, to adopt the language of the US Supreme Court in a different context, 'a discrete and insular minority'.[115] Comparative research pointed to a mixed approach on the part of European states, with 20 permitting prisoners to vote and eight refusing them permission to do so. Voluntary and detained mental patients were no longer denied the vote in this way.[116] The administrative inconvenience caused by facilitating the prisoners' right to vote would not be great; indeed such an opportunity for civic engagement might even be thought a useful stimulus to societal rehabilitation. Despite all this, and relying on a scattering of decisions by the former Commission of Human Rights, the Divisional Court found that Article 3 had not been breached. Deprivation of the right to vote was in these circumstances not so disproportionate a punishment as to attract the strictures of the Convention.

There is a stark contrast to be drawn between this decision and *R (Robertson) v Wakefield Metropolitan District Council*[117] in which Kay J stamped very hard on the suggestion that the right to vote should depend on agreeing that one's details in the electoral register could be sold to the highest commercial bidder.[118]

---

[112] [2001] EWHC 239 (Admin). The decision also includes *Hirst v Attorney General*. See H Lardy, 'Prison Disenfranchisement: Constitutional Rights and Wrongs' [2002] *PL* 524; S Foster, 'Prisoners' Rights, Freedom of Expression and the Human Rights Act' (2002) 7 *Journal of Civil Liberties* 53.

[113] Representation of the People Act 1983, s 3(1).

[114] See n 34 above, para [52].

[115] See *US v Carolene Products* 304 US 144 (1937), 152, n 4 *per* Stone J.

[116] See Representation of the People Act 2000, adding a new s 7 to the 1983 Act; *Moore v United Kingdom*, European Court of Human Rights, 30 May 2000.

[117] [2001] EWHC 915 (Admin), [2002] QB 1052.

[118] Ibid, particularly paras [40]–[42]. Cf *R (Robertson) v Secretary of State for the Home Department* [2003] EWHC 1760 (Admin) where sale of the electoral register to credit agencies was not regarded as unlawful because the rationale for the transaction lay in the control of fraud rather than solely or primarily in the interests of commercial gain.

A particularly disappointing feature of the court's reasoning in the *Pearson and Martinez* case is its large but (in this instance) misplaced reliance on judicial deference to the will of the legislature. As Kennedy LJ put it in that case, 'Parliament in this country could have provided differently in order to meet the objectives which it discerned, and . . . [his lordship] would accept that the tailoring process [in relation to the extent of the right to vote] seldom admits of perfection, so the courts must afford some leeway to the legislator.'[119] This may be true where important matters of an economic, cultural, or broadly political nature are involved, a point which from the perspective of this book is sufficiently important to warrant a whole chapter being devoted to it.[120] But as counsel for the claimants pointed out to the court, though the issues before it did involve matters of social policy, 'the right to vote, even if under used, is of high constitutional importance and in so far as disenfranchisement is regarded as a punishment the courts may be said to be as well placed to assess the need for protection as they would be in relation to any other sentence in the armoury which the legislature controls'.[121] The court however was not persuaded. The tone of the judgment does seem to assume that a decision the other way would have given prisoners the right to vote, when of course all it would have done would have been to have produced an unenforceable declaration of incompatibility. We should not forget that the whole procedure of such declarations is precisely designed to ensure that Parliament's judgment is deferred to: there was accordingly no need for the court to add its extra layer of deference when identifying the limits of the right before it. From the perspective of principle, not to say that of the disenfranchised prisoners in this jurisdiction, numbering (we should not forget) in the tens of thousands, the case must rank as a profound disappointment, and a depressing way in which to end a chapter that has been generally upbeat about the capacity of the Convention and the Human Rights Act to promote respect for and the protection of civil liberties.

---

[119] n 112 above, paras [16]–[17].   [120] See chapter 6 below.   [121] n 112 above, para [10].

4

The Principle of Legality

A. Legality and the 'rule of law'

In the last chapter, I briefly mentioned the importance of the principle of legality to the model of representative government that underpins the approach to civil liberties (and therefore to human rights) that has been taken in this book. The subject is so fundamental that it deserves to be regarded as a principle in itself and to have a chapter dedicated to its exposition. For while it is true to say that there can be legality without civil liberties, it is clear that there can be no civil liberties without a commitment to legality: the concept is as basic to civil liberties as is the right to vote. The version of legality that will be identified and defended here as integral to the Convention system (and therefore to the Human Rights Act) is one that requires all official action in a democratic state to be positively authorized by law. Though sometimes (as we shall see) considered by legal philosophers and proponents of judicial activism to be a rather narrow approach to legality, the connection with and dependence upon a properly functioning system of representative democracy saves it from (potentially authoritarian) aridity. Indeed the concept as I develop it here is democracy-reinforcing in the sense that it *requires* that all legal authority come only from the elected branch, in other words the legislature. Viewed in this light, it can be seen as intimately connected with the approach to representative democracy outlined in chapter two. In a perfectly functioning system of government of this type, the only source of law would be an elected legislature, whether directly by statute or at various removes via delegated legislation or the exercise of executive discretion under law.

In this chapter I will argue that the version of legality which is to be found in the European Convention on Human Rights and the Human Rights Act fits very well with the democracy-oriented model of legality set out above, and in particular that adherence to this approach to legality permits me to make some quite strong observations about the appropriate impact of the Convention on both the common law and the royal prerogative. Before I turn to the Convention and the Act, however, there is preparatory theoretical work to be done. I have to recognize that the principle of legality to which I have just committed myself is regarded by many lawyers as weak and inadequate. It is also clear that it is rooted in a conception of representative democracy that is itself highly contested. The battle is joined in the scholarly legal literature over the phrase 'the rule of law'. I have managed to avoid the term entirely up to now in this book, but it cannot be circumvented forever; it has a long and influential pedigree in British law and is regarded by many as the key to a proper understanding of the UK constitution and therefore to a correct appreciation of the place of the judges within it.[1] As such its intimate connection with the Human Rights Act will be immediately obvious. The difference between the principle of legality developed here and the concept of the rule of law needs to be unravelled before we can turn with confidence to the substance of the law, and in particular to a description of how the principle of legality (as opposed to what is meant today by the phrase 'the rule of law') is deeply entrenched within the substance and the case law of both the Convention and the Human Rights Act.

The most eloquent contemporary writer on the rule of law is without question the Cambridge academic Trevor Allan, and among his most articulate expositions of the subject are two of his most recent, in a chapter in a book celebrating the great jurist Sir William Wade in 1998[2] and in an article published in the *Law Quarterly Review* the following year.[3] Allan identifies 'two radically contrasting conceptions of the British Constitution or of British democracy' that 'compete for allegiance'.[4] The first of these, the '*majoritarian* theory gives pride of place to majority rule'.[5] This view reflects the approach to legality which we have just been discussing. In analysing it Allan develops a version of representative democracy which is implicit in the approach to legality that I have just outlined:

The legal process is clearly subservient to the political process, the latter constituted by the clash of conflicting interests and struggle for power characteristic of pluralist democracy; and the legislative outcome of the political battle derives its moral authority entirely from its pedigree as the product of a decision-making procedure to which all parties and interest-groups have access, according to their numbers and strength. In this conception, legislation enjoys primacy: statutory rules are ultimately expressions of power, and the common law should defer to the result of the political struggles, duly enacted. The intrusion of judicial values, rooted in the common law tradition, when the consequence is to fetter the execution of policies or implementation of measures sanctioned by Parliament, is generally an illegitimate usurpation of democratic authority. Statutes enjoy an independent status, not a 'parasitic and contingent existence within the body of the

[1] See generally M Elliott, *The Constitutional Foundations of Judicial Review* (Oxford: Hart Publishing, 2001); CF Forsyth (ed), *Judicial Review and the Constitution* (Oxford: Hart Publishing, 2000).

[2] TRS Allan, 'Fairness, Equality, Rationality: Constitutional Theory and Judicial Review' in CF Forsyth and I Hare (eds), *The Golden Metwand and the Crooked Cord* (Oxford: Oxford University Press, 1998), 15.

[3] TRS Allan, 'The Rule of Law as the Rule of Reason: Consent and Constitutionalism' (1999) 115 *LQR* 221. See for a general overview of his position, TRS Allan, *Constitutional Justice. A Liberal Theory of the Rule of Law* (Oxford: Oxford University Press, 2001). This book is in turn subjected to a most interesting criticism in T Poole, 'Dogmatic Liberalism? TRS Allan and the Common Law Constitution' (2002) 65 *MLR* 463. For a recent contribution to administrative law scholarship see TRS Allan, 'Doctrine and Theory in Administrative Law: An Elusive Quest for the Limits of Jurisdiction' [2003] *PL* 429.

[4] Allan, n 2 above, 15.

[5] Ibid 17 (emphasis in original).

common law'; and even indications of majority support for particular measures, which fall short of formal enactment, can justify (or require) judicial deference to that opinion.[6]

On this view, it can be seen immediately that '[j]udicial review, whether of legislation or administrative action, threatens the sovereignty of the majority will', and '[c]onstraints of fairness or reasonableness, as grounds for quashing administrative decisions, can be justified (though sometimes implausibly) only as an expression of implicit parliamentary intention.'[7] In this framework,

[t]he importance of the rule of law is not denied. There must be formal equality, in the sense that all are equally subject to the law, government ministers as much as ordinary citizens. There must be proper respect for the rules of natural justice and the precept, *nulla poena sine lege*; administrative discretion must, so far as possible, be exercised within clear boundaries given by legislation. But all such expectations and requirements are, in the end, subject to contrary legislative intent. Obedience to parliamentary sovereignty, benignly construed, exhausts the requirements of the rule of law.[8]

Such a view of the rule of law does not appeal to Allan. Under it, he believes that the 'grant of unlimited discretion to officials to pursue their own ideas of the public good, unfettered by legislative guidance or judicial review, would be consistent with the rule of the law',[9] and 'every dictatorship whose authority is acknowledged by the courts would be a *Rechtsstaat*'.[10] In fact, Allan asserts, it is 'widely understood that the bare notion of formal legality cannot furnish a useful conception of the rule of law'.[11]

In opposition to it, he turns to a radically different approach, rooted in what he calls communitarianism.

The rule of law, under this communitarian conception, is not the faithful application of whatever rules emerge from the political battle, regardless of content, but rather the subjection of government (and other significant sources of power) to principles of justice and fairness which express the community's enduring commitment to fundamental ideas of human freedom and human dignity. Allegiance to the rule of law, by citizens and judges, consists not merely in unquestioning obedience to the legislative command, or administrative order, oblivious of its moral quality, but in a more discriminating response, respectful of the constitution as a source of moral constraints on those in power. Ideas of citizenship and the common good generate standards to govern both the interpretation of statute and the appraisal of executive action. These ideas necessarily impose ultimately binding, if rarely analysed, limits on the permissible content of legislation (limits generally hidden, with characteristic British reserve, behind a scheme of principle for the interpretation of statutes expressed in the common law). From this more idealistic perspective, the common law is not viewed as wholly subservient to statute because it embodies, albeit

[6] Allan, n 2 above, 15, 16 omitting footnotes (though the remark in quotes is that of HW Arthurs 'Rethinking Administrative Law: A Slightly Dicey Business' (1979) 17 *Osgoode Hall LJ* 1, 22.
[7] Ibid 17.
[8] Ibid.
[9] Allan, 'The Rule of Law as the Rule of Reason', n 3 above, 221–222.
[10] Ibid 221.
[11] Ibid 222.

imperfectly, a set of constitutional values transcending the ordinarily more transient, and particular, rules enacted by the legislature.[12]

This 'substantive rule of law' incorporates 'principles of good government which transcend the supremacy of majority rule'.[13] Since 'equality before the law is regarded as an aspect of *equal citizenship*, an ideal of the moral equality or equal dignity of all those subject to governmental power, it must be supplemented by independent principles of justice or fairness'.[14] On this view, the rule of law 'insists that all governmental acts and decisions affecting the fortunes of particular persons should be capable of justification, and be explicitly defended, on the basis of a publicly avowed, even if politically contentious, view of the common good'.[15] When '[f]ully articulated' in this way, 'the rule of law amounts to a sophisticated doctrine of constitutionalism, revealing law as the antithesis of arbitrariness or the assertion of will or power'.[16]

Allan is quite right that his communitarian approach 'ultimately reflects a different conception of law from that which informs the majoritarian view'.[17] Its view of democracy is also different; it 'treats the equality of political power expressed in equal adult suffrage as only one, albeit important, feature of a more thorough-going and fundamental equality' in which 'the individual citizen's dignity and moral autonomy constitute essential components of the common good, which provides the ultimate touchstone for the validity of legislation and the legality of governmental action'.[18] From the communitarian perspective, 'democracy involves the participation of every citizen in decisions which foster and embody a collective sense of justice, founded on open debate and full deliberation'.[19] This approach to democracy is, in comparison with the majoritarian view, 'the superior interpretation' precisely because the outcomes it can produce are constrained by principle:

It is more attractive as a matter of political morality, resolving the latent contradiction between Dicey's principles of parliamentary sovereignty and the rule of law in favour of the latter. It also provides a more coherent and convincing account of the nature of modern public law, in which the doctrine of *ultra vires*, characterized by the limits of *Wednesbury* review, has lost its dominance. I shall not deny the propriety of allowing Parliament to determine, in broad outline, the great majority of the social and political questions confronting a modern liberal democracy. I shall argue only that the recognition of some limits on the powers of a parliamentary majority, however tentatively identified, is implied in such a description of the British state. Parliamentary sovereignty is ultimately a legal doctrine whose precise meaning and full implications depend, like such equally fundamental doctrines as the rule of law and the separation of powers, on detailed analysis of the constitutional scheme as a whole. Moreover, such doctrines acquire determinate meaning in specific contexts only on the basis of a scheme of constitutional values: the limits of public powers will necessarily reflect our fundamental commitment to principles of liberty and equality.[20]

---

[12] Allan, n 2 above, 16–17 (footnote omitted).   [13] Ibid 19.   [14] Ibid 17.
[15] Allan, n 3 above, 231–232.   [16] Ibid 223.   [17] Allan, n 2 above, 19.
[18] Ibid 17.   [19] Ibid 19.   [20] Ibid 18.

It will be obvious that the conception of democracy outlined in each of the last two chapters and which defines the approach taken to the principle of legality in this chapter is far removed from Allan's model.[21] Here the emergence of law from the representative legislature is the high point of our theory, with the legitimacy of such laws being contingent not upon their content but rather upon their having undergone an agreed transformative procedure which has translated them from mere aspirations on bits of paper into enforceable laws. In chapter two I described the traditional British constitutional system in exactly these terms, and not at all uncritically. The version of the rule of law proposed here is designed to reinforce this democratic framework, mainly by guaranteeing the 'sovereignty' of its legislative outcomes, but also—by ensuring through its underlying commitment to civil libertarian principle—that the democratic arena on which all the factions are competing is a level playing field. There is plenty of room for morality and ethics in this approach, for talk of justice, fundamental values and the like, but the space for it is to be found *within* the legislative branch, at the stage of law-making rather than law-enforcing. On our playing field, all the various groups are vying for the crowd's attention with their talk of right and wrong, of the interests of the nation, of security and the like. But when the whistle blows at the end of this legislative match, there is a winner, and to that victor go the spoils of the game, in the form of the power to make legally enforceable pronouncements. Of course the defeated factions can immediately try to undo this work and win authority from the crowd for their own brand of truth. But until they succeed in this they have to abide by past outcomes, neither refusing to obey them nor challenging their validity elsewhere.[22]

The core difference between this approach and that adopted by Allan lies in its rejection of objective values separate from the process it describes and in its consequent acceptance—celebration even—of the inevitability of conflict in all free societies. If there is one thing that the communitarian perspective favoured by Allan seems to fear most of all, it is the possibility of dispute. It has a horror of the 'political battle', of the 'the assertion of will or power'. The correct democratic model channels political debate into 'the great majority of the social and political questions confronting a modern liberal democracy' but requires and expects of such discussion that it should accept that it must defer to what Allan claims are objective and agreed values that lie outside it and against which its outcomes must be tested for legitimacy. Variously expressed in the extracts quoted above, these values are the 'independent principles of justice or fairness', the 'principles of justice and fairness which express the community's enduring commitment to fundamental ideas of human freedom and human dignity,' and a society's 'fundamental commitment to principles of liberty and equality'. How true is it that these are words represent agreed-upon values? Of course as basic

---

[21] See for a very strong critique of Allan's approach, echoes of which are to be found in what follows, R Ekins, 'Judicial Supremacy and the Rule of Law' (2003) 119 *LQR* 127.

[22] Begged here is the question of the democratic effectiveness (or lack of effectiveness) of the legislative chambers, a point to which we return in our concluding chapter.

principles they are unexceptional; in contemporary politico-legal western culture, everybody is dedicated to the pursuit of justice, fairness, and equality. It is however when an attempt is made to translate these concepts into conceptions on the ground, into legally enforceable rules giving substance to their ethical claims, that the cracks in the consensus start to show. Much parliamentary time is taken up not with whether we should pursue the goals of justice, equality, and liberty but with whether this or that measure before the legislature supports or subverts one or all of these ideals. There is agreement about concepts but often very little about how to realize them in law. Since the proper manifestation of these values in law is bound to be contested, it follows that the power to decide which conceptions of justice, equality, and liberty are right and which are wrong in particular situations is a political power (in the broadest sense) of the highest significance.

Now consider again Allan's majoritarian and communitarian models. The first—our principle of legality—leaves the conception of the values of justice, liberty and equality to the legislative branch. The second in contrast requires the principle of the rule of law to circumscribe the range of possible legislative outcomes by reference to these abstract concepts. In practice this means that the judges get to check the parliamentary conceptions of justice, equality, and liberty against their own version of what these concepts should entail. Once this concept/conception distinction is made, and the reality of dispute recognized as regards the latter if not (necessarily) the former, then it becomes clear that Allan's theory is as much about power as it is about principle. Allan believes in the capacity of the common law to deliver the kind of safeguards of justice, equality, and liberty that he believes are woefully lacking in the majoritarian model. As we have already noted above, he regards it as important that 'the common law is not viewed as wholly subservient to statute because it embodies, albeit imperfectly, a set of constitutional values transcending the ordinarily more transient, and particular, rules enacted by the legislature'[23] The 'special strength of the common law, as a foundation for constitutional government, lies in its inherent commitment to rationality and equality'.[24] Furthermore, in the absence (as in Britain) of a written constitution which enjoys the status of fundamental law, the common law must serve as a constitutional framework and expression of the community's most important values. It therefore enjoys a superiority to legislation in the sense that a statute must be interpreted consistently with deep-rooted common law principles even where the consequence is some dimunition in its efficacy. When an Act of Parliament contradicts 'common right and reason', as Coke C J expressed it, it must be appropriately 'controlled'.[25]

The authority cited in this reference to Coke is *Dr Bonham's Case*,[26] which dates from 1609, 90 years *before* the parliamentary revolution which conclusively (or so it was thought) established parliamentary sovereignty. In this and

[23] n 12 above.   [24] Allan, n 3 above, 239.   [25] Ibid 241–242.
[26] (1609) 8 Co Rep 107, 27 ER 638.

other respects, Allan manages at the same time to be both historically-rooted and yet profoundly ahistorical. His theory of the rule of law is doubly conservative in being rooted in the established values of the common law and also (on account of these roots) in being profoundly antagonistic to radical change. Yet the lack of historical grasp shines through in his reliance on a pre-revolutionary case like *Dr Bonham's*. The judges of the seventeenth century rowed in behind the Stuart monarchy in the main and more often than not legitimized its extra-parliamentary excesses.[27] Are these many cases bowing before executive power less reflective of enduring common law values than *Dr Bonham's*? How can we tell? In the three centuries or so since the parliamentary revolution of 1689, the conceptions of justice, equality and liberty extolled by the common law judges have often been profoundly out of kilter with contemporary opinion. We have already seen in chapter three how as late as 1907, it was, as far as at least one judge was concerned, 'a principle of the unwritten constitutional law of this country that men only were entitled to take part in the election of representatives to Parliament'.[28] Presumably then on Allan's theory the judges (or at least this judge) should have struck down as invalid the later law giving women the right to vote? If some judges would have done so and others not, how can we tell which fundamental value is right and which wrong? Likewise, when the anti-trade union decision of *Amalgamated Society of Railway Servants v Osborne*[29] was overridden by the Trade Union Act 1913, Lords Shaw and James would have been right on Allan's view then to have struck down that measure, as their reasoning in the original case had been that trade union support for parliamentary representation had been 'unconstitutional and illegal' as subversive of the first principles of representative government. It is surely no answer to say that their version of what the constitution entailed was, we can now see, wrong or misguided. It was what they believed then that mattered, and only parliamentary sovereignty prevented the escalation of their error into anti-democratic catastrophe.

Fine though the rhetoric of justice and equality is, the application of this language to particular situations reveals the judges in a somewhat less attractive light. Illuminated in the act of translating lofty principle into practice, they often resemble the grubby political warriors from whom theory requires that they should remain grandly apart. The record of the judges in the democratic era has been discussed in an earlier chapter;[30] it does not inspire confidence in their capacity to serve as guardians of anything other than the values of the generation just past. Allan believes that his theory means that '[d]raconian legislative solutions to short-term problems, which may represent an exaggerated response to public agitation for immediate results, must be integrated with settled legal

---

[27] See J Goldsworthy, *The Sovereignty of Parliament* (Oxford: Clarendon Press, 1999).
[28] *Nairn v The University Court of the University of St Andrews* 1907, 15 SLT 471, 473 *per* Lord McLaren.
[29] [1910] AC 87.
[30] See above chapter three.

doctrine which expresses more enduring principles of justice'[31] and that the failure of the majoritarian approach to address this kind of problem means that, to quote for a second time one of his characteristically striking phrases, 'every dictatorship whose authority is acknowledged by the courts would be a *Rechtsstaat*'.[32] It is implicit in all this that armed with the kind of power for which Allan argues, the judges of twentieth century Britain, for example, would have acquitted themselves better than the record suggests they did and on the basis of which I have earlier criticized them. Can this be true? Or is it not more likely that their perspective on justice, equality and, particularly, liberty would have led them into conflict with the lower house much as the values profoundly believed in by members of the House of Lords provoked the parliamentary crisis of 1909-11 and the commitment to a partisan version of freedom held by the US Supreme Court led it into a collision with the Roosevelt administration in the 1930s?

The experience of Nazi Germany is instructive in this regard. During the 1930s, as is well known, Hitler's Nazi regime was able to rely on a tenuously-rooted legality as the basis for its power in Germany, such that it was indeed in formal terms a *Rechtstaat*. But it was far more than that as well, with the executive arm and paramilitary elements associated with it frequently engaging in criminal and lawless activity, assault, criminal damage, murder, the setting aside of contracts and the like. Such wrongful behaviour was on the whole either tolerated or legitimized by the courts; nobody would ask us to believe, presumably, that had they had a fundamental power to strike down laws by reference to abstract concepts such as justice or liberty their conduct would have been different?[33] Or, closer to home, could it really be the case that the record of the United Kingdom judiciary in relation to Northern Ireland would have been different and better had there been a human rights charter (or some recovered principles of the common law) readily to hand?[34] Judges are exactly the wrong people to depend upon in a political crisis, a fact recognized by the judges themselves if not by the theorists who desire them to assert ever greater power. In an important and unanimous terrorism case the outcome of which was favourable to government, and in which the speeches were given shortly after the events of 11 September 2001, Lord Hoffmann put the point succinctly:

I wrote this speech some three months before the recent events in New York and Washington. They are a reminder that in matters of national security, the cost of failure can be high. This seems to me to underline the need for the judicial arm of government to respect the decisions of ministers of the Crown on the question of whether support for terrorist activities in a foreign country constitutes a threat to national security. It is not only that the executive has access to special information and expertise in these matters. It is also that such decisions, with serious potential results for the community, require a legitimacy which can be conferred only by entrusting them to persons responsible to the community through

---

[31] Allan, n 2 above, 242.   [32] Ibid 221.

[33] For a brilliant study, see M Mandel, 'A Brief History of the New Constitutionalism, or "How We Changed Everything So That Everything would Remain The Same"' (1998) 32 *Israel Law Review* 250.

[34] See S Livingstone, 'The House of Lords and the Northern Ireland Conflict' (1994) 57 *MLR* 333.

the democratic process. If the people are to accept the consequences of such decisions, they must be made by persons whom the people have elected and whom they can remove.[35]

It might be that Allan agrees with these sentiments, indeed that they are a practical example of the 'fine balance' that 'must be maintained between the power of an elected majority of representative legislators and the ability of legal and constitutional tradition to tame its excesses'.[36] It may be that all the decisions inimical to civil liberties in the twentieth century were correctly decided on the basis that they arose in areas within the exclusive remit of the executive and/or legislative branches. But if this is the case, the values of the common law are at risk of looking more ideologically partisan than ever, with a commitment to liberty combined with an acceptance of authoritarianism that would have made Margaret Thatcher an ideal appointment to the Bench.

B. Representative democracy, the European Convention and the principle of legality

I now return to the 'representative' model of the rule of law (the principle of legality), undeterred by the Allan critique and with a different dimension to history on my side. Freed from the temptations of its ambitious sibling the rule of law, the principle of legality has much to contribute to our analysis of the Human Rights Act. It certainly connects more easily than Allan's rule of law with the framework of law that had grown up in the twentieth century. On the domestic front, there is a strong democracy-reinforcing aspect to the way in which the courts have developed the principle of legality in the 70 or so years that the United Kingdom has been a full representative democracy. This can be seen particularly clearly if the civil liberties cases are left to one side and the general relationship between the legislative and judicial branches is analysed without the expectation (invariably as we have seen disappointed in the civil liberties context) of strong and principled judicial activism. For all its negative potential to underpin dictatorship elsewhere, the requirement for legality usefully emphasizes that the exercise of state authority in a democracy must be backed by law. The principle of *ultra vires* has been deployed by the courts as a safeguard against any temptation that the executive might have to exercise power above and beyond that which it has been given by the legislature. Sometimes this can lead to quite dramatic results as in the *Fire Brigades* decision. Here, an attempt by the then Home Secretary Michael Howard indefinitely to postpone the bringing into force of an Act of Parliament was held unlawful on account of his refusal even to consider exercising the powers of implementation that Parliament had given him.[37] The doctrine of *ultra vires* can also on occasion be seen to complement

---

[35] *Secretary of State for the Home Department v Rehman* [2001] UKHL 47, [2002] 1 AC 153, para [62].

[36] Allan, n 3 above, 242.

[37] *R (Fire Brigades Union) v Secretary of State for the Home Department* [1995] 2 AC 513.

the democratic process, as in the short line of cases showing that the courts can be induced in appropriate circumstances to insist upon a process of consultation before secondary legislation can be said validly to have taken effect.[38] Of course the judges have sometimes deployed their *ultra vires* powers in a partisan way, in the pursuit of their brand of justice or fairness, and this has got the courts into trouble with both the legislative and executive branches.[39] But at the abstract level of principle, the requirement that a power be in an Act of Parliament before it can be exercised is not a recipe for authoritarianism; rather it is a profoundly democratic safeguard against just such a dismal eventuality. (It is recognized that this requires an act of faith in the democratic body that it will not enact truly draconian and illiberal legislation, a belief that is constantly tested and exposed by events, but—unlike those whose faith lies with the courts—it is at least a belief that the ordinary citizen can seek through ongoing political activity to render more real: I address this point directly in the concluding chapter to this book.)

There is no point in having a law in place if the executive can breach it with impunity. Mindful of this, the principle of legality goes further than *ultra vires*, with the courts in recent years having extended the tentacles of the law to reach the executive with ever-increasing confidence. Stimulated by the European Court of Justice, the House of Lords has held that Community law may require the making available of injunctive relief against the Crown.[40] In 1993, the same judicial body found the Home Secretary liable for contempt of court for having refused to return to the United Kingdom a Zairean teacher who was claiming refugee status in this country and whose return had been ordered by a high court judge.[41] Another logical dimension to the principle of legality relates to access to the courts. The judges have had to be on permanent guard against the temptation of the executive to insulate some of its actions from judicial review altogether, in so-called 'ouster' clauses or through the denial or restriction of court oversight by other means.[42] Another strand of cases emphasizes the necessity for an access to justice which is real and not just linked to a potential litigant's financial resources.[43] The courts have been similarly robust in protecting the lawyer-client relationship, seeing the integrity of this connection as a pre-requisite for a properly functioning system of adjudication.[44] The independence of the judiciary has long been emphasized as an important guarantor of the impartiality of

---

[38] Usually there will be some indication in the primary legislation of the need for some kind of consultation: the leading case is *Agricultural Horticultural and Forestry Industry Training Board v Aylesbury Mushrooms Ltd* [1972] 1 WLR 190. See for a recent example *Howker v Secretary of State for Works and Pensions* [2002] EWCA Civ 1623.

[39] See eg *Secretary of State for Education and Science v Tameside Metropolitan Borough Council* [1977] AC 1014.

[40] *R (Factortame) v Secretary of State for Transport (No 2)* [1991] 1 AC 603.

[41] *Re M* [1994] 1 AC 377.

[42] See *Anisminic v Foreign Compensation Commission* [1969] 2 AC 147.

[43] *R (Witham) v Lord Chancellor* [1998] QB 575.

[44] *General Mediterranean Holdings SA v Patel* [2001] 1 WLR 272. This has been especially important in the context of prisoners' rights: see *Leech v Deputy Governor of Parkhurst Prison* [1988] AC 533.

those involved in adjudication, and a vital aspect of the principle of legality (and indeed of 'the rule of law' howsoever defined). Though with long roots in the common law,[45] this concept has received an added and very public impetus from the controversy caused by Lord Hoffmann's failure to declare a certain interest in the course of the *Pinochet* extradition proceedings during 1998-9.[46]

All of these various case law developments reflect the commitment of the common law to the idea that the law should be objective, accessible, and independently and impartially applied. Combined with the concept of *ultra vires*, they reflect the success of a mature system of law in putting the principle of legality into practical operation. In recent years, these streams of authorities have become intertwined with those emerging from the European Court of Human Rights at Strasbourg. In the solicitor-client case referred to above, for example, *General Mediterranean v Patel*,[47] Mr Justice Toulson drew extensively on the European authorities in support of his conclusion that a provision on wasting costs in the new civil procedure rules was not only *ultra vires* its parent Act in the ordinary way but also infringed Convention rights to privacy under Article 8. The *Pinochet* litigation also involved a ready interaction between the old rules on judicial impartiality and their new form in Article 6(1) of the Convention, and this has been the subject of a later, very important ruling from a strengthened Court of Appeal.[48] Indeed it is arguable that some at least of the recent domestic developments in this general area would not have occurred were it not for the Convention.[49] This intermingling of authorities should not in the least surprise us. Just as the common law has long been committed to and robust in its defence of the principle of legality, so too has the concept been at the core of the Convention since its inception after the Second World War.

The Statute of the Council of Europe which launched the whole enterprise on 5 May 1949 makes clear the centrality of the principle of legality to the project, with the Member States of the Council collectively:

[r]eaffirming their devotion to the spiritual and moral values which are the common heritage of their peoples and the true source of individual freedom, political liberty and the rule of law, principles which form the basis of all genuine democracy.[50]

In a similar vein, Article 3 of the Statute insisted that '[e]very Member of the Council of Europe must accept the principle of the rule of law and of the enjoyment by all persons within its jurisdiction of human rights and fundamental freedoms ....'[51] It is true that the term 'rule of law' is being used here, but the deployment of it in association with such other phrases as 'human rights' and

---

[45] *Dimes v Grand Junction Canal (Proprieters of)* (1852) 3 HLC 759, 10 ER 301.
[46] *R (Pinochet Ugarte) v Bow Street Metropolitan Stipendiary Magistrate (No 2)* [2000] 1 AC 119.
[47] n 44 above.
[48] *Locabail (UK) Ltd v Bayfield Properties Ltd* [2000] QB 451.
[49] See the cases at n 63 below.
[50] See European Commission of Human Rights, *Documents and Decisions* (The Hague, Martinus Nijhoff, 1959), 2.
[51] Ibid.

'fundamental freedoms' shows that it is intended to have a more restricted remit than that for which Allan later contends; in other words that it is one of a range of ways of achieving justice rather than being itself coterminous with the idea as Allan seems to believe. This key point is made clear in the preamble to the Convention itself, where the signatory governments first reaffirm 'their profound belief in those fundamental freedoms which are the foundation of justice and peace in the world and which are best maintained on the one hand by an effective political democracy and on the other by a common understanding and obser-vance of the human rights upon which they depend', and then go on to resolve 'as the governments of European countries which are like-minded and have a common heritage of political traditions, ideals, freedom and the rule of law, to take the first steps for the collective enforcement of certain of the rights stated in the Universal Declaration'. The rights are not part of the rule of law but exist side by side with legality in the same basket of benefits.

The fundamental basis of legality is established in Article 34:

The Court may receive applications from any person, non-governmental organisation or group of individuals claiming to be the victim of a violation by one of the High Contract-ing Parties of the rights set forth in the Convention or the protocols thereto. The High Contracting Parties undertake not to hinder in any way the effective exercise of this right.

This commitment to law is then carried forward into the domestic jurisdictions themselves via Article 6(1):

In the determination of his civil rights and obligations or of any criminal charge against him, everyone is entitled to a fair and public hearing within a reasonable time by an independent and impartial tribunal established by law.

In an early and very important decision of the European Court, *Golder v United Kingdom*,[52] Article 6(1) was held to embrace an underlying general right of access to the courts. The applicant, who had been a prisoner at the relevant time, was denied permission to consult a solicitor with a view to launching legal proceedings against a prison officer whom he believed had libelled him. This made it impossible for his case to get off the ground. Of course, had he made it to court, his 'civil right' to damages for injury to reputation would have been 'determined' by an entirely independent and impartial tribunal in proceedings which would have been manifestly fair to all concerned. The problem was that there was no chance of reaching this point of departure into Article 6. On these facts, the court found by a vote of six to three that Article 6(1) had indeed been breached:

The principle whereby a civil claim must be capable of being submitted to a judge ranks as one of the universally 'recognised' fundamental principles of law; the same is true of the principle of international law which forbids the denial of justice. Article 6(1) must [be] read in light of these principles.

[52] (1975) 1 EHRR 524.

Were Article 6(1) to be understood as concerning exclusively the conduct of an action which had already been initiated before a court, a Contracting State could, without acting in breach of that text, do away with its courts, or take away their jurisdiction to determine certain classes of civil actions and entrust it to organs dependent on the Government. Such assumptions, indissociable from a danger of arbitrary power, would have serious consequences which are repugnant to the aforementioned principles and which the Court cannot overlook.

It would be inconceivable, in the opinion of the Court, that Article 6(1) should prescribe in detail the procedural guarantees afforded to parties in a pending law suit and should not first protect that which alone makes it in fact possible to benefit from such guarantees, that is, access to a court. The fair, public and expeditious characteristics of judicial proceedings are of no value at all if there are no judicial proceedings.

... Taking all the preceding considerations together, it follows that the right of access constitutes an element which is inherent in the right stated by Article 6(1). This is not an extensive interpretation forcing new obligations on the Contracting States: it is based on the very terms of the first sentence of Article 6(1) read in its context and having regard to the object and purpose of the Convention, a lawmaking treaty, and to general principles of law.[53]

Of course the risk in such grand claims to a right to a court is that they lead to a judicialization of disputes that are far better off resolved outside the arena of litigation. Though the *Golder* decision did try to limit the breadth of the right that it was implying into Article 6(1),[54] this has been a route down which some subsequent lines of authority have been unable to resist going, leading to a degree of analytical confusion that I shall consider in a later chapter.[55] But the basic sentiment behind the *Golder* decision, that the Convention requires access to courts as well as procedural safeguards within them, is of fundamental importance. In *Airey v Ireland*,[56] this idea was pushed even further, to encompass an obligation on the part of a state to render such access practically possible by providing legal aid for litigants in appropriate cases. The decision involved a woman whose desire to petition for a judicial separation in the local high court was stymied by her lack of means and her consequent inability to secure the services of a lawyer to act on her behalf. While rejecting the argument that Article 6 requires the provision of free legal aid for every dispute relating to a civil right, but nevertheless finding (by five votes to two) that the applicant before it had had her own right of access wrongly impeded by her lack of funds, the court in a famous passage declared that:

the Convention is intended to guarantee not rights that are theoretical or illusory but rights that are practical and effective. This is particularly so of the right of access to the courts in view of the prominent place held in a democratic society by the right to a fair trial.... The Court ... considers ... that the mere fact that an interpretation of the Convention may extend into the sphere of social and economic rights should not be a

---

[53] (1975) 1 EHRR 524, paras [35]–[36] (footnotes omitted).
[54] See in particular ibid paras [37]–[40].
[55] See chapter eight below.
[56] (1979) 2 EHRR 305.

decisive factor against such an interpretation; there is no watertight division separating that sphere from the field covered by the Convention.[57]

There can be few passages in the court's jurisprudence so frequently quoted and yet so invariably distinguished. The prospect of securing from the European Court a human rights-mandated obligation on the part of contracting states to provide improved levels of legal aid in civil matters has been salivating to lawyers ever since the judgment first appeared over two decades ago, but the court has resolutely refused to build such a right off the back of this dicta.[58] Nor has the potential for socio-economic rights been much developed; it may be that the *Airey* case is at the very outer edge of a human rights court's proper remit in a system of government still firmly rooted in the principles of representative democracy. This is part of a more general question of the appropriateness of judicial activism to which I shall return in a later chapter.[59]

It is perhaps best, then, to view the *Airey* case as an indication, with the *Golder* case, of quite how indelibly imprinted the Convention has been from the very earliest days of the Strasbourg court's jurisprudence with the importance of access to justice. In the same vein are two other reasonably early cases, *Silver v United Kingdom*[60] and *Niemietz v Germany*.[61] In the first of these, the court found a violation of Article 8 of the Convention in various restrictions that had been placed on prisoners' access to their lawyers. In the second, it was the search of a lawyer's office (albeit under the authority of a court warrant) that was held unanimously to have infringed Article 8, with the profession of the applicant being regarded as of particular importance:

The warrant was drawn in broad terms, in that it ordered a search for and seizure of 'documents', without any limitation, revealing the identity of the author of the offensive letter; this point is of special significance where, as in Germany, the search of a lawyer's office is not accompanied by any special procedural safeguards, such as the presence of an independent observer. More importantly, having regard to the materials that were in fact inspected, the search impinged on professional secrecy to an extent that appears disproportionate in the circumstances; it has, in this connection, to be recalled that, where a lawyer is involved, an encroachment on professional secrecy may have repercussions on the proper administration of justice and hence on the rights guaranteed by Article 6 of the Convention.[62]

It is clear therefore that, both in its emphasis on access to justice and in its respect for the sanctity of the solicitor-client relationship, the European Convention case law echoes the common law's commitment to these dimensions of the principle of legality, and adds to it where gaps in common law protection are revealed, as

[57] Ibid paras [24] and [26].
[58] See most recently *A v United Kingdom* [2002] 36 EHRR 917, esp paras [90]–[100] on this point.
[59] See chapter six below.
[60] (1983) 5 EHRR 347.
[61] (1992) 16 EHRR 97.
[62] Ibid para [37].

was the case in the *Golder* and *Silver* decisions.[63] But the resemblance between the two systems on this point is most marked, and the democracy-reinforcing qualities of the Convention most to the fore, in the way in which the Convention insists that any exceptions or qualifications to the rights within its remit be achieved only via the positive authority of domestic law.

C. The importance of legality in the 'trumping' of rights

We have already seen in an earlier chapter that only a very few of the Convention rights are absolute in their terms.[64] For those that are not, the question arises as to what the circumstances are in which these rights can be required to give way to other interests. As we have already observed, the Convention is littered with many such exceptions and provisos, rooted in a wide variety of legitimate aims, and we have earlier analysed one of the most common requirements of such exceptions, namely the insistence that the exception be 'necessary in a demo-cratic society'. We now turn our attention to an even more pervasive Convention requirement, namely that any exception to a right be explicitly mandated by law. In Article 5, for example, the right to liberty may be removed by reference to various matters but only 'in accordance with a procedure prescribed by law'. Article 7(1) is about precisely this requirement:

No one shall be held guilty of any criminal offence on account of any act or omission which did not constitute a criminal offence under national or international law at the time when it was committed. Nor shall a heavier penalty be imposed than the one that was applicable at the time the criminal offence was committed.[65]

The right to respect for private and family life permits of various interferences where these are 'in accordance with the law'. The freedom of thought, con-science and religion in Article 9 refers to limitations which are 'prescribed by law'. Article 10's right to freedom of expression also uses the phrase 'prescribed by law', as does the limitations paragraph in the right to freedom of assembly and association in Article 11.

These various clauses all impose an *ultra vires* style requirement on states, and therefore on public authorities via the Human Rights Acts 6(1). All restrictions on Convention rights have to be justified by reference to some law. They cannot be invented out of thin air or imposed by the authority as a matter of brute executive force. The concept of 'prescribed by law/in accordance by law' in Articles 8–11 goes beyond the mere requirement for some law somewhere; to this extent it reaches into the substance of the law but not generally, as far as

---

[63] A neat combination of the two approaches is evident in the well known decision of *R (Daly) v Secretary of State for the Home Department* [2001] UKHL 26, [2001] 2 AC 532. Also of interest in this context is *R (Van Hoogstraten) v Governor of HMP Belmarsh* [2002] EWHC 1965 (Admin), [2003] 1 WLR 263.

[64] See chapter two above.   [65] See *Streletz, Kessler and Krenz v Germany* (2001) 33 EHRR 751.

these articles are concerned, to impose a requirement for justice or fairness (as perhaps Allan would want or expect), but rather—in perfect accord with the principle of legality—to ensure that the law is properly available to and capable of being understood by those subject to it. To pick just one of the many decisions on the point, the court has stressed:

that one of the requirements flowing from the expression 'prescribed by law' is forseeability. A norm cannot be regarded as a 'law' unless it is formulated with sufficient precision to enable the citizen to regulate his conduct. At the same time, whilst certainty in the law is highly desirable, it may bring in its train excessive rigidity and the law must be able to keep pace with changing circumstances. The level of precision required of domestic legislation—which cannot in any case provide for every eventuality—depends to a considerable degree on the content of the instrument in question, the field it is designed to cover and the number and status of those to whom it is addressed.[66]

Citing earlier Convention case law, Lord Hope of Craighead noted in a UK case decided in July 2000 that to meet this requirement, domestic law 'must be sufficiently accessible to the individual and that it must be sufficiently precise to enable the individual to foresee the consequences of the restriction' on the right in question.[67]

Thus we can see that, as far as Articles 8–11 are concerned, the Convention broadly favours what we might call (using Allan's terminology) a majoritarian rather than a communitarian view. Of course it can do this in these articles because the other controlling phrase, 'necessary in a democratic society' that exists in all of them permits substantive evaluation of the rightness of an executive action, by reference in particular to the concept of proportionality. So the principle of legality does not need here to be stretched in the way favoured by Allan. Interestingly however, in the one non-absolute article dealing with a core civil liberty which does not contain this controlling requirement that all exceptions be 'necessary in a democratic society', the right to liberty in Article 5, the European Court has read far more into the concept of legality than it has needed to do (or has done) in relation to the other freedoms. As early as 1976, the court was stressing that the aim of Article 5 was 'to ensure that no one should be dispossessed of [his or her] liberty in an arbitrary fashion'.[68] In *Tsirlis and Kouloumpas v Greece* in 1997,[69] the court was to be found reiterating its by now settled case law in relation to Article 5 'that the Convention here essentially refers back to domestic law and states the obligation to conform to the substantive and procedural rules thereof; but it requires in addition that any deprivation of liberty should be consistent with the purpose of Article 5, namely to protect individuals from arbitrariness'.[70] The remarks of Lord Hope quoted in the

---

[66] *Hashman and Harrup v United Kingdom* (1999) 30 EHRR 241, para [31] (footnote omitted).
[67] *R (Evans) v Governor of Brockhill Prison (No 2)* [2001] 2 AC 19, 38, citing *Sunday Times v United Kingdom* (1979) 2 EHRR 245 and *Zamir v United Kingdom* (1983) 40 DR 42, paras [90]–[91].
[68] *Engel and others v The Netherlands (No 1)* (1976) 1 EHRR 647, para [58].
[69] (1997) 25 EHRR 198.
[70] Ibid para [56] (footnote omitted).

preceding paragraph were drawn from an Article 5 case, and his lordship continued that, in relation to detention, there was a third question (apart from the accessibility and forseeability of the law), namely 'whether, ... assuming that the detention is lawful under domestic law, it is nevertheless open to criticism on the ground that it is arbitrary because, for example, it was resorted to in bad faith or was not proportionate'.[71] To this qualified extent, therefore, the Convention does take Allan's expansive line on the rule of law.

It should be stressed that Article 5 is unusual in the scheme of the Convention in allowing such substantive issues to be dealt with under the principle of legality, and I do need to return to the mainstream of legality in a moment. But first we should notice an English decision under Article 5 which was one of the earliest and most dramatic examples of the revolutionary impact that the Human Rights Act was likely to have on UK law. *R v Offen*[72] concerned five appeals all involving the same point, the extent to which the legislature could consistently with Article 5 require courts automatically to mete out life terms of imprisonment to certain offenders. Under the Crime (Sentences) Act 1997, s 2 (subsequently re-enacted as the Powers of Criminal Courts (Sentencing) Act 2000, s 109), a sentencing court was required to impose an automatic life sentence on a person convicted of a serious offence, committed after the commencement of that provision, and when he or she was 18 years of age or older, where that person had previously been convicted of another serious offence, unless the court was of the opinion that there were exceptional circumstances relating to either of the offences which justified its not doing so. This legislative dictate was very unpopular with the judiciary, which had long cherished and sought to protect the discretion its members traditionally enjoyed to take into account all relevant circumstances when deciding upon the punishment of offenders. Yet here was the legislature seeking, apparently successfully if the early, pre-Human Rights Act case law was taken into account, to tie judicial hands. Many cases quickly occurred in which, judged by traditional standards, the sentence of life imprisonment appeared ludicrously harsh.

One of the most extreme of these was the *Offen* case itself, in which the hapless defendant had wholly ineffectually and as a clear result of mental deficiencies twice robbed building societies with an imitation firearm. On the first occasion he had given himself up to the police. On the second, an irate customer at the building society had simply grabbed his loot from him, with his friends later telephoning the police to tell them what he had done. On these facts, having pleaded guilty to the second offence, Offen was sentenced to life imprisonment. In the Court of Appeal, giving the judgment of the court, the Chief Justice Lord Woolf characterized the sentencing of offenders to life in the circumstances envisaged by the Act as a punishment that was so severe in its effect that the rigorous application of the section could on occasion be out of all

---

[71] *Evans*, n 67 above, 30 citing both *Engel*, n 68 above and *Tsirlis and Kouloumpas*, n 69 above.
[72] [2001] 1 WLR 253.

proportion to its purpose, namely the protection of the public. Where this was the case, the sentence would according to Lord Woolf infringe the substantive safeguard of legality set out in Article 5 and should not therefore be imposed, whatever Parliament might otherwise seem to have required. Lord Woolf avoided any overt challenge to parliamentary sovereignty by using the Human Right Act, s 3 to give fresh and Convention-compatible content to the meaning of 'exceptional circumstances' in the section. Offen himself and one of the other defendants in the appeal had their life sentences set aside in favour of much shorter periods of incarceration.

The *Offen* case is an unusual one from the perspective of the principle of legality since it is concerned with the one article in which, as I have earlier explained, this concept in the Convention is given (by the Strasbourg Court if not explicitly in the original wording of the provision itself) a strong, substantive meaning. But as I have also noted above, this is clearly because of the absence of any alternative route in for judicial review in such cases. The case is a challenging one for those who desire to restrict the judicial role under the Human Rights Act and who (flowing from this initial position) want to see the principle of legality applied in a narrow, democracy-reinforcing way. The decision is right in the sense that the Strasbourg case law clearly envisaged the notion of legality in Article 5 being deployed in an expansive fashion. It may also be right in the sense that it correctly applies Parliament's intention to the facts, a point of which Lord Woolf himself makes much in his judgment. But however it is dressed up or explained away, the *Offen* case has effectively disembowelled a particularly savage legislative intervention, passed at the height of a panic about crime and (if its words were to be believed) designed to inflict exactly the kind of punishment that was originally imposed on Offen and his fellow appellants.[73] Even opponents of judicial activism find themselves applauding the result while diverting their eyes from how it was brought about. Certainly the right to liberty is dear to the hearts of the judges and involves a subject, criminal justice and sentencing, which is at the centre of their adjudicative function. If Allan-style judicial activism has to be allowed anywhere, then it is more legitimate in this sphere than in any other.

Let us conclude this section of the chapter by returning briefly to the mainstream legality cases. A classic illustration of the less ambitious, and more democracy reinforcing, way in which the requirement of legality works in the rest of the Convention is afforded by the well-known decision in *Malone v United Kingdom*.[74] The applicant, an antique dealer, was prosecuted for offences relating to the dishonest handling of stolen goods. At his trial it emerged that his telephone had been tapped by the police acting on a warrant from the Home Secretary, issued without any explicit legal authority but on the basis of criteria that had been determined in advance by the government and which had then

---

[73] See for an application of the *Offen* case in the House of Lords *R v Drew* [2003] UKHL 25, [2003] 1 WLR 1213.   [74] (1984) 7 EHRR 14.

been applied by the relevant government officials so as to sanction the interception in this particular case. Various statutes appeared to recognize that such a power existed, without in any explicit case establishing or authorizing it. Manifestly there was an interference with the applicant's privacy of a type that engaged Article 8(1). Whether that interference was justifiable as being 'necessary in a democratic society' was a subject of some dispute when the case reached the European Court but before this exculpatory formula could be brought into play, the restriction on the right had first to be found to be 'in accordance with the law'. It was at this hurdle that the government's case collapsed. The relevant law was 'somewhat obscure and open to differing interpretations'.[75] It could not 'be said with any reasonable certainty what elements of the powers to intercept are incorporated in legal rules and what elements remain within the discretion of the executive'.[76] The court concluded that:

> ... the law of England and Wales does not indicate with reasonable clarity the scope and manner of exercise of the relevant discretion conferred on the public authorities. To that extent, the minimum degree of legal protection to which citizens are entitled under the rule of law in a democratic society is lacking.[77]

Shortly after the *Malone* decision, Parliament did enact the Interception of Communication Act 1985 which put the whole issue of tapping on a statutory basis for the first time. The way in which Parliament did this was itself controversial, with there being much concern at the time that the executive had persuaded the legislative branch to enact a measure which conceded only the most minimal of oversight in this sensitive area, and which allowed surveillance to continue without effective protection for the individual.[78] But if this was the case, it is a problem with regard to the functioning of the legislative rather than the judicial branch. This is not to say that the matter is not an important one; its centrality to the argument in this book about the value of representative democracy will be obvious. But the courts can only at best require the legislative branch to act; they cannot themselves draft the legislation. This is where Allan's critique of the majoritarian approach to the rule of law is credible to the extent that it is not a perspective which gives courts as much power as Allan would like to sketch out exactly how gaps in the law should be filled. But in a properly-functioning representative democracy this is exactly as it should be.

D. The common law

The *Malone* case is a good example of a gap in our legislative code which the European Convention required to be filled. There are many Strasbourg decisions

---

[75] (1984) 7 EHRR 14, para [79].   [76] Ibid.   [77] Ibid.
[78] *Halford v United Kingdom* (1997) 24 EHRR 523 is of interest in this regard. For a critique of the 1985 Act see KD Ewing and CA Gearty, *Freedom under Thatcher. Civil Liberties in Modern Britain* (Oxford: Clarendon Press, 1990), ch 3.

in a similar vein.[79] Further spaces surely await to be discovered now that the Convention is part of UK domestic law. Old assumptions about uncontrollable executive power clearly have to be rethought. The constitutional heresy of Sir Robert Megarry VC in the *Malone* case in the English Chancery Division, that the executive can do anything which is not prohibited by law, has been laid to rest, at least as far as conduct impinging on Convention rights is concerned.[80] Similarly problematic in the new legal order is the royal prerogative. The Human Rights Act does bind the Crown[81] but orders in council under the exercise of the prerogative are assimilated to primary legislation for the purposes of the Act.[82] Direct exercises of the prerogative, manifesting themselves as executive orders without any other hook of law upon which to hang themselves may be very exposed on legality grounds however.[83] Then if we move beyond government into the quasi-government or regulatory sector, we find many bodies engaged in decision-making affecting rights but which draw their authority from non-statutory sources; these too need to be prepared to defend the legality of their decision-making remit, as the Advertising Standards Authority successfully did when one of its adjudiciations was challenged under Article 10.[84]

Through its insistence on legality, the Human Rights Act has the potential to be a pervasive legal instrument, colonizing discrete areas of law with its ethical values. To the extent that these parts of our legal system have hitherto received no attention at all from the legislature, then this is a situation which is to be welcomed on broadly democracy reinforcing grounds. A particularly fascinating question concerns the impact of the Act on the common law. Not having the codes that are mainly to be found in continental Europe, we take for granted that the judges in this jurisdiction occasionally make law by 'developing' the common law when the opportunity arises in the course of litigation suitable to this purpose. But what about the losing parties in such cases who have been surprised in this way? It might cost them a small (or indeed a large) fortune, or even their liberty. Where such cases impact adversely on interests that can be characterized as Convention rights, in what sense can such changes/developments be regarded as 'prescribed by law' or 'in accordance with law'? The matter arose in acute form in 1995, in the cases of *SW and CR v United Kingdom*.[85] The applicants had been found guilty of, respectively, rape and attempted rape. In each case the

---

[79] See for eg *Halford v United Kingdom*, ibid; *Khan v United Kingdom* (2000) 31 EHRR 1016; *Armstrong v United Kingdom* (2002) 36 EHRR 515; *Taylor-Sabori v United Kingdom* (2002) 36 EHRR 248; *Lewis v United Kingdom*, European Court of Human Rights, 25 November 2003.

[80] *Malone v Metropolitan Police Commissioner* [1979] Ch 344, 366–367.

[81] s 22(5).

[82] See s 21(1).

[83] See D Squires 'Judicial Review of the Prerogative after the Human Rights Act' (2000) 116 *LQR* 572; P Billings and B Pontin, 'Prerogative Powers and the Human Rights Act; Elevating the Status of Orders in Council' [2001] *PL* 21.

[84] *R (Matthias Rath BV) v Advertising Standards Authority* [2001] HRLR 22. Note that in the case of the advertising code there is some statutory recognition—and therefore indirect underpinning—of its existence.

[85] (1995) 21 EHRR 363.

assault had been carried out not against a stranger or acquaintance but against the applicant's wife. Historically the common law had granted husbands immunity from prosecution for such offences on the basis that the wife on marriage by definition consents to such sexual intercourse for the rest of her life. This harsh and outdated rule had been modified around the edges by subsequent case law but had not been entirely removed. The case of CR provided the English courts with an opportunity finally to jettison the defence, which it duly did when his appeal came before first the Court of Appeal and afterwards the House of Lords.[86] This legal development having taken place, SW then found his own conviction on similar facts now to be unchallengeable in domestic law. The rules of the legal game appeared to have changed around both men, retrospectively transforming the conduct in which they had engaged into criminally punishable acts.

In such circumstances it is hardly surprising that both men took their cases to Strasbourg, arguing that the way the common law had been applied to them violated the prohibition against retrospective punishment which was contained in Article 7 of the Convention. No doubt the court was anxious to avoid headlines of the 'Euro Court saves rapists' type in the British tabloid press. There was also the respect that the Strasbourg judges no doubt felt was owed to the ancient system of the common law, the health of which entirely depended on finding new ways of expressing ancient ideas, of moving while pretending to stand still. At the same time, the applicants had been jailed, for five years in SW's case and three years in CR's. The court's solution was to emphasize the need not for the law to be clearly set out in statutory or code-like form but for its content to be accessible, and for any possible changes to it to be reasonably foreseeable. The court drew upon its approach to the 'prescribed by law/in accordance with law' requirement to be found in other articles:

> When speaking of 'law' Article 7 alludes to the very same concept as that to which the Convention refers elsewhere when using that term, a concept which comprises written as well as unwritten law and implies qualitative requirements, notably those of accessibility and forseeability.... Article 7 of the Convention cannot be read as outlawing the gradual clarification of the rules of criminal liability through judicial interpretation from case to case, provided that the resultant development is consistent with the essence of the offence and could reasonably be foreseen.[87]

Thus in the instant cases, the 'evolution' of the common law 'had reached a stage where judicial recognition of the absence of immunity had become a reasonably foreseeable development of the law'.[88] In particular, 'given the recognition of women's equality of status with men in marriage and outside it and of their autonomy over their own bodies, the adaptation of the ingredients of the offence of rape was reasonably foreseeable, with appropriate legal advice, to the

---

[86] *R v R* [1992] 1 AC 599.
[87] n 85 above, paras [35]–[36] (*SW v United Kingdom*); paras [33]–[34] (*CR v United Kingdom*).
[88] Ibid para [43] (*SW v United Kingdom*); para [41] (*CR v United Kingdom*) (footnote omitted).

applicant'.[89] The idea that the men should have sought legal advice in advance of their attacks is inherently absurd, but it is a necessary absurdity, avoiding the even greater nonsense that the Human Rights Act has frozen for ever the common law in the form that it happened to be in on the day of the Act's implementation.

The opposite possibility has also been unlocked by the Human Rights Act. Far from rigidifying the common law, the Act has the potential capacity to broaden its current, rather narrow ethical base.[90] The human rights set out in the Convention include values that have long been part of the fabric of the common law, such as the right to property in the first article of the first protocol and the guarantees of due process and of free speech in Articles 6 and 10 of the Convention itself. This close connection between the common law and the rights to be found in the Convention is not at all surprising given the influence that UK lawyers had over its drafting, a point I have discussed in an earlier chapter. Indeed as Martin Loughlin has astutely observed of those who pushed so hard for incorporation during the 1990s, the 'rights movement seems to be rooted ultimately in an attempt to rationalise the common law'.[91] There is more to the Convention however than the values which have long enjoyed pre-eminence in the common law. In particular Article 8's qualified guarantee that everyone has the 'right to respect for his private and family life, his home and his correspondence' has the capacity to add an undoubtedly fresh dimension to the common law. Article 11's guarantee of freedom of assembly and association and Article 14's prohibition of discrimination have the same potential to intrude into the pre-existing ethical structure of the common law. The values of the Convention are broader than those of the old common law, emphasizing a more rounded person than the property-owning, contract-concluding autonomous agent that the common law has historically favoured.

In the period between incorporation and implementation, a small school of thought argued that the Human Rights Act had no impact at all on common law adjudication between private parties, and that its only importance was as a guide to the interpretation of statutes and as a controller of the actions of public authorities.[92] This view of the Act could not survive the simple but devastating fact that Parliament had specifically included courts and tribunals in its definition of what a public authority was, and had therefore made absolutely certain that judges were also bound by s 6(1)'s injunction that such bodies should not

---

[89] Ibid para [40] (*SW v United Kingdom*); para [38] (*CR v United Kingdom*). See in the post Human Rights Act context *R v Goldstein, R v R* [2003] EWCA Crim 3450 (common law offence of causing public nuisance continues to exist notwithstanding the Act).

[90] On which see KD Ewing, 'The Unbalanced Constitution' in T Campbell, KD Ewing and A Tomkins (eds), *Sceptical Essays on Human Rights* (Oxford: Oxford University Press, 2001), ch 6. I return to this point in chapter seven.

[91] M Loughlin, 'Rights Discourse and Public Law Thought in the United Kingdom' in G Anderson (ed), *Rights and Democracy: Essays in UK-Canadian Constitutionalism* (London: Blackstone Press, 1999) 193, 201. The essay is a very useful summary of the writings of many British proponents of rights in the run-up to enactment of the Human Rights Act.

[92] R Buxton, 'The Human Rights Act and Private Law' (2000) 116 *LQR* 48 is a good example.

'act in a way which is incompatible with a Convention right'.[93] The fact that the parties before the courts might not be public authorities did not therefore seem to matter to Parliament as far as the application of the Human Rights Act was concerned: it was the judges themselves who were the relevant public authority for the purposes of the Act. But this raised another, intriguing possibility: could any person simply show up in court, assert against another private individual (whether natural or artificial) that his or her Convention rights had been infringed, and then demand from the court a remedy in discharge of its s 6(1) duty to act compatibly with the Convention?[94] This argument surely pushes the point too far. Parliament may have intended to bring the courts within the Human Rights Act but it could hardly have intended the 10 words it deployed to achieve this also (and without any notice) to lead to the abolition of the common law. The structure of the Human Rights Act, with its emphasis on proceedings against public authorities and its explicit linkage to the pre-existing system of judicial review, did seem to suggest that the distinction between private parties and public authorities was one that in some way or another was required to matter. And from the perspective of this chapter, there are obvious problems of foreseeability and accessibility in permitting the detailed and slowly built common law to be entirely supplanted by rights as vague as those that are set out in the European Convention.

This question of the exact remit of the Human Rights Act vis-à-vis the common law was the one that was perhaps most eagerly debated during the period between enactment of the Act and its implementation, and I consider it in further detail in chapter seven. As we shall see, the issue has yet to be conclusively resolved in the case law. An early and celebrated decision suggested that the Convention may prove to be the midwife to the new tort of privacy which the common law was already expecting.[95] However, the courts have proved less enthusiastic than might have been expected.[96] The fear of a breach of Articles 2 and 3 has also been held to be capable of underpinning controls on press freedom that might not have been possible in the absence of the Human Rights Act.[97] These developments have occurred in litigation between exclusively private

[93] See s 6(3)(a) for the reference to the courts (where tribunals are also included).

[94] See HWR Wade, 'Horizons of Horizontality' (2000) 116 *LQR* 217 for a taste of the kind of arguments that have been made along these lines.

[95] *Douglas v Hello! Ltd* [2001] QB 967. The academic literature on the *Douglas* case is already substantial: see N Moreham, '*Douglas and others v Hello! Ltd*—the Protection of Privacy in English Private Law' (2001) 64 *MLR* 767; AL Young, 'Remedial and Substantive Horizontality: the Common Law and *Douglas v Hello! Ltd*' [2002] *PL* 232; J Morgan, 'Privacy, Confidence and Horizontal Effect: "Hello" Trouble' (2003) 61 *CLJ* 444; G Phillipson, 'Transferring Breach of Confidence? Towards a Common Law Right of Privacy under the Human Rights Act' (2003) 66 *MLR* 726.

[96] *Wainwright v Home Office* [2003] UKHL 53, [2003] 3 WLR 1137; *X v Y* [2001] 1 WLR 2341 and especially *Douglas v Hello!* [2003] EWHC 786 (Ch), (2003) 153 NLJ 595 in which Lindsay J found that 'no relevant hole' existed in English law into which a new action for privacy needed to be inserted: para [84(ii)]. But the uncertainty of the law seems to have been an incentive to out-of-court settlements: see 'Friends star wins topless damages' *Guardian* 11 July 2003.

[97] *Venables and another v News Group Newspapers Ltd and others* [2001] Fam 430. See also *X (formerly Mary Bell) v O'Brien and others* [2003] EWHC 1101 (QB).

parties but in each case there has been a cause of action (for example breach of confidence) upon which to hang, however loosely, the Convention argument: it has not been simply a matter of turning up and waving the relevant right in the face of the judge. The same has been true in a celebrated nuisance case where the claimants' distress at the noise caused by low-flying military aircraft was usefully but not indispensably characterized as a breach of their Article 8 rights.[98] However in another case, where a strong attempt was made by counsel to persuade the Court of Appeal to apply the Convention in a case between private parties by dint of a broad application of s 6(1) read with s 6(3)(a), the judges— led by the Lord Chief Justice Lord Woolf—showed themselves notably reluctant to seize the initiative.[99]

The approach which the courts are in the main adopting, and which focuses on identifying an underlying cause of action[100] seems to be exactly right.[101] It requires the common law to develop in accordance not only with its old values but now also in line with the broader set of principles and rights, set out in the Convention, that Parliament has decreed should henceforth be taken into account. The common law is not in any sense superseded by the Human Rights Act, an event the destabilizing effect of which would greatly outweigh any notional good that it might achieve. Rather it is invigorated by the Act's injection into its rather stale circulatory system of a new (and it has to be said long-awaited) supply of fresh blood. Viewed in this way, the jaded 'horizontality/verticality' debate disappears and the Human Rights Act can be seen for what (at least partly) it was designed by its drafters to be, an Act aimed at the democratization of the common law, achieved by an articulation by the legislature (in the form of the Convention rights set out in the Act) of the values that should henceforth underpin the adjudicative process. The challenge to legality posed by the common law is met without the need exclusively to rely on a rights' statute so broad that to do so would raise its own issues of legitimacy from the legality perspective.

[98] *Dennis v Ministry of Defence* [2003] EWHC 793 (QB).

[99] *Jones v University of Warwick* [2003] EWCA Civ 151, [2003] 1 WLR 954, esp paras [26] and [30] *per* Lord Woolf, giving the judgment of the court.

[100] Based on an influential article by Murray Hunt: M Hunt, 'The "Horizontal Effect" of the Human Rights Act' [1998] *PL* 423.

[101] N Bamforth, 'The True "Horizontal Effect" of the Human Rights Act 1998' (2001) 117 *LQR* 34. But compare two articles arguing for stronger horizontality: J Morgan, 'Questioning the "true effect" of the Human Rights Act' (2002) 22 *LS* 259; and D Beyleveld and S D Pattinson, 'Horizontal Applicability and Direct Effect' (2002) 118 *LQR* 623.

5

The Principle of Human Dignity

A. 'Human dignity' in its legal context

We concluded the last chapter on an optimistic note, with Parliament legislating through the Human Rights Act to guide the common law towards a new and broader set of ethical principles and standards. In that chapter we also saw how, properly understood, the principle of legality can be seen as a vital adjunct to representative democracy and that it is consistently viewed as such in the European Convention. In this chapter I am concerned with probing more deeply into the nature of the wider set of values that I say is to be found in the Convention. It is clear that respect for civil liberties and adherence to the principle of legality only take us part of the way to a proper understanding of this document. The third of our triad of principles, which combine with each other and with the aspirations to which I turn in the next part of this book to make (I hope) sense of the Human Rights Act, needs now directly to be addressed. This is an idea that is less obviously rooted than either of my first two principles in the British legal tradition. It is the most human-rights-specific of our principles, and reflects most clearly the insights that were forced upon the world in the aftermath of the Second World War. It can best be expressed as an unwavering commitment to the principle of respect for human dignity.[1] Though not specifically mentioned in the preamble to the European Convention, the notion that each person matters in view of his or her humanity is a core sentiment that lies behind and explains much of the language actually deployed in the Convention.

There is a potentially hazardous conceptual trap lurking along this journey which I now need to spring and disarm. As I went to some pains to point out in chapter two, the idea of 'human rights' is somewhat vacuous. Are we not now letting in via this third principle all the vague 'nonsense upon stilts' about human rights that we thought we had expunged? After all, there would seem to be a kind of platitudinous kinship between 'human rights' and 'human dignity': it is impos-

---

[1] For the purposes of this book, the idea of human dignity can be conveniently understood as embracing within it respect for the autonomy of the person. Of course the two can and do lead in different directions but in a book of this nature it is suggested that they are sufficiently close to be linked together under this single principle rather than allocated their own separate ethical spaces. It is appreciated that as a result a large number of the medical ethics cases are not discussed in the text; from the perspective of this book these can be regarded as applications of the principle of human dignity in the sphere of human autonomy. Cases like *Evans v Amicus Health Care Ltd*; *Hadley v Midland Fertility Services Ltd* [2003] EWHC 2161 (Fam), [2003] 4 All ER 903 (on consent to IVF treatment) raise human rights points that, though important, are not directly discussed in this book.

sible to be against either or to explain in any kind of satisfactorily specific sense what they mean. As Deryck Beyleveld and Roger Brownsword have remarked, 'the concept of human dignity . . . . is something of a loose cannon, open to abuse and misinterpretation'.[2] This is not to imply that philosophers like Immanuel Kant and those writing more specifically in the legal tradition like Ronald Dworkin and Alan Gewirth may not have many interesting things to say about the intrinsic value of the person and about how dignified conduct is a special kind of virtue.[3] But to understand the principles underpinning the adjudicative process in human rights law we need to connect with how ideas apply on the ground; theoretical frameworks, however complete in the abstract they might be, are not our main interest. For similar reasons, Michael Perry's argument that a religious foundation to human rights is essential, with religion being understood widely to embrace the sacredness and the inviolability of the other, may seem exactly right to many, but it is not an argument for human dignity so much as it is (from a rational perspective blind) an assertion of a belief in its existence.[4]

Mention of religion reminds us of how contested the idea of human dignity can be when applied to different situations: a fundamentalist Christian's view of what human dignity entails is likely to differ markedly from that of the secular human rights activist. Metaphorically resembling members of the society in which they must operate, conceptions of human dignity are born, grow, and die, their influence sometimes enduring for generations, but occasionally being cast off well before death by a different brand of dignity. In the West, as Richard Rorty has noted in a remark I have already quoted in an earlier chapter, our improvement over the past 200 years, has been 'more easily understood not as a period of deepening understanding of the nature of rationality or of morality, but rather as [a time] in which there [has] occurred an astonishingly rapid progress of sentiments in which it has become easier for us to be moved to action by sad and sentimental stories'.[5] In other words we have noticed people more as people, and connected more to the (different) needs of those we might already have seen but never bothered to understand. First, in the nineteenth century it was the locally destitute and women. Then in the twentieth century, our hitherto blinkered view of what it meant to be human widened sufficiently to catch sight of persons of different colour to ourselves, and then later to see those with different sexual

---

[2] D Beyleveld and R Brownsword, 'Human Dignity, Human Rights, and Human Genetics' (1998) 61 *MLR* 661, 662.

[3] See ibid 663, 666. I have always found Alan Gewirth a difficult writer to follow: see his *Human Rights. Essays on Justification and Applications* (Chicago: University of Chicago Press, 1982). For a good summary, see R Plant, *Politics, Theology and History* (Cambridge: Cambridge University Press, 2001), ch 9.

[4] G Filibeck, *Human Rights in the Teaching of the Church: from John XXIII to John Paul II* (Vatican City: Libreria Editrice Vaticana, 1994) is a comprehensive guide to Catholic teaching on the subject within a specific time frame. The book referred to in the text, MJ Perry, *The Idea of Human Rights. Four Inquiries* (New York: Oxford University Press, 1998), is a hugely stimulating study of the subject and much to be recommended. Cf on the religious dimension to rights C Dwyer, 'Human Rights—Values for a Godless Age?' (2001) 146 *Law & Justice* 28; N Bobbio, *The Age of Rights* (Cambridge: Polity Press, 1996), ch 5.   [5] See above p 18.

orientations and then (even more recently) to confront the desires of those with physical impediments to lead a full life.

In the 1980s, a great surge of moral energy reflected the Western public's realization that the poor and starving of the developing world were, after all, people like us. So successful has this process been that new movements such as those campaigning for animal or environmental rights have also tried to jump aboard the moving wagon of human dignity, sometimes rather successfully. The story so far would appear largely a happy one, with ever-widening circles of persons being brought within the warm embrace of our dynamic perception of what it means to respect the dignity of the person. But it has been accompanied by continuing high levels of brutality, of genocide on occasion, in a not insignificant number of countries. Even in the West there has been talk of 'compassion fatigue', and a new harshness towards asylum seekers has become evident as the scale of those seeking such protection from the West has mounted. Above all, after the events of 11 September 2001 there has been a new kind of brutal utilitarianism in the air. It is too early to tell whether any or all of this will have an effect on how we discharge our obligation to respect human dignity in the future. Without doubt the obligation will remain, but will it (as in the past) extend only to family, friends, and our racial or national kin? The goal remains the same, but achieving it can be made a lot less demanding.

David Feldman is therefore right to remark that respect for human dignity is a 'notion which is culturally dependent and eminently malleable'.[6] As such it is something on which a consensus is particularly 'difficult to maintain in a pluralist society'[7] for in such a community no single vision of the person predominates and as a result different versions of dignity, drawn from different historical traditions, compete for our attention and approbation. But as Feldman also observes, '[n]evertheless it is important that we strive to uphold a consensus, because without it we would lose one of the bases for mutual respect.'[8] The issue for this ultimate 'floating signifier' (as Costas Douzinas would surely call the principle of human dignity)[9] becomes the highly practical one of how you flesh out its meaning. What is the right mechanism to get from the idea of respect for human dignity (with which everyone agrees) to the manifestation of this idea on the ground (in ways that are bound to be controversial)? As Jack Donnelly has observed, '[l]ists of human rights emerge out of the political struggle for human dignity and indicate the principal directions of that struggle.'[10] The work of Christine Sypnowich is particularly valuable in answering this question. In her important book, *The Concept of Socialist*

---

[6] D Feldman, 'Human Dignity as a Legal Value' [1999] *PL* 682, 698.

[7] Ibid 686 citing A Macintyre, *After Virtue: A Study in Moral Theory* 2nd edn (London: Duckworth, 1985).

[8] Ibid.

[9] See above p 19 n 54.

[10] *Universal Human Rights in Theory and Practice* (Ithaca: Cornell University Press, 1989), 27.

Law,[11] she offers a robust defence of human rights which nevertheless takes into account and largely accepts the validity of the Marxist critique of the idea.

Sypnowich's argument depends on regarding 'human rights' as little more than propaganda talk, as an open vessel into which meaning is poured. The first part of what she has to say rehearses ground we have already covered. Because it 'is difficult to provide an immutable definition of human dignity that is not vacuous',[12] it is not surprising that 'the question of what counts as human dignity [has varied] from epoch to epoch and from society to society'.[13] It follows that 'what it is to actually live a life of dignity undergoes a process of evolution. While human dignity seems a constant value, what gives human beings dignity will be constituted by social and historical factors.'[14] Human rights are 'constructed in a process of insurgence, so that we come to understand them in the changing social context of new political projects'.[15] Thus is man indeed a 'species-being', the phrase used by Marx to capture the same basic point.[16] It follows from this that human rights are 'not natural rights; they seek to protect human dignity, a concept which, while seemingly constant and eternal (thus "natural"), changes in its meaning from one society to the next'.[17] It follows from this that for Sypnowich, human rights cannot be separated from their political context; they are 'not only conditioned by history; they are an historical achievement, made possible by political conquest'.[18] Taking the critique further than we have yet gone, Sypnowich then observes that the health of the concept of human rights depends 'on certain political considerations about citizenship, on the reciprocal relation between individual and collective which comes from man's capacity to be a member of a political community'.[19] It follows that:

The kinds of human rights valued by socialists reflect a socialist conception of human dignity. In this conception, human dignity requires a minimum of material well-being: an individual who lives a degraded physical existence, who has no access to the means of life let alone those cultural resources that enrich it, cannot be said to live a life of dignity.[20]

Socialists from Marx to the old British Labour Party historically viewed human rights and human dignity with suspicion because they saw these ideas as essentially liberal in design, intended to buttress rather than to subvert the prevailing, capitalist, status quo. The leadership of the now disappeared USSR was motivated by the same scepticism when it fought a rearguard action against the ascendancy of human rights principles in the second half of the twentieth century. This did not mean that any of these sceptics were opposed to the concept of human dignity as such, a point we have already made in chapter two in relation to Marx.[21] Rather it was that they did not trust how the term was

---

[11] Oxford: Clarendon Press, 1990. An earlier, very valuable work is T Campbell, *The Left and Rights. A Conceptual Analysis of the Idea of Socialist Rights* (London: Routledge and Kegan Paul, 1983), esp ch 6.

[12] Sypnowich, n 11 above, 100.   [13] Ibid 100–101.   [14] Ibid 101.

[15] Ibid 105.   [16] Ibid 101. For Marx's approach to human rights see pp 15–16 above.

[17] Ibid 112.   [18] Ibid 107.   [19] Ibid 108.

[20] Ibid 109.   [21] Above p 16.

then understood, the meaning that was universally accorded to it: as Douzinas might put it, it was a 'floating signifier' which signified the wrong thing. Sypnowich's particular achievement is to show that socialists need not on this account be frightened off the concept altogether, but rather they need to enter (to use a deliberately provocative metaphor) the marketplace of ideas, and fight for the supremacy of their version of human rights. In this battle all options are open: '[i]f human rights are shaped by social factors, there can be no ultimate, timeless "core" of negative human rights, to which positive rights stand as dispensable extras.'[22] The political 'marketplace' in which to resolve these rival (though at times complementary) visions of the person is ideally the legislative assembly in which the representatives of the people meet to make rules for their society, pluralist or otherwise. In this way does Sypnowich connect with the writings of Eduard Bernstein (whom we discussed in chapter two) to provide us with a democratic theory of human rights which seeks to embrace and turn to good use, rather than to oppose and ignore, the concept of human dignity. Far from being antagonistic to our first two principles, respect for human rights is seen to be complementary to and dependant upon a properly functioning democratic process. The triad of principles that underpin the European Convention are mutually reinforcing of rather than antagonistic to each other.

B. Human dignity and the British parliamentary tradition

When we locate the idea of human dignity in its historical and political context in this way, it becomes possible for us to see that, far from being hostile to the concept, the UK Parliament has over the years been one of its staunchest friends, promoting various versions of human dignity through legislation as the mood of the times has allowed. I traced in an earlier chapter how the legislature has from time to time been engaged in the promotion of civil liberties, which term covers many of the traditional (that is to say 'negative') human rights that are at the core of the orthodox liberal's understanding of the term. But the broader, more socialistic version of human dignity has also been the focus of parliamentary intervention. Such legislation may not be presented in explicitly 'human rights' terms but it is none the less real for that. To trace the history of twentieth century interventions on this subject is to recount the story of the welfare state, with the people of Britain choosing through their elected representatives to enact laws designed to ensure a certain basic minimum dignity for all within the jurisdiction. Highlights in any such narrative would include the Education Act 1944, the National Health Service Act 1946, and the New Towns Act 1946, all of which initiatives came with the radical impetus of war behind them, demanding a better deal for those who had taken such risks in combat, and for the families they had left behind at home.

---

[22] Sypnowich, n 11 above, 111.

But the commitment to human dignity shown by the British Parliament has been more than merely reactive. Indeed from the landslide election of Henry Campbell-Bannerman's Liberals in 1905, it could be said that the dignity of the person was, with the defence of the realm, one of the two great legislative preoccupations of the twentieth century. The famous Trade Disputes Act of 1906 made possible trade union activism which transformed the lives of many working men and women, and legislation of this type continued until the mid 1970s. Winston Churchill's initiatives on national insurance and hours of work in 1911 were similarly radical for their day.[23] The trend persisted into the immediate post-war period, and came to fruition with the establishment of the welfare state after 1945, though other, even bolder assertions of dignity were to follow, such as the Housing (Homeless Persons) Act, enacted in 1977. Of course none of these (as we would call them) human dignity-oriented initiatives might have happened, or flourished as they did, had it not been for the emergence of the Labour Party or had there not developed an apparent challenge to capitalism in the Soviet Union with which for seven decades it was thought vital to compete. Nor was it the case that Parliament's commitment to human dignity was unwavering. We have already noted in passing a rival concern (defence of the realm) which has never fitted comfortably with the idea of human dignity, and a version of it now pushes hard for a perspective on human dignity which would exclude from the category of visible humanity asylum seekers and suspected 'terrorists' of many shapes and sizes.[24] Even apart from such a natural, albeit disapproving, bedfellow as national security, human dignity has also had in the last quarter of the century to cope with an attack on its whole underlying premise, namely that the electors have (through their government) any responsibility at all for the welfare of their neighbours and co-nationals.

If we move into areas of legislative activity more focused on the individual, and therefore closer to what we would normally expect to consider when dealing with issues of human dignity, we find that, here too, successive British parliaments have not been inactive. In the 1960s, reforming legislation on homosexuality[25] and capital punishment[26] could be said to have drawn their inspiration from a recognition of a certain kind of human 'dignity' or personhood which had hitherto been unnoticed or ignored by the state. The same is true of legislation passed in that and succeeding decades on issues such as racial and gender equality.[27] The British parliamentary tradition has been particularly favoured in this regard by the possibility of enactment of private members' (as opposed to government) bills. These are measures on which the established Parties quite deliberately take no line, thereby permitting legislators the luxury—and the

[23] Shops Act 1911; National Insurance Act 1911.
[24] See eg Anti-Terrorism, Crime and Security Act 2001, part 4; Nationality, Immigration and Asylum Act 2002, part 3.
[25] Sexual Offences Act 1967.
[26] Murder (Abolition of the Death Penalty) Act 1965.
[27] See eg Sex Discrimination Act 1975 and the Race Relations Act 1976.

onerous responsibility—of voting in accordance with their consciences rather than the relevant central office dictate. Many sensitive moral issues relating to matters of human dignity, often concerned with issues of autonomy, have been confronted and settled via this route. But that such resolutions are both always contingent and often controversial can be seen from the Abortion Act, a hotly debated measure enacted as a private members' Bill in 1967, and never since without its vehement critics, with the measure being subsequently partly revised in 1990.[28] Abortion is of course the quintessential hard case but it makes the point that the transition from the principle of human dignity (with which we all agree) to its manifestation on the ground is invariably a difficult one, involving sharp differences of opinion.

As is to be expected in a system which has long favoured legislative sovereignty, the courts in the British constitutional tradition have taken second place to Parliament in the definition of human dignity and in its promotion through law. There are advantages in this which lawyers may be slower than others to appreciate. An explicit legislative intervention is a more effective way of achieving change than is the isolated case, both in terms of enforcement and consciousness-raising. Parliament may have been wrestling with the abortion conundrum for over 35 years, but at least this has saved the judges from the crisis of legitimacy faced by many of their brethren in other jurisdictions who have been drawn into attempts conclusively to resolve the issue via litigation.[29] Certainly there are some judicial highlights, such as early common law initiatives on slavery and Lord Denning's work on behalf of separated wives in the third quarter of the twentieth century.[30] More recently, there have been judges willing to take robust and courageous stands to protect the humanity of asylum seekers in the face of attack from the two other branches of the state. Particularly remarkable in this regard was the decision of the Court of Appeal in which by a majority the court simply refused to regard as lawful delegated legislation the effect of which was to deprive asylum seekers of the means to live.[31] But the overall impression, viewed historically, is of a judicial branch that has been rather passive when it has come to the assertion of conceptions of human dignity in opposition to the other organs of the state. Indeed this may be just as well, since an activist judiciary in this sphere might find itself imposing a version of dignity far removed from that shared by the community as a whole, of which of course the judges are not representative and to which they are not accountable. A case like *Shaw v DPP*, in which in 1962 a majority of the House of Lords asserted 'a residual power to enforce the supreme and fundamental purpose of the law, to conserve not only the safety and order but also the moral welfare of the State', is

---

[28] Human Fertilisation and Embryology Act 1990, s 37.
[29] A rare judicial intervention in the English courts is *R v Bourne* [1939] 1 KB 687.
[30] See eg *Appleton v Appleton* [1965] 1 WLR 25.
[31] *R (Joint Council for the Welfare of Immigrants) v Secretary of State for Social Security* [1997] 1 WLR 275. See further *R (Q, D, J, M, F and B) v Secretary of State for the Home Department*, n 74 and 81 below.

now remembered—if it is remembered at all—with embarrassment as an example of wholly inappropriate judicial legislation.[32] Professor David Feldman is surely right, perhaps even understating the point, when he concludes the first part of his study of human dignity as a legal value by observing that 'the notion of a right to protection of dignity is so lacking in substantial and determinate content as to be unhelpful as a guide to judicial decision-making'.[33]

C. Human dignity, the Human Rights Act and the judges: a review of the case law

The Human Rights Act is not judicial legislation; rather it is an entirely proper Act of the UK legislature. It does not promulgate a right to dignity as such, but its effect is to infuse into British law a wide-ranging and general commitment to respect for the human person, and to locate that person in various guises not previously explicitly recognized by the courts. As mentioned earlier, this is the fresh dimension that the principle of respect for human dignity brings to the legislation. The statute which established the Council of Europe required the acceptance by all member states not only, as we saw in chapter four, of the principle of the rule of law, but also of the fact that all persons within every such state should be able to enjoy 'human rights and fundamental freedoms'.[34] The first of these phrases is suggestive of human dignity, the second of civil liberties. The preamble to the Convention affirms the 'profound belief' of signatory states in 'fundamental freedoms which are the foundation of justice and peace in the world' and 'are best maintained on the one hand by an effective political democracy and on the other by a common understanding and observance of the human rights upon which they depend'. Many of the central provisions of the Convention can best be understood not as assertions of the importance of civil liberties or legality but as manifestations of this underlying commitment to human dignity. This is particularly the case with the non-derogable right to life in Article 2,[35] and the prohibition of torture, inhuman, and degrading treatment or punishment and slavery and servitude in Articles 3 and 4(1) respectively. Article 4(2)'s prohibition on 'forced or compulsory labour' falls most readily into this category, as does the otherwise mysterious guarantee of the right to marry in Article 12. None of these rights exist solely to foster an effective representative democracy. As I briefly mentioned at the start of this chapter, they much more directly recall the origins of the Convention in the immediate post-war period, when memories were fresh as to the brutal extremism into which even Enlightenment cultures were capable of sinking. Article 8's guarantee

---

[32] [1962] AC 220, 267 *per* Lord Simonds. See also *Knuller Ltd v DPP* [1973] AC 435.

[33] Feldman, n 6 above, 698.

[34] Article 3 of the Statute: see European Commission of Human Rights, *Documents and Decisions* (The Hague, Martinus Nijhoff, 1959), 2.

[35] Subject as we have already seen to killing in the course of lawful acts of war; see p 42 above.

of the right 'to respect for [a person's] private and family life, his home and his correspondence' falls into the same category, albeit, as we have seen in chapter four, this provision has also proved its importance in the field of legality. The open texture of Article 8, its potential breadth, and the relative novelty of the concept vis-à-vis pre-existing forms of legal rights makes it the most obvious channel through which to infuse the bulk of the fresh ethical blood with which the drafters of the Human Rights Act hoped to revitalize the body of established law.

In incorporating these dignity-oriented aspects of the European Convention into domestic law, the Human Rights Act is squarely within the spirit of the kind of legislation that as we saw in the last section the British parliament has been producing over the past 100 years. Of course it is a dramatic piece of legislation, wider and more general than its predecessors, but viewed as a contribution to the conceptualization of human dignity it is neither unique, nor even such a large break with the past. The Act has the potential to force a radical revision of the way in which the law views the human person, by insisting on the ethical primacy of the individual in many arenas in which no such priority has ever previously been considered, much less accorded. But has the Act made any kind of difference to the way society collectively, its members individually, or the government corporately view the person? In particular has it unblinkered the law as to the range of persons within its reach, forcing a new awareness of people on the margins of our society? For advocates of the new 'culture of rights' that it was hoped the Human Rights Act would introduce,[36] this is a crucial issue; the Act fails if it is only about reinforcing the dignity of those (natural and legal) persons whose rights were already well seen and catered for by the law.[37] This critical point can only be addressed empirically, so it is to the case law on the human dignity oriented articles that I now turn.

1. Articles 2 and 3

It will be remembered that Article 2 is the provision that promises that '[e]veryone's right to life shall be protected by law.' In the hands of the European Court of Human Rights, this guarantee has been given a capacity to bite which has gone far beyond what its bare words would seem to encompass. Under it, each signatory state has found itself obliged 'not only to refrain from the intentional and unlawful taking of life, but also to take appropriate steps to safeguard the lives of those within its jurisdiction.'[38] A breach of the article occurs if it is established to the court's satisfaction:

---

[36] Eg F Klug, *Values for a Godless Age. The Story of the United Kingdom's New Bill of Rights* (London: Penguin, 2000); M Hunt, 'The Human Rights Act and Legal Culture: The Judiciary and the Legal Profession' (1999) 26 *JLS* 86.

[37] See GW Anderson, 'Review Article: Rights and the Art of Boundary Maintenance' (1997) 60 *MLR* 120 where this point is made very well.

[38] *Osman v United Kingdom* (1998) 29 EHRR 245, para [115].

that the authorities knew or ought to have known at the time of the existence of a real and immediate risk to the life of an identified individual or individuals from the criminal acts of a third party, and that they failed to take measures within the scope of their powers which, judged reasonably, might have been expected to avoid that risk.[39]

In another important strand to its case law, the European Court has used Article 2 on numerous occasions as a platform for the examination of killings by the police and security forces of member states. The key authority establishing this stream of decisions was the highly controversial one of *McCann v United Kingdom*[40] in which the court ruled by the narrowest of majorities (10 votes to nine) that the planning of a counter-terrorism operation by the UK authorities which led to the shooting dead of three unarmed IRA members in Gibraltar had been so conducted that the killings could not be said to have been 'absolutely necessary in defence of persons from unlawful violence within the meaning of Article 2(2)(a) of the Convention'.[41] In four decisions in May 2001, also arising from the conflict in Northern Ireland, the court extended this interpretation of Article 2 to include a requirement for member states to have proper, and in particular in these cases independent, investigating procedures where deaths at the hands of officers of the state occurred within their jurisdiction.[42]

These cases reflect the European Court's view that Article 2 'ranks as one of the most fundamental provisions in the Convention' which together with Article 3 'enshrines one of the basic values of the democratic societies making up the Council of Europe'.[43] As they seep their way into UK law via the Human Rights Act, they can be expected greatly to upgrade the law's perception of the value of each and every person whose plight is forced into judicial view by the vagaries of litigation. Already they have done important work, equipping Butler-Sloss LJ with a legal rationale with which to seek to protect from the attentions of an hysterical and vindictive media the notorious killers of the infant James Bulger on their release from prison.[44] There is some evidence that that decision has been subsequently used to protect the identities of persons accused of criminal or disciplinary offences against children where the disclosure of such persons' names could be shown to be enough to put their lives at risk.[45] The opportunity for the courts to rule on the effectiveness of the state's investigative process for killings by the police has not yet arisen, though clearly the Human Rights Act

---

[39] Ibid para [116].

[40] (1995) 21 EHRR 97.

[41] Ibid para [213].

[42] *Jordan and Others v United Kingdom* (2001) 37 EHRR 52. See further *McShane v United Kingdom* (2002) 35 EHRR 593 and *Finucane v United Kingdom* (2003) 37 EHRR 656.

[43] *McCann v United Kingdom*, n 40 above, para [147].

[44] *Venables and Thompson v News Group Newspapers and others* [2001] Fam 430.

[45] One such case certainly occurred in early 2001 in the context of disciplinary proceedings against a member of the nurses' profession: author's personal knowledge.

offers new ways—given the judicial energy—for such matters to be far more carefully scrutinized than in the past.[46]

There are, however, natural limits to the extent of the duties that can, through Article 2, be imposed on the executive branch. In *Orange v Chief Constable of West Yorkshire*[47] the Court of Appeal ruled that the police and prison authorities did not owe a duty of care to all prisoners to prevent them committing suicide. It would not 'be fair, just and reasonable to impose upon either the police or the Prison Authorities a general obligation to treat every prisoner as if he or she were a suicide risk. The consequence would be an unacceptable level of control and precaution, not only as an obligation placed upon the authorities, but also as an imposition on the individual prisoner.'[48] The Convention jurisprudence was not extensively relied upon and did not affect the outcome of the case.[49] It was however central to the decision of the Court of Appeal in *Lord Saville of New-digate v Widgery soldiers and others*[50] that British soldiers involved in the inquiry into the 'Bloody Sunday' killings of January 1972 did not need to go to Derry in order to give evidence lest by going there they would expose themselves to the possibility of attack. This case, a stark reminder to human rights activists in Northern Ireland that 'human rights' cuts both ways, also neatly illustrates that the decision as to who is a vulnerable person for the purposes of Article 2 can itself be perceived as (and indeed sometimes be) a highly political one.

A frequent comment from the European Court of Human Rights, and one quoted in the last paragraph, assimilates Article 3 with Article 2 as two provisions which together enshrine one of the 'basic values' that underpin the Convention. The absolute and non-derogable prohibition on torture and inhuman or degrading treatment or punishment is probably the single most human dignity-oriented of all the clauses in the Convention. The cases from Strasbourg on the article have been among the most well-known of the court's whole jurisprudence, from the finding of an abuse by the United Kingdom authorities in the context of the interrogation of suspected terrorists in Northern Ireland[51] to the assertion of its extra-jurisdictional reach in *Soering v United Kingdom*[52] and later (even more controversially) in *Chahal v United Kingdom*.[53] These are all cases in which the Convention draws to the centre of law's discourse the kind of

---

[46] See on the procedure at coroners' inquests: *R (Wright and another) v Secretary of State for the Home Department* [2001] EWHC 520 (Admin); and *R (Amin) v Secretary of State for the Home Department* [2001] EWHC 719 (Admin). The second of these was appealed to the Court of Appeal with *R (Middleton) v West Somerset Coroner* [2002] EWCA Civ 390, [2003] QB 581. The effect of developments under the Human Rights Act for coroners' courts is further considered in *Sacker v HM Coroner for County of West Yorkshire* [2003] EWCA Civ 217, [2003] 2 All ER 278 and by the House of Lords in the *Amin* case: [2003] UKHL 51, [2003] 3 WLR 1169.
[47] [2001] EWCA Civ 611, [2002] QB 347.
[48] Ibid para [42].
[49] Ibid paras [45]–[47].
[50] [2001] EWCA Civ 2048.
[51] *Ireland v United Kingdom* (1978) 2 EHRR 25.
[52] (1989) 11 EHRR 439.
[53] (1996) 23 EHRR 413.

person—the suspected terrorist, the alleged murderer, the immigrant—who is usually consigned to the margins and rarely seen or otherwise noticed. The domestic potential of the article in light of implementation of the Human Rights Act is well illustrated by three Strasbourg cases decided during the first seven months of 2001. In the first of these, *Keenan v United Kingdom*,[54] the court found that the treatment by prison officials of a mentally ill detainee in the weeks leading up to the young man's suicide, and in particular the failure to provide adequate medical care, amounted to a breach of Article 3. In its decision in *Z v United Kingdom* on 10 May 2001,[55] the court found a breach of Article 3 in the failure by a local authority to act to prevent the children in a family from being subjected to ongoing abuse and neglect. Both cases show how dynamic the jurisprudence of the European Court can be, particularly where, as with Article 2, a key Convention right can be seen to be in issue.[56] This is also clear from the third of these 2001 decisions, *Price v United Kingdom*.[57]

In that case, the applicant was a severely disabled person who had been consigned to prison without much thought being given as to how she would be able to cope physically with her incarceration. Before considering the facts, the court took the chance to summarize the way in which its thinking on the article has developed:

The Court recalls that ill-treatment must attain a minimum level of severity if it is to fall within the scope of Article 3. The assessment of this minimum level of severity is relative; it depends on all the circumstances of the case, such as the duration of the treatment, its physical and mental effects and, in some cases, the sex, age and state of health of the victim.

In considering whether treatment is 'degrading' within the meaning of Article 3, one of the factors which the Court will take into account is the question whether its object was to humiliate and debase the person concerned, although the absence of any such purpose cannot conclusively rule out a finding of violation of Article 3.

In this case the applicant, a four-limb-deficient thalidomide victim with numerous health problems including defective kidneys, committed contempt of court in the course of civil proceedings and was ordered by a judge to be detained for seven days (although, as a result of the rules on remission of sentences, she was in fact detained for a total of three nights amounting to four days). It appears that, in accordance with English law and practice, the sentencing judge took no steps, before committing the applicant to immediate imprisonment, a particularly harsh sentence in this case, to ascertain where she would be detained or to ensure that it would be possible to provide facilities adequate to cope with her severe level of disability.[58]

---

[54] (2001) 33 EHRR 913. To similar effect is *McGlinchey v United Kingdom* (2003) 37 EHRR 821.

[55] (2001) 34 EHRR 97.

[56] See further *E and Others v United Kingdom* (2002) 36 EHRR 519. Cf *DP and JC v United Kingdom* (2002) 36 EHRR 183. Deaths in custody have been particularly controversial in the UK: see GS Vogt and J Wadham, 'Deaths in Custody: Redress and Remedies' (London: The Civil Liberties Trust, 2003).

[57] European Court of Human Rights, 10 July 2001.

[58] Ibid paras [24]–[25] (case citation omitted).

The court accepted that there was 'no evidence in this case of any positive intention to humiliate or debase the applicant'[59] but nevertheless found a violation, considering 'that to detain a severely disabled person in conditions where she is dangerously cold, risks developing sores because her bed is too hard or unreachable, and is unable to go to the toilet or keep clean without the greatest of difficulty, constitutes degrading treatment contrary to Article 3'.[60]

There could hardly be a series of more explicit indications from the Strasbourg court about the expansive stage upon which Article 3 is now permitted to act. Gone are the days (if they ever existed) when the provision was a mere long-stop against unthinkably appalling systematic state violence.[61] Instead Article 3 now clearly catches all sorts of arbitrary attacks on the person, and covers not only the direct actions of state authorities but also their culpable omissions. This is a respect for human dignity, that is on the move, expanding the moral dictates of civilized society ever outwards, bringing more and more persons within its field of vision. Despite this potential, clearly evident in the Strasbourg case law, the Article 3 case law took a little while to catch fire in the domestic courts. In the early decision of *R v H*,[62] the Court of Appeal rightly insisted that the reasonable chastisement defence to the prosecution of a parent for an assault upon his or her child should now take into account the limitations on that line of argument which flow from the European Court's ruling in 1998 that the leniency of the domestic law on this matter infringed Article 3.[63] Another strong ruling in the early days came from Scotland, and raised the question of the incompatibility with Article 3 of the way in which a remand prisoner was being treated in that jurisdiction, a case with potential implications for the whole prison system north of the Border.[64] Despite these two cases, however, the approach in the first couple of years of the Act's life can be characterized as having been rather cautious.

In *R (Russell) v Governor of Frankland Prison*,[65] the issue was concerned with the lawfulness of the respondent governor's policy that any prisoner placed in the segregation unit of the prison who refused to wear prison clothes was not to be allowed to collect his or her meals from the servery but was rather to be restricted to one meal per day (instead of the usual three) brought directly by staff to the prison cell. Clearly here was a dispute that had spiralled out of control into a battle over authority, and the Divisional Court duly found a breach of the relevant prison rule that adequate food should be supplied to all prisoners. The judge also found that 'the policy... (in view of the possible indefinite duration of a segregation of the prisoner in the unit) may well breach the fundamental rights protected by article 3',[66] but said no more on the subject, and it is clear that the case would have been decided the same way even in the absence of the Human Rights Act. It is regrettable that the opportunity for some strong judicial guidance on Article 3 was not taken. In *X v Secretary of State for*

---

[59] European Court of Human Rights, 10 July 2001, para [30].   [60] Ibid.
[61] See *Donnelly v United Kingdom* (1975) 4 DR 4.
[62] [2001] EWCA Crim 1024.   [63] *A v United Kingdom* (1998) 27 EHRR 611.
[64] *Napier v Scottish Ministers* Outer House, Court of Session, 26 June 2001. See below pp 138–139.
[65] [2000] 1 WLR 2027.   [66] Ibid para [19].

the Home Department,[67] the Court of Appeal declined to find any breach of Article 3 in the decision to deport a mentally ill but illegal immigrant to Malta. The claimant relied upon a supportive but highly unusual decision of the European Court of Human Rights which had held on the particular facts before it that although it could not 'be said that the conditions which would confront [the applicant] in the receiving country [were] themselves a breach of the standards of Article 3, his removal would expose him to a real risk of dying under the most distressing circumstances and would thus amount to inhuman treatment'.[68] The risk of dying was not as obvious in the X case as it had been in that Strasbourg decision (which had involved a person suffering from AIDS), and the Court of Appeal had little trouble in distinguishing it, albeit in a rather pre-emptory fashion.[69]

The subject matter of the cases of *Russell* and *X*, prison and immigration law respectively, is not at all surprising since it is in our treatment of prisoners and asylum seekers that we are most likely to be tempted to gloss over our human rights obligations. When it comes to interpreting Article 3, it would seem that the judiciary is wavering between, on the one hand, accepting the moral imperative to accord all persons before them this most basic of human rights, and on the other hand an appreciation that the Convention cannot and should not be used to restructure Britain's penal and immigration policies, matters that clearly belong in the political domain and are indeed highly controversial within it. In the asylum and deportation cases epitomized by its decision in *X*, this perspective produces a reluctant recognition that the whole world cannot live in Britain and just managing to get here should not bring automatic jurisdictional salvation. While 'out of sight, out of mind' is too narrow a rule to apply, something more that being physically seen is required before the Convention can be marshalled to do its beneficial work. The dilemma is neatly caught in *R (Turgut) v Secretary of State for the Home Department*,[70] where the Court of Appeal found itself stressing both that the Secretary of State remains the primary finder of fact even in immigration cases with an Article 3 component but also (and at the same time) that the zone of judicial deference to the executive in this field is very narrow. Torn between their ethical and their professional selves, the judges cannot help but try to have it both ways.

Having said all this, however, it may be that as the Human Rights Act beds down, a stronger, more spirited interpretation of Article 3 is beginning to emerge. In a case decided in January 2003, *A v Home Secretary*,[71] the Court of Appeal allowed an appeal against a decision to remove a woman to a place where it was likely she would be exposed to a risk of gang violence and sexual

---

[67] Court of Appeal, 7 December 2000.

[68] *D v United Kingdom* (1997) 24 EHRR 423, para [53].

[69] *X v Secretary of State for the Home Department*, n 67 above, para [14]. See also *R (Mian) v Secretary of State for the Home Department* [2002] EWHC 2191 (Admin).

[70] [2001] 1 All ER 719.

[71] [2003] EWCA Civ 175.

abuse because of her previous involvement as a police informer. The court was emphatic that where Articles 2 and 3 were involved, the factual record required 'most anxious scrutiny' from the relevant decision-makers, including the courts.[72] It was clear that a 'contracting state, such as the United Kingdom, [would] ... be in breach of the European Convention if it expel[led] or remove[d] a person to a state where there [was] a real risk to that person from people who [were] not public officials'.[73] The following month came the remarkable Administrative Court decision of *R (Q, D, J, M, F and B) v Secretary of State for the Home Department*.[74] The claimants challenged a recently enacted asylum law[75] which prohibited the provision of support for asylum seekers whose claims for asylum were judged by the Secretary of State not to have been made as soon as was reasonably practicable. The claimants—all adversely affected by the new law—argued that this meant that they would have no food or shelter nor any means of obtaining them and that their consequent destitution would necessarily involve a breach of their Convention rights.

The Act which had promulgated this harsh rule had itself asserted that its terms should not be interpreted so as to infringe Convention rights.[76] Collins J deployed the freedom of manoeuvre that this chink in the legislative armoury had left him to hold that there would 'normally be a real risk that to leave someone destitute [would] violate'[77] not only Article 3 but Article 8.1 as well. Therefore the authorities had to give much closer consideration than they had done in these cases to the consequences of the decision to withdraw or to refuse to extend support. His Lordship recognized that this ruling would 'weaken the anticipated effect'[78] of the provision before the court but, remarking that it 'would be surprising if the standards of the ECHR were below those believed 200 years ago to be applicable as the law of humanity',[79] he suggested that 'Parliament [could] surely not have intended that genuine refugees should be faced with the bleak alternatives of returning to persecution ... or of destitution.'[80] The Court of Appeal unanimously dismissed the government's expedited appeal, albeit on a somewhat different basis than had originally found favour before Mr Justice Collins. The appellate body found that it was 'not unlawful for the Secretary of State to decline to provide support unless and until it is clear that charitable support has not been provided and the individual [was] incapable of fending for himself,' but that the Secretary of State had to be 'prepared to entertain further applications from those to whom he has refused support who

---

[72] [2003] EWCA Civ 175, para [20] *per* Keene LJ. The phrase 'most anxious scrutiny' is drawn from the speech of Lord Bridge in *Bugdaycay v Secretary of State for the Home Department* [1987] AC 514, 531.

[73] Ibid para [25].   [74] [2003] EWHC 195 (Admin).

[75] Nationality, Immigration and Asylum Act 2002, s 55.

[76] s 55(5)(a).

[77] n 74 above, para [72].

[78] Ibid para [74].

[79] Ibid. The implied reference is to *R v Inhabitants of Eastbourne* (1803) 4 East 103, discussed by Collins J at ibid para [59].

[80] Ibid para [74].

have not been able to find any charitable support or other lawful means of fending for themselves'.[81] At an intuitive level, it is surely hard to argue with the proposition that deliberately rendering people destitute infringes their human rights; and there is, as Collins J and the Court of Appeal amply demonstrated, plenty of Strasbourg case law connecting that insight with Convention rights. The reaction of the government of the day to the Administrative Court ruling was one of extreme anger,[82] a response which was fortunately not repeated when the decision of the lower court was vindicated on appeal.

2. Article 8 and the principles of judicial review

The construction of Article 8's guarantee of respect for privacy has been somewhat less problematic for the UK judiciary in the aftermath of incorporation, not only because the right guaranteed is less fundamental than are those to be found in Articles 2 and 3 but also (and mainly) because the variety of exceptions to the right set out in paragraph 2 of the provision leave plenty of room for executive manoeuvre and therefore for judicial deference. Though we have seen a passing reference to the provision in the asylum case on Article 3 that we have just discussed, the overall impact of Article 8 has, from the perspective of vulnerable groups and individuals, proved a tantalizing disappointment: it allows all sorts of speculative arguments to be made but has then doomed most of them to failure. The most important Article 8 case however, and one of the handful of key decisions so far handed down under the Human Rights Act, did produce a remarkable victory for the claimant. This was *R (Daly) v Secretary of State for the Home Department*,[83] in which the complaint was that the standard cell searching procedure, to which the claimant in common with other prisoners had been regularly subjected, infringed his right to privacy to the extent that it invariably involved the scrutiny—in his absence—of (among other documents) his privileged legal correspondence. The relevant prison policy ostensibly limited the amount of scrutiny of the documentation allowed, but it was obvious that there would be a high temptation for the prison officers involved in the search to go further. It was the absolute nature of the rule that particularly offended their lordships when the case reached them in spring 2001. As Lord Bingham put it, while '[a]ny search policy must accommodate' the 'inescapable fact' that 'the prison population include[d] a core of dangerous, disruptive and manipulative

---

[81] *R (Q and others) v Secretary of State for the Home Department* [2003] EWCA Civ 364, [2003] 3 WLR 365, para [63] of the judgment of Lord Phillips of Maltravers MR, giving the judgment of the court. The thoughtful discussion of Art 3 and of the role of positive and negative obligations at paras [44]–[63] repays careful study. See *R (S T and D) v Secretary of State for the Home Department* [2003] EWHC 1941 (Admin) where an Art 3 challenge was successful on the basis of the decision in the Q case.

[82] Press coverage of the decision on the day after it was handed down, 20 February 2003, was extensive: among other reactions it provoked a hostile front-page story in the *Daily Mail*. See also *The Guardian*, 20 February 2003, p 2. The government's approach to asylum has precipitated many appeals: see *R(T) v Secretary of State for the Home Department* [2003] EWCA Civ 1285.

[83] [2001] UKHL 26, [2001] 2 AC 532.

prisoners, hostile to authority and ready to exploit for their own advantage any concession granted to them', it was equally clear that there were other means of dealing with such persons without the imposition of the policy under scrutiny 'in its present blanket form'.[84] It followed that, while any prisoner 'who attempts to intimidate or disrupt a search of his cell, or whose past conduct shows that he is likely to do so, may properly be excluded even while his privileged correspondence is examined so as to ensure the efficacy of the search', there could be 'no justification...for routinely excluding all prisoners, whether intimidatory or disruptive or not, while that part of the search is conducted'.[85]

Lord Bingham's view was supported by the rest of their lordships hearing the case. His judgment was largely based on the common law, and the subsequent fame of the decision rests more on some general remarks made by Lord Steyn on the nature of judicial review in light of the Human Rights Act than it does on the resolution of the precise issue before the court. Speaking for the whole tribunal, Lord Steyn analysed the approach that had been taken to the review of administrative discretion in three earlier decisions of lower courts under the Human Rights Act,[86] and went on to consider how the new emphasis on proportionality inherent in the Act was properly to be connected to the pre-existing approach of the law, rooted as it had been in the principles set out in the well-known case of *Associated Provincial Picture Houses Ltd v Wednesbury Corporation*[87]:

The starting point is that there is an overlap between the traditional grounds of review and the approach of proportionality. Most cases would be decided in the same way whichever approach is adopted. But the intensity of review is somewhat greater under the proportionality approach. Making due allowance for important structural differences between various convention rights, which I do not propose to discuss, a few generalisations are perhaps permissible. I would mention three concrete differences without suggesting that my statement is exhaustive. First, the doctrine of proportionality may require the reviewing court to assess the balance which the decision maker has struck, not merely whether it is within the range of rational or reasonable decisions. Secondly, the proportionality test may go further than the traditional grounds of review inasmuch as it may require attention to be directed to the relative weight accorded to interests and considerations. Thirdly, even the heightened scrutiny test developed [for cases involving human rights issues] .... is [now] not necessarily appropriate to the protection of human rights.[88]

With implementation of the Human Rights Act, 'the intensity of the review' of administrative action was now 'guaranteed by the twin requirements that the limitation of the right was necessary in a democratic society, in the sense of

---

[84] Ibid para [19].

[85] Ibid.

[86] *R (Mahmood) v Secretary of State for the Home Department* [2001] 1 WLR 840; *R (Isiko) v Secretary of State for the Home Department* 20 December 2000 (Court of Appeal); *R (Samaroo) v Secretary of State for the Home Department* 20 December 2000 (High Court).

[87] [1948] 1 KB 223.

[88] *Daly* n 83 above, para [27], citing the 'gays in the military' case *R (Smith) v Ministry of Defence* [1996] QB 517 as the key authority, pre the Human Rights Act, for the proposition that human rights cases required close scrutiny.

meeting a pressing social need, and the question whether the interference was really proportionate to the legitimate aim being pursued'.[89]

Needless to say these dicta have had public lawyers enthusiastic about the prospect of vastly increased litigation, with their lordships through Lord Steyn seeming to sanction far more robust judicial engagement in the exercise of administrative action than has ever been contemplated—much less sanctioned—in the past. Certainly the language is more expansive than that to be found in the *Wednesbury* line of cases. But this does not mean that the outcome of cases is bound to change. As Lord Steyn goes on to remark, his comments do not 'mean that there has been a shift to merits review. On the contrary . . . the respective roles of judges and administrators are fundamentally distinct and will remain so.'[90] And then, he chooses to conclude his speech with the powerful but cautionary remark that '[i]n law context is everything.'[91] The three cases whose earlier, more deferential, approach to executive power had been what had led to Lord Steyn's statement of general principle[92] had all arisen in the context of immigration law, and it is by no means obvious that the approach in *Daly* would have made very much difference to them. Indeed one of these cases, *Samaroo v Secretary of State for the Home Department*, did go on appeal to the Court of Appeal on this very point, but without any success.[93] The claimant was a foreign national resident in the UK who had been convicted of a serious crime and who was on that account to be deported. Giving the lead judgment, Lord Justice Dyson considered that 'the function of the court in a case such as this [was] to decide whether the Secretary of State has struck the balance fairly between the conflicting interests of Mr Samaroo's right to respect for his family life on the one hand and the prevention of crime and disorder on the other. In reaching its decision, the court must recognise and allow to the Secretary of State a discretionary area of judgment.'[94] The *Daly* decision did 'not assist' Samaroo's argument.[95] The dilemma identified earlier in relation to Article 3, concerning the proper remit of judicial involvement, was not abolished by the *Daly* case; rather it (merely) framed the issue in a different way.[96]

3. Article 8 and the rules/discretion distinction

In the *Samaroo* case only the individual and his family were involved. It was not the rule itself which underpinned the action against the claimant that was being challenged; rather it was the exercise of a discretion under that rule. Judges are

---

[89] Ibid.   [90] Ibid para [28].   [91] Ibid.   [92] See text at n 88 above.
[93] [2001] EWCA Civ 1139.   [94] Ibid para [35].   [95] Ibid para [19].
[96] To similar effect is *R (Ponting) v Governor of HMP Whitemoor* [2002] EWCA Civ 224. In *Edore v Secretary of State for the Home Department* [2003] EWCA Civ 716, [2003] 1 WLR 2979, the Court of Appeal emphasized the 'discretionary area of judgment' that was inherent in Art 8 which meant (quoting from the 'enormously helpful' (para [16]) judgment of Moses J in *R (ALA) v Secretary of State for the Home Department* [2003] EWHC 521 (Admin)) that the Secretary of State was 'bound to be better placed to take a wider overall view as to what [was] needed to ensure that immigration control [was] effective'.

more comfortable with the latter kind of review than with the former. This is hardly surprising: rules have a greater aura of legitimacy than have individual decisions by public officials. In the context of the exercise of discretion under the Human Rights Act, the courts have also shown themselves reluctant wholly to overturn executive policies on privacy grounds, even where they have been convinced that a true issue of human rights has been in issue. In such cases, the judges have been diffident about reaching past the concrete exercise of discretion in an individual case (such as we saw attempted, albeit unsuccessfully, in the *Samaroo* case) in order (by implication) to rule on an executive practice applicable to a whole class of persons. Thus in *R (Kozany) v Secretary of State for the Home Department*,[97] a policy in relation to where to hear asylum cases distinguished between claimants with and claimants without families in the UK. In refusing an application for judicial review by an individual claimant, Mr Justice Gibbs confirmed the appropriateness of exercising the relevant statutory discretion by reference to the policy that had been established. Any argument to the contrary was 'doomed to fail'.[98] It was 'indisputable...that the Secretary of State [could] set a policy to guide decisions on immigration matters where Article 8 rights may be engaged', the policy being 'itself...designed to conform to Article 8'.[99] However, in making his decisions by reference to his policy on this provision of the Convention, the Secretary of State was of course 'susceptible to judicial review for failure to conform to the policy in a given case'.[100]

In both the *Kozany* and *Samaroo* cases, we have a variant of the ethical struggle that we earlier saw arising in the context of Article 3. Judicial diffidence in the context of challenges to rules and policies is unsurprising: the wider the range of cases affected by a court ruling, the more the judge's intervention cannot help but take on a legislative rather than an adjudicative colour. And the closer to a legislative act the ruling becomes, the more likely it is to be unacceptable on constitutional grounds. The impasse here is between the moral imperative of human dignity in the individual case and the executive entitlement ('right' is too strong a word in the context) to have regard to the wider public interest. It is a version of the war between rights and utility that is waged on all fronts throughout the Human Rights Act and indeed in the European Convention itself, an important topic to which I turn in the next chapter. The *Daly* case is a good indicator of how the courts have sought to resolve this tension. The case's concern with legal professional privilege makes it more a legality than a human dignity decision and perhaps therefore one that belongs more comfortably in the last chapter than in this one. What is important about the *Daly* case in the present context is that, as we have seen, the law lords there showed a strong distaste for the over-rigid application of a policy invasive of privacy. Lord Bingham and Lord Steyn were both particularly strong on this point. It was not the *idea* of a policy as such that excited their lordships' indignation; rather it was the unyielding and

---

[97] [2002] EWHC 2830 (Admin).   [98] Ibid para [11].   [99] Ibid.
[100] Ibid.

over-prescriptive nature of the *application* of the policy in question. As a rule, judges like inflexible policies which permit no exceptions for the individual case even less than they like striking down executive policies. This antipathy to blanket policies is derived from a tendency on the part of the courts to regard each individual case as special. In the Article 3/Article 8 context, we have already seen that one of the things that Collins J and after him the Court of Appeal disliked most about the withdrawal of support from 'late' asylum seekers was the apparently blanket assumption, made *in every case*, that no Convention issue related to destitution would arise. Their lordships insisted that more attention needed to be given to the point on an individual basis.

This distaste for general rules is deeply entrenched in the common law culture, where the assumption that every individual has a right to put his or her side of the story is centuries old. This institutional bias towards natural justice found a ready echo in post-*Daly* cases dealing directly with matters of dignity and personal autonomy. In a way reminiscent of the *Turgut* decision which we discussed in the context of Article 3, the courts have been tempted to escape the dilemma of having to choose between expediency and utility on the one hand (suggesting the inflexible application of general policies) and human dignity/ human rights on the other (suggesting that every case be treated as a single matter to be viewed entirely on its own terms) by accepting *in principle* that a policy is necessary while at the same time stressing *the need for flexibility* on the part of the primary decision maker in the application of that policy. It is a nice way of, as the cliché goes, having your cake and eating it at the same time: the judge accepts the policy and also the need for every case to receive potentially individual attention. The administrator might respond that it is then left to the primary decision maker to square the circle by managing to be both efficient and open-minded at the same time. But by then the law has moved on and the official is left with the unglamorous task of cleaning up.

Much inevitably depends on the kind of policy that is in issue, how inflexible it is, and how many decisions fall to be taken under it.[101] *R (Mellor) v Secretary of State for the Home Department*[102] concerned a prisoner's desire to be given access to artificial insemination facilities to start a family. The relevant prison service policy allowed such permission in exceptional circumstances and explicitly asserted that 'each case [was to be] considered on its own facts'.[103] This was enough for the Court of Appeal which, in rejecting the claimant's arguments stressed that it did 'not follow from [the ruling] that it will always be justifiable to prevent a prisoner from inseminating his wife artificially,

---

[101] Very useful is C Hilson, 'Judicial Review, Policies and the Fettering of Discretion' [2002] *PL* 111, an article which comes to broadly similar conclusions to mine on the human rights point being discussed here: 'it seems fair to say that blanket policies *generally* violate the spirit of human rights law in failing to provide a sufficient proportionality-based balancing between the general interest aims served by the policy and the merits of an individual's case': ibid 128.
[102] [2001] EWCA Civ 472, [2002] QB 13.
[103] Ibid para [17] of the judgment where the policy is set out in detail.

or indeed naturally'.[104] In *R (Hirst) v Secretary of State for the Home Department*[105] permission to prisoners to telephone representatives of the media was given only in 'wholly exceptional circumstances'[106] which could never include commenting on matters of interest and concern to prisoners generally. In judicial review proceedings, Mr Justice Elias condemned such a policy as insufficiently flexible; while a policy that allowed a right to contact the media 'only exceptionally'[107] was appropriate, the policy before the court amounted to 'effectively a blanket ban on media interviews in matters of this kind'[108] and was for this reason impermissible. In *R (M L) v Secretary of State for Health*[109] the challenge was to a health service circular which set out directions and guidance for visits by children to patients in three high security hospitals. The patients in these institutions suffered from mental disorders and needed to be treated and cared for in conditions of special security because of their dangerous, violent, or criminal tendencies. The policy was not to permit visits from children other than in certain particular circumstances, but it was not an inflexible rule and permission for particular visits to be made could be sought. Noting that a 'cursory glance at Article 8(2) [of the European Convention was] enough to see that a balancing exercise [was] required'[110], Mr Justice Scott Baker went on to say:

The words *necessary in a democratic society* flag up proportionality and the reference to *the protection of the rights and freedoms of others* shows that in drafting these Directions the Secretary of State has to weigh the interests of children on the one hand against those of patients on the other.[111]

This had been done in the circular before him, with its elaborate system for the processing of requests for exemption. The judge was alive to the possible inflexibility of the policy:

At one time I was concerned that the Directions might absolutely exclude visits by a child who did not fall within the categories [permitted under the policy directive] but nevertheless was well acquainted with the patient, for example a godchild or a neighbour. The answer however is that no child is absolutely excluded. There is always the fallback of an application to the court for a contact order under Sections 8–10 of the Children Act 1989.[112]

What problems there were lay with the apparently inefficient administration of the scheme, but any 'unreasonable delay in that regard [could] not be laid at the

---

[104] [2001] EWCA Civ 472, [2002] QB 13, para [45].
[105] [2002] EWHC 602 (Admin), [2002] 1 WLR 2929.   [106] Ibid para [6].   [107] Ibid para [77].
[108] Ibid para [78]. Cf *R (Gilbert) v Secretary of State for the Home Department* [2002] EWHC 2832 (Admin); *R (Williams) v Secretary of State for the Home Department* [2002] EWCA Civ 498, [2002] 1 WLR 2264.
[109] High Court, 11 October 2000.
[110] Ibid 13 of the transcript.
[111] Ibid (emphasis in the original).
[112] Ibid 10.

door of the Secretary of State and [did] not go to the lawfulness of the circular with which this case [was] concerned'.[113]

It is interesting to compare these decisions with yet another prison case, *R (P and Q) v Secretary of State for the Home Department*.[114] Here the issue was the extremely tricky one of whether and if so for how long new born babies could be left with their mothers in prison. The relevant prison service policy prohibited such babies from remaining with their mothers after they had reached the age of 18 months. Clearly there was an Article 8 issue, in the sense both that the privacy of the mother and child was affected by the policy and that the policy could be described as being, in the language of Article 8(2), 'in accordance with the law and... necessary in a democratic society' for (among other possibilities) 'the prevention of disorder or crime' and the 'protection of the rights and freedoms of others' (including the rights of the 'child vis-à-vis her mother').[115] After a close analysis of the Strasbourg case law, the Court of Appeal accepted that the prison service was entitled to have a policy and that the 'only question' it had to decide was whether it was permissible for that policy to be operated 'in a rigid fashion, insisting that all children leave by the age of 18 months at the latest (give or take a few weeks if their mother is about to be released), however catastrophic the separation may be in the case of a particular mother and child, however unsatisfactory the alternative placement available for the child, and however attractive the alternative solution of combining day care outside prison with remaining in prison with the mother'.[116]

With the issue phrased in this way, there could be little doubt as to the outcome. The court considered that 'the policy must admit of greater flexibility' than was currently allowed.[117] The court then set out various guidelines which it considered should properly guide the prison service in the exercise of its judgment on these matters, relating to the fact that a woman's rights when in prison did inevitably need to be limited, the risk to order within the prison from any relaxation of the policy and the welfare of the child. Turning to the facts before it, the court approved the separation of mother and child in one of the cases but not in the other. As is usual in decisions of this nature, the judges were at pains to stress that they were not engaged in second-guessing the expertise of the relevant public authority.[118] On the other hand the case illustrates the momentum towards judicial intrusion into the public sphere that has been built up under the Human Rights Act, and particularly as a result of the *Daly* decision. Giving the judgment of the court, Lord Phillips MR noted that as a result of that decision he had had 'to set out the facts and the reasons underpinning the Prison Service's current policies in much greater detail than the Divisional Court [had

[113] Ibid 6.
[114] [2001] EWCA Civ 1151, [2001] 1 WLR 2002.
[115] Ibid para [66] *per* Lord Phillips MR giving the judgment of the court.
[116] Ibid para [100].
[117] Ibid para [101].
[118] Ibid para [64].

pre-*Daly*) considered necessary'.[119] Then in what from the perspective of this chapter was a highly significant paragraph, Lord Phillips went on to address the anxieties that the prison authorities had expressed about any relaxation in the policy, concerns that were rooted not in a blind disregard for the dignity of the prisoner but rather in the need for administrative efficiency:

> We understand that the Prison Service must usually operate along clearly defined and clearly understood lines which leave little room for individual discretion, but the policy itself emphasises the need for individual consideration, so there can be no insuperable objection to a discretionary element in these decisions. In the great majority of cases, almost all of these considerations would point to separating mother and child at or before the age of 18 months. After that age the harm to the mother's family life could not normally outweigh the harm to the welfare of the child or to the good order of the prison. But there may be very rare exceptions where the interests of the mother and child coincide and outweigh any other considerations. *The mother must be given a fair opportunity to argue that that is so.*[120]

We have emphasized the last sentence in order to make perfectly clear what the human right is in this case. It is not to keep one's baby in prison but rather to have the opportunity to be able to argue that one is within the exceptional category of mothers who should be allowed this privilege. The policy is required more closely to resemble those to be found in the *Mellor* and *M L* cases or it will be struck down. Steeped as they are in the adjudicative process, the judges almost instinctively turn even basic questions of human dignity into matters of due process. In the course of their training for the Bar, their professional lives and then finally in the discharge of their judicial responsibilities they have had inculcated into them a respect for the value of case-by-case adjudication that borders on the sacramental. Stuck at that sometimes nasty intersection where a society's core values collide with the interests of its citizenry, the administrator frequently sees things rather differently. Confronted by hordes of supplicants, all trying to grab the public servant's eye, all with a hard luck story to tell or with a special set of facts to plead, the official would not be human if his or her heart did not sometimes harden. Now the Human Rights Act insists that the public official must listen, must see the person in the office and not just the statistic on the graph. When it is right to demand such attention, a right to be heard, and when it would come at too high an administrative price is a matter we consider at length in a later chapter. But the issue that arose in the *P and Q* case was central to a mother's dignity, and it is not likely to arise so often as to cause adminis-trative chaos. The court was surely right, therefore, to insist upon the individual mother's right to be seen and therefore heard. But had there been the right kind of flexibility built into the policy, of the sort that there was in the *Mellor* and *M L* cases, it is doubtful that the governor's decision in either case would have been

---

[119] [2001] EWCA Civ 1151, [2001] 1 WLR 2002, para [60].   [120] Ibid para [106].

overturned, even if both had been negative from the perspective of the claimants.[121]

4. *Article 1 of the first protocol: the rights of the 'possessive individual'*[122]

So far in this chapter I have been concerned with the impact of the Human Rights Act on the dignity of those who before the Act were only infrequently seen, and therefore went largely unprotected, by the law. I have noticed in the Act a strong impetus towards greater judicial activism than in the past and an increased emphasis on requiring public officials to be flexible in their application of rules and policies invasive of human dignity. But we should remember that the Act's availability is not restricted solely to those most in need. It is a liberal axiom that human rights legislation should be available to all, including those to whom life has already been kind. It is artificial therefore to restrict our scrutiny of the principle of human dignity to the marginalized categories of persons that have up to now been the focus of my attention. The reach of the Act is far wider than this, and consequently more controversial. In particular, we cannot leave the subject of human dignity without asking about the location of the property-owning individual in the Convention's ethical pecking order. There is no use pretending that such persons are not at the heart of our systems of law, both ancient and modern, and that their interests have not vitally moulded the content of human rights law.

The connection between individual, or as we would now say 'human', rights and property is a very old one, making a brief excursion back in time, and into some political philosophy, necessary before I return to the case law. Whereas the French revolution produced a commitment to various rights included amongst which was (as we have seen)[123] a very strong right to property, an earlier generation of English philosophers had made the connection between the individual and the ownership of property absolutely integral to their version of the political person. Thus for Thomas Hobbes, writing in the middle of the seventeenth century, the state of nature that he describes as having (whether hypothetically or otherwise) existed in advance of civil society was an arena of competing possessive individuals. Writing a little later, John Locke asserted as self-evident the proposition that every man had a natural right to possessions; the condition all men are naturally in is 'a *State of perfect Freedom* to order their Actions, and dispose of their Possessions, and Persons as they think fit, within the bounds of the Law of Nature, without asking leave, or depending upon the Will of any other Man'.[124] On Locke's view men had 'a natural right to property, a

---

[121] See further *R (CD and AD) v Secretary of State for the Home Department* [2003] EWHC 155 (Admin).

[122] See GL Gretton, 'The Protection of Property Rights' in A Boyle, C Himsworth, A Loux and H MacQueen (eds), *Human Rights and Scots Law* (Oxford: Hart Publishing, 2002), ch 13.

[123] Above p 15.

[124] Quoted in CB Macpherson, *The Political Theory of Possessive Individualism* (Oxford: Oxford University Press, 1962), 199 and see generally ch 5 for his discussion of John Locke.

right prior to or independent of the existence of civil society and government'.[125] It was the emergence of money which transcended the natural right to property and made accumulation possible, and it was the rationality of such accumulation which in turn created the moral framework for capitalist society.

The power and depth of Locke's political philosophy makes it wholly unsurprising that he should for so long have been regarded as the intellectual Godfather of liberal capitalism. He was writing at a time when the conflict between the Stuart kings and the English House of Commons was coming to a head, and indeed it was during his lifetime that Parliament's victory was finally assured with its final triumph over King James II and the invitation of William and Mary to take the throne on the legislature's terms. John Locke's engagement with all this was as a powerful exponent of the doctrine of parliamentary sovereignty, and in this context also his influence has been profound. But how did Locke reconcile his commitment to property, the 'human right' to property as we would call it today, with his devotion to the authority of the majority in Parliament? In his famous study of the period, Professor C B Macpherson articulates the dilemma in graphic terms and then suggests a likely answer:

The contradiction . . . was between the assertion of majority rule and the insistence on the sanctity of individual property. If the men of no property were to have full political rights, how could the sanctity of existing property institutions be expected to be maintained against the rule of the majority? This was no fanciful problem. When it had been raised during the Civil War all the men of property had seen the impossibility of combining real majority rule and property rights. And Locke assumed, correctly, that the propertyless were a majority in England at the time he wrote. But we can now see that there is no conflict between Locke's two assertions, of majority rule and of property right, inasmuch as Locke was assuming that only those with property were full members of civil society and so of the majority.[126]

There was no need to prioritize the individual over the interests of the majority in Parliament since the two amounted to the same thing:

No individual rights are directly protected in Locke's state. The only protection the individual has against arbitrary government is placed in the right of the majority of civil society to say when a government has broken its trust to act always in the public good and never arbitrarily. Locke could assume that this supremacy of the majority was a sufficient safeguard of the rights of each, because he assumed that all who had the right to be consulted were agreed on one concept of the public good, ultimately the maximization of the nation's wealth, and thereby (as he saw it) of the nation's welfare. He could assume this agreement only by virtue of his assumption that the labouring class was not among those who had the right to be consulted.[127]

Now as we have seen in chapter three, the beauty of Locke's notion of parliamentary sovereignty, and its durability, has depended on its capacity to be expanded so as to include the 'labouring class', that is, to develop into a system of representative democracy. But this was surely unthinkable to Locke.

---

[125] Quoted in CB Macpherson, *The Political Theory of Possessive Individualism* (Oxford: Oxford University Press, 1962), 198.
[126] Ibid 252 (footnote omitted).   [127] Ibid 257.

He literally did not see the majority of Englishmen (much less women) as people to whom his ascription of natural rights applied. Marginalized though it now has been by this triumph of democracy, Locke's emphasis on the right to property has nevertheless survived intact as an important feature of modern democratic states, revealing (perhaps more clearly than anything else) the extent to which liberal democracy and capitalism remain—despite the political power now enjoyed by the 'labouring class'—two sides of the same coin. This is not to say that individuals enjoy absolute rights to their property; not even Locke went that far, as Michael Taggart has convincingly demonstrated in a recent essay.[128] But the liberal democrat will be inclined if at all possible to protect individual property rights if this can be done without too much damage to the public good. The social democrat in contrast will be far more impatient of property rights, more inclined to remove or at least heavily regulate them, and likely to vigorously assent to Jeremy Waldron's powerful assertion in his exhaustive study of the subject that:

[u]nder serious scrutiny, there is no right-based argument to be found which provides an adequate justification for a society in which some people have lots of property and many have next to none. The slogan that property is a human right can be deployed only disingenuously to legitimise the massive inequality that we find in modern capitalist countries.[129]

If the right to property takes us to the ideological frontier between democratic socialism/social democracy on the one hand and liberalism on the other, on which side have the massed legal battalions of the European Convention on Human Rights and the Human Rights Act pitched their tent? The historical commitment to property of both the English and the continental jurisdictions is clear, as we saw in relation to continental Europe when we looked in chapter two at the constitution-building that followed the second world war, and as Professor KD Ewing has convincingly demonstrated in his study of the politics of the British constitution.[130] The experience in the United States is similar with the finest scholar on the subject concluding that the 'Constitution and Bill of Rights, as interpreted by the Supreme Court, have done much to safeguard property ownership, investment capital, the business corporations, and the national market in the face of hostile governmental actions'.[131] Neither as a document in itself nor as a basis for aggressive judicial interpretation has the Convention operated in quite such a robustly partisan way. Its army is parked somewhere in

---

[128] M Taggart, 'Expropriation, Public Purpose and the Constitution' in C Forsyth and I Hare (eds), *The Golden Metawand and the Crooked Cord. Essays on Public Law in Honour of Sir William Wade QC* (Oxford: Oxford University Press, 1998), 91. And see TH Green, 'Liberal Legislation and Freedom of Contract' in D Miller (ed), *Liberty* (Oxford: Oxford University Press, 1991) for an ambitious late Victorian attempt, by a considerable thinker, to redefine liberty in broader terms than property and freedom of contract.

[129] J Waldron, *The Right to Private Property* (Oxford: Clarendon Press, 1988), 5.

[130] 'The Politics of the British Constitution' [2000] *PL* 405.

[131] J W Ely Jr, *The Guardian of Every Other Right. A Constitutional History of Property Rights* 2nd edn (New York: Oxford University Press, 1998), 162.

no-man's land, probably closer to the liberal than the socialist forces but in a way that is not emphatically visible to the naked eye. The key provision on property, Article 1 of the first protocol, could hardly be described as over-assertive:

Every natural or legal person is entitled to the peaceful enjoyment of his possessions. No one shall be deprived of his possessions except in the public interest and subject to the conditions provided for by law and by the general principles of international law.

The preceding provisions shall not, however, in any way impair the right of a State to enforce such laws as it deems necessary to control the use of property in accordance with the general interest or to secure the payment of taxes or other contributions or penalties.

This is more a presumption in favour of, rather than a right to, private property and even as a presumption it is not particularly strong or (so far as settled law is concerned) intrusive. Many aggrieved owners have challenged the expropriation or regulation of their property before the Strasbourg court, but few have succeeded. The trustees of the Grosvenor estate failed in 1986 to persuade the European judges that the statutory right of leaseholders to buy the freehold in their properties amounted to an infringement of the estate's right to property, notwithstanding that many of its properties were affected by the legislation in question.[132] Later the same year the owners of extensive interests in the aircraft and shipbuilding industries were similarly unsuccessful in their challenge to the nationalization of their property by the state.[133] In the latter case, the applicants 'did not contest the principle of the nationalisation as such'; rather it was the 'grossly inadequate' compensation that excited their indignation and led to their complaint.[134] Though the court found against these applicants on the point, it is as a guarantor, or near-guarantor, of compensation that the right to property in the first protocol has come closest to flexing its Lockyean muscles. The settled case law of the court has unsurprisingly applied a test of proportionality in its effort to interpret the first protocol so as to 'strike a fair balance between the demands of the general interest of the community and the requirements of the protection of the individual's fundamental rights'.[135] In this context it has made clear that 'the taking of property without payment of an amount reasonably related to its value will normally constitute a disproportionate interference and a total lack of compensation can be considered justifiable under Article 1 of Protocol No 1 only in exceptional circumstances'.[136] Not only should there generally be compensation, but it must also be 'reasonably related' to value—a powerfully abstract stipulation for national governments to allow courts to require of them.

---

[132] *James v United Kingdom* (1986) 8 EHRR 123.
[133] *Lithgow v United Kingdom* (1986) 8 EHRR 329.
[134] Ibid para [105].
[135] *Former King of Greece and others v Greece* (2000) 33 EHRR 516, para [89]. For a recent illustration of the operation of the Protocol in favour of a United Kingdom applicant, see *Stretch v United Kingdom*, European Court of Human Rights, 24 June 2003.
[136] Ibid.

The cases have sometimes proved controversial and expensive. In November 2000, the European Court found a law passed by the Greek Parliament in April 1994 settling matters relating to the property of the deposed royal family (which had been confiscated during the military dictatorship in the country) to be a breach of the family's right to property,[137] with the Greek authorities having to compensate their former king to the tune of €12 m.[138] In *Pine Valley Developments Ltd v Ireland*, the respondent government was ordered to pay a sum well in excess of IR£1 m.[139] In that case, the applicants were able to connect their property argument to one based on the right to non-discrimination in the enjoyment of their Convention rights to be found in Article 14 of the Convention. This is the equality provision of the Convention which, as we have seen in an earlier chapter, has no independent existence but is instead parasitic on the other substantive rights in the Convention, only being capable of being called into action when the fact situation under scrutiny reveals itself to be within the ambit of the other right. Thus various taxation allowances that have been available to widows but not widowers in the United Kingdom have been challenged in Strasbourg as involving an interference with property rights (very broadly interpreted) which has then been argued not to have been justified under Article 14.[140]

Despite the apparent potential of Article 14, however, it has been the first sentence of Article 6(1) that has proved of most significance as an indirect guarantor of the Convention's right to property; indeed it could be argue that it has functioned as a more effective protection of property rights than the first protocol itself. So far as is relevant, that sentence asserts that:

In the determination of his civil rights and obligations . . . everyone is entitled to a fair and public hearing within a reasonable time by an independent and impartial tribunal established by law.

This is the Convention's 'due process' clause and as such it has of course attracted a huge amount of case law, with the great body of which we are for present purposes entirely unconcerned. What is interesting in relation to this discussion about property rights is that early on in the jurisprudence on this provision, it was clearly established that the 'right to property' was a civil right for the purposes of the article[141] and that the effect of this in many cases has been

---

[137] *Former King of Greece and others v Greece*, n 135 above.

[138] *Former King of Greece v Greece (no 2)*, European Court of Human Rights, 28 November 2002.

[139] (1993) 16 EHRR 379. The case involved a breach of Art 14 taken in conjunction with the first protocol. On the general question of damages under the European Convention, see Law Commission, *Damages under the Human Rights Act 1998* (Cm 4853, The Stationery Office, 2000). For the still uncertain role of damages awards under the Human Rights Act, see *R (KB) v South London and South and West Region Mental Health Review Tribunal and Secretary of State for Health* [2003] EWHC 193 (Admin), [2003] 3 WLR 185; *Annfriejeva v Southwark London Borough Council* [2003] EWCA Civ 1406.

[140] See *Willis v United Kingdom* (2002) 35 EHRR 547 and the friendly settlements in *Crossland v United Kingdom* (1999) 29 EHRR CD 34 and *Cornwell v United Kingdom* (2000) 29 EHRR CD 30.

[141] The key authority is *Sporrong and Lönnroth v Sweden* (1982) 5 EHRR 35.

an insistence on due process which has had the effect of inhibiting the regulation of property by the state.[142] Here the possessive individual has been in full flow and the litigants before the court have often been quite unlike those that one would generally expect to find throwing themselves at the mercy of a tribunal of human rights lawyers.[143] Indeed the Article 6 concept of a 'civil right' has grown into a fully-fledged notion of a financial right, with the court admitting within the protective remit of Article 6(1) actions that are '"pecuniary" in nature' or which are 'founded on an alleged infringement of rights which were likewise pecuniary rights'.[144] (In contrast, and paradoxically, the assertion of political rights has been excluded from the article.)[145]

The Human Rights Act has inherited the Convention's ambiguous solicitude for property rights that I have been describing in the preceding paragraphs. It is early days and the authoritative stamp of the British judges has yet to be placed on this sphere. Pure Article 1 victories are few and far between.[146] In the well-known decision of *Ghaidan v Godin-Mendoza*[147] the discrimination against homosexual couples in relation to the succession to statutory tenancies was held to infringe the Convention, but Articles 8 and 14 were the provisions principally relied upon.[148] An early case from Scotland found a breach of Article 6(1) in relation to a planning matter, with the status of the applicant as a limited company having caused surprise in uninformed circles.[149] In *R (BBC) v Broadcasting Standards Commission*[150] Lord Woolf left open the question of whether corporations could rely on the Convention's right to privacy.[151] The two leading cases on the right to property so far have been *Wilson v First County Trust (No 2)*[152] and *Aston Cantlow and Wilmcote with Billesley Warwickshire v Wallbank and Another*[153] and in both cases decisions favourable to the property owner were overturned in the House of Lords. In the first of these, the issue was

---

[142] For the historical development of the right see CA Gearty, 'Unravelling Osman' (2001) 64 *MLR* 159.

[143] Plenty of companies for example, including majority shareholders: *G J v Luxembourg* (2000) 36 EHRR 710.

[144] *Editions Periscope v France* (1992) 14 EHRR 597, para [40].

[145] *Pierre-Bloch v France* (1997) 26 EHRR 202.

[146] One such case, on unusual facts, is *N Harding v Customs and Excise Commissioners* VAT and Duties Tribunal, 4 August 2003. Defeats include *R (M W H and H Ward Estates Ltd) v Monmouthshire CC* [2002] All ER (D) 463; *Hughes v HM Customs and Excise* [2002] EWCA Civ 734, [2003] 1 WLR 177; *R (Peart) v Secretary of State for Transport, Local Government and the Regions* [2002] EWHC 2964 (Admin); *Holder v Law Society* [2003] EWCA Civ 39, [2003] 1 WLR 1059; and *Duggan v Governor of Full Sutton Prison* [2003] EWHC 361 (Ch), [2003] 2 All ER 678; cf *Crompton v Department of Transport North Western Area* [2003] EWCA Civ 64.

[147] [2002] EWCA Civ 1533, [2003] Ch 380.

[148] See ibid para [14] for a brief discussion by Buxton LJ of Art 1. Cf *R (Wilkinson) v Commissioners of Inland Revenue* [2003] EWCA Civ 814, [2003] 1 WLR 2683. At the time of writing, the *Ghaidan* case is on appeal to the Lords.

[149] *County Properties Ltd v The Scottish Ministers* 2000 SLT 965.

[150] [2001] QB 885.   [151] Ibid para [17].

[152] [2001] EWCA Civ 633, [2002] QB 74; reported in the Lords as *Wilson v Secretary of State for Trade and Industry* [2003] UKHL 40, [2003] 3 WLR 568.

[153] [2001] EWCA Civ 713, [2002] Ch 51, [2003] UKHL 37, [2003] 3 WLR 283.

primarily one of legality, with the statutory bar on the enforcement of certain credit agreements contained in the Consumer Credit Act 1974, s 127(3) being held by the House of Lords not to involve an infringement of either Article 6(1) or the first protocol. In the second, the defendant freehold owners of former rectorial land ultimately failed in their attempt to resist efforts by the parochial church council to make them meet the full repairs of the chancel of the local church. The Court of Appeal had held that the parish body had had a discretion (rather than a duty) to proceed against the defendants for compensation, and that the discretion was not one which should have been exercised in this case, since so to act would have unlawfully interfered with the defendants' peaceful enjoyment of their possessions and discriminate between landowners in the area in a way which both had no reasonable or objective justification and would have been disproportionate in its effect. But the House of Lords saw the liability as a mere incident of ownership, with some of their lordships giving the rather brutal impression (for the losing litigants) of wondering what all the fuss was about.[154]

D. Conclusion

The *Cantlow* decision is a disappointing one for defenders of the rights of the possessive individual, a property-owning David against a parsimonious local Goliath. The pawnbroker litigant in *Wilson v First County Trust* and the commercial interest that generated the *Broadcasting Standards Commission* case are more typical of the kind of clients that seek to characterize damage to their commercial interest as an infringement of their human rights. The spate of celebrity law suits rooted in the Convention's right to privacy that disconcerted the press in the months following implementation of the Act[155] is a reminder that similar issues can arise in other Convention articles as well. The point, and it is a fundamental one, is about the effect of the insertion of a code of human rights in a society in which resources are distributed in a highly unequal way. The honest liberal democrat recognizes that the inevitable result of such a disparity is that any new code of human rights, however designed, will be deployed by the rich and the powerful as a new weapon in the various legal campaigns in which such persons (often 'legal' rather than truly human, as was the case in *Wilson v First County Trust* and *County Properties*) are frequently engaged. If he or she is being adventurously straightforward, the liberal will accept this as morally right and point out that the poor and the disadvantaged can benefit from the legal droppings from the rich man's litigious table. The democratic socialist cannot logically square his or her determination to transform society with a belief that the forces of reaction should be equipped with a new set of legal weapons—

---

[154] [2003] UKHL 37, [2003] 3 WLR 283, para [72] (Lord Hope of Craighead) and para [91] (Lord Hobhouse of Woodborough).

[155] See esp *Douglas and another v Hello! Ltd* [2001] QB 967; *A v B plc* [2001] 1 WLR 2341 (DC), [2002] EWCA Civ 337, [2003] QB 195.

including due process and property rights—with which to resist change. The relics of this perspective are to be seen in the Human Rights Act's strong ongoing solicitude for parliamentary sovereignty. Somewhere in the middle are the social democrats, who hate the poverty, want equality very badly and would much prefer a Human Rights Act which does not offer quite so many temptations to the powerful. Such a charter has proved, however, impossible to design.[156]

The practising commercial lawyer Michael Smyth ended his excellent study *Business and the Human Rights Act 1998*[157] with the remark that 'it would not be remotely surprising if, in the early years after the Act's wholesale introduction, a considerable proportion of the landmark cases emanated from the commercial sector'.[158] As we have seen this has to some extent proved true, but pure human rights victories for such entities have not been as many as Smyth might perhaps have expected. While those who are already clearly seen by the law have been able to use the Human Rights Act as a magnifying glass with which to make themselves even larger in the eyes of the judges, it has not meant that they have always got their way. In this chapter approaching the subject from the perspective of human dignity, I have argued that one of the main tests of the Human Rights Act has been in the degree to which it has offered protection for groups and individuals in our society whose political power has traditionally been slight and who have as a result been rarely seen by the law. As we noted in our analysis of Articles 2, 3, and 8, the way the judges have approached these articles has had the effect of equipping many such individuals with rights to be heard that would not otherwise have been available, and with good arguments to put to the authorities when their time to speak comes around. To this extent the United Kingdom judges have risen to the challenge of the Human Rights Act. Could the judges have done more? This takes us into the issue of how far the courts can legitimately go in their assertion of human rights without trespassing on the authority of other branches of the state or overextending themselves in other ways. These are the topics that concern us in part three of this book.

---

[156] But for one such attempt see Art 21 of Liberty's 1991 draft bill of rights: Liberty, *A People's Charter* (London: NCCL, 1991), 82.

[157] Bristol: Jordan Publishing, 2000.

[158] Ibid 362.

PART THREE
APPLYING THE CORE PRINCIPLES

6

The Aspiration of Institutional Competence

A. Separation of powers and the Human Rights Act

In the last three chapters I have analysed the principles that I say should underpin an activist judicial approach to the Human Rights Act. I have argued that where any one or more of my three principles—respect for civil liberties, legality, and human dignity—are directly engaged, then the courts should be inclined to give effect to the Act if this is what is required to protect or affirm the principle under scrutiny. The approach that I have taken so far has been suggestive of a lively and creative judicial branch, determined to do justice under the Human Rights Act when principle demands that such justice be done. But this is only half the story of judicial responsibility under the Act. The judges make up an important branch of the state but it is no more than one branch, with there being two others, the legislative and the executive, towards both of which the courts must show sensitivity and understanding. Each part of the apparatus of government clearly has different spheres of influence. It is through this jurisdictional divide, this allocation of different ambits to each element, that the three branches can individually do what they are best at, and thereby collectively add to the health of the body politic viewed as a whole. In this chapter we are concerned with analysing the proper bounds of judicial power. Always an important topic in public law, it has been made even more so by enactment of the Human Rights Act. Very many cases since the measure came into effect have been concerned not so much with principle directly as with the question whether the case before the court is one in which the judges should get involved.

The well-known decision in *R (Pretty) v Director of Public Prosecutions*[1] serves well as an introduction to what lies ahead. The case grew out of one of those tragic sets of facts that the adjudicative process throws up from time to time. Mrs Pretty suffered from motor neurone disease, which is a progressive degenerative illness carrying with it no hope of recovery. The disease had reached an advanced stage, with Mrs Pretty paralysed from the neck down, but with her intellect and her capacity to make decisions as yet unimpeded. In this physical limbo on the verge of total incapacitation, Mrs Pretty desired to control how and when she died. In particular, not being capable any longer of ending her own life

---

[1] [2001] UKHL 61, [2002] 1 AC 800. See A Pedain, 'The Human Rights Dimension of the *Diane Pretty* case' (2003) 62 *CLJ* 181.

herself, she wished her husband to assist her, and he agreed. A legal obstacle to their last project together then emerged, in the form of the Suicide Act 1961, s 2(1) under which a person who 'aids, abets, counsels or procures the suicide of another, or an attempt by another to commit suicide' remains liable to prosecution. The husband faced a jail sentence of up to 14 years for this offence if he acted as his wife wished. Under s 2(4) of the same Act, however, no prosecution for such a crime can be instituted without the consent of the Director of Public Prosecutions. When this officer refused to promise not to prosecute, Mrs Pretty turned to the courts, arguing that this omission to give an advance undertaking of inactivity amounted to an infringement of her Convention rights, and was therefore unlawful under the Human Rights Act, s 6(1).

As was to be expected, the case travelled through the English legal system with compassionate expedition, but at every stage it was unsuccessful. When the matter reached the House of Lords, the Convention rights that were mainly in issue were Article 2 (the right to life), Article 3 (the prohibition of torture and inhuman or degrading treatment or punishment), Article 8 (the right to respect for privacy), and Article 14 (the prohibition of discrimination). Weighty arguments were marshalled on both sides but their lordships were unanimous that Mrs Pretty could successfully rely on none of these fundamental guarantees. This is of course the core of the case, and each speech in the Lords has much to offer in terms of understanding the breadth as well as the limitations to the guarantee of human dignity that is, as we saw in the last chapter, one of the essential features of the Convention viewed as a whole. What is of particular interest in the context of this chapter is the wider background against which the analysis of the Convention rights took place. The senior law lord, Lord Bingham started his speech by recognizing the seriousness of the 'frightening ordeal' to which Mrs Pretty was being subjected as a result of her terrible disease,[2] but he then went on to put what the judges were being asked to do its constitutional context:

In discharging the judicial functions of the House, the Appellate Committee has the duty of resolving issues of law properly brought before it, as the issues in this case have been. The committee is not a legislative body. Nor is it entitled or fitted to act as a moral or ethical arbiter. It is important to emphasise the nature and limits of the committee's role, since the wider issues raised by this appeal are the subject of profound and fully justified concern to very many people. The questions whether the terminally ill, or others, should be free to seek assistance in taking their own lives, and if so in what circumstances and subject to what safeguards, are of great social, ethical and religious significance and are questions on which widely differing beliefs and views are held, often strongly. Materials laid before the committee (with its leave) express some of those views; many others have been expressed in the news media, professional journals and elsewhere. The task of the committee in this appeal is not to weigh or evaluate or reflect those beliefs and views or give effect to its own but to ascertain and apply the law of the land as it is now understood to be.[3]

---

[2] [2001] UKHL 61, [2002] 1 AC 800, para [1].
[3] Ibid para [2].

Unsurprisingly in light of this dictum, Lord Bingham concluded that this was not an appropriate case for the courts to intervene. The remaining law lords took broadly the same line. Even the usually robustly activist Lord Steyn considered that in 'our parliamentary democracy...such a fundamental change' as that required by the claimant could not 'be brought about by judicial creativity. If it is to be considered at all, it requires a detailed and effective regulatory proposal.'[4] To Lord Hope, the case had raised '[i]mportant questions of medical ethics and of morality' but that, while these were 'of great interest to society', they were 'not the questions which [had] brought this matter before the court.'[5] To Lord Hobhouse, the 'conclusion [was] inescapable that both the nature of the questions raised by assisted suicide and the formulation of any new policies must under our system of Parliamentary democracy be a matter for the legislature not the judiciary'.[6] There can be little doubt that the judges' perception of the limits of their judicial powers informed their analysis of the Convention rights and their application of those rights to the facts before them. Though deference to Parliament was of course a relevant dimension to the case, being explicitly referred to in the comments of Lord Hobhouse and Lord Steyn quoted above and also being mentioned by other of their lordships, this was not a case in which the fundamental question was the proper application of the Human Rights Act, ss 3 or 4. The reasoning in the speeches in the House did not get that far. Their lordships were not assuming breach of the Convention, and then considering whether this state of affairs was one that Parliament had explicitly, or by necessary construction, authorized. Rather as we have already noted, they were finding that no breach of the Convention had occurred, and the result of this was that no question of interpretation under s 3(1) arose.

There is a deeper constraint in operation here than respect for legislative sovereignty *simpliciter*; in the *Pretty* case a prior question is being asked, about the appropriateness of deploying the Convention to the factual matrix before the court. This question concerns the competence of the judicial forum for the resolution of the issue before it, whether or not Parliament has spoken on the matter. The point is clearer in the later case of *re Campaign for Nuclear Disarmament*,[7] albeit this was a decision not directly involving the Human Rights Act. In that case the Administrative Court declined to be drawn into an analysis of UN resolution 1441 and in particular on whether its terms were sufficient to authorize military action against Iraq. The court made its decision about the inappropriateness of its getting involved quite independently of Parliament: indeed there was no statutory guidance on the issue before the court in that case. The judges hearing the case considered that the courts were not the right forum in which to determine these matters; whether there was a statute on the question was neither here nor there. It will be clear, therefore, that the competence of the judicial branch to adjudicate on a matter is (theoretically at least) a separate issue from the requirement that that branch defer to the elected

---

[4] Ibid para [57].   [5] Ibid para [72].   [6] Ibid para [120].
[7] [2002] EWHC 2759 (Admin).

legislature in the appropriate case: the first of these, *judicial restraint*, is not precisely the same idea as the second, *judicial deference*. Thus, we can see that if Parliament were to legislate unambiguously on a specific subject central to the court's normal zone of operations, then judicial deference would be called for, but there would be no place for the operation of any autonomous notion of judicial restraint, since without the relevant legislation the subject matter would have been well within the jurisdiction (broadly defined) of the judicial branch. Equally, some subjects are just not suitable for judicial intervention, whether or not Parliament has spoken on them (with *re Campaign for Nuclear Disarmament* being—to the judges who decided the case at any rate—a particularly good example of this). It is clear that the two ideas frequently overlap, as they did in the *Pretty* case, and combined they set limits to the role of the adjudicative branch. It may be that judicial restraint relates to areas where the executive is rightly the lead agent (eg foreign policy), and judicial deference to those subject matters that Parliament has taken onto itself. But I do not need to develop the distinction here or maintain that it is pure and clear; it is enough for the purposes of this chapter to appreciate that it exists.[8]

Heard at the same time as the *Pretty* case in another committee room in the House of Lords is a third case illustrating the point I am making in these introductory remarks to this chapter. *Re S (FC)* involved a challenge by two local authorities to a dramatic but unanimous Court of Appeal decision, the effect of which was greatly to increase the role of the courts in the oversight of child care plans agreed under the Children Act 1989 (by means of a system of regular review of starred milestones in such plans).[9] A unanimous House of Lords expressed great concern at the failure of successive governments 'to attend to the serious practical and legal problems' which had been identified by the Court of Appeal[10] but was nevertheless emphatic that the case was not appropriate for judicial intervention. In this 'sensitive and controversial field which [Parliament] may be said to have taken to itself', the Court of Appeal had 'exceeded the bounds of its judicial jurisdiction ... in introducing this new scheme'.[11] Whatever the limits of the judicial function were, the Court of Appeal had gone beyond them, both because the matter was one that Parliament had identified as its own and because the remedies that were being sought took the judges far beyond the court-room into the realm of policy and enforcement. Again in this case we see an interaction between judicial restraint (what the court is not equipped to do) and judicial

---

[8] Professor Jeffrey Jowell developed similar ideas in the course of a lecture entitled 'Due Deference under the Human Rights Act', delivered on 25 June 2002 as part of the UCL/Justice *Delivering Rights* programme of lectures at UCL; see also his 'Judicial Defence: Serrility, Civility or Institutional Capacity?' [2003] *PL* 592, and his 'Beyond the Rule of Law: Towards Constitutional Judicial Review' [2000] *PL* 671.

[9] *In re S (Minors) (Care Order: Implementation of Care Plan); in re W (Minors) (Care Order: Adequacy of Care Plan)* [2002] UKHL 10, [2002] 2 AC 291.

[10] Ibid para [106] *per* Lord Nicholls of Birkenhead, with whom Lords Mackay of Clashfern, Browne-Wilkinson, Mustill and Hutton agreed.

[11] Ibid para [44], with the first extract quoted in the text to this note being a quote from Cooke P in the New Zealand case of *R v Stack* [1986] 1 NZLR 257, 261–262.

deference (what the court should not do because what is proposed trespasses on the legislative role).

In the days before enactment of the Human Rights Act it was unusual to come across many frank reflections on the proper exercise of judicial power in the English law reports. The absence of a written constitution or a bill of rights meant there was no fundamental document through which such issues could be flushed to the surface of a judgment. A combination of the supremacy of parliamentary legislation, the control enjoyed by the executive over the legislative branch, and the lack of judicially enforceable constitutional safeguards capable of being deployed by the courts had over many decades contributed to an atmosphere of judicial deference in this country which was so pervasive that it has rarely needed to be judicially noted. Now, as the cases of *Pretty, re Campaign for Nuclear Disarmament* and *re S* show us, a new kind of human rights-based discourse about judicial power has begun to infiltrate the law. To some extent this had already commenced in advance of implementation of the 1998 Act, in a series of decisions in the 1990s in which the courts had set about 'rapidly developing a jurisprudence of fundamental rights in public law'.[12] With the coming into force of the Human Rights Act, the issue of judicial competence can no longer be avoided; nor can it be adequately resolved by ringing (albeit somewhat vacuous) endorsements of 'human rights', or by glib assumptions about a 'discretionary area of judgment' or by asserting the need for judicial deference to the wishes of the legislative branch. The former are too question-begging to be of any use while the latter fail to address what it is courts should do apart from defer to Parliament, which as the *Pretty* and *re S* cases show us amounts to only half the picture in terms of identifying limits on the adjudicative power: judicial deference does not tell you all you need to know about judicial restraint.

The key issue for this chapter concerns the approach that should be adopted when the case before the courts is one in which a Convention right is plausibly engaged. Should judges be super-vigilant on behalf of the right, inclined to vindicate it if at all possible, or should they consider its application to the facts before them with a degree of circumspection, even diffidence? This question is not about the application of the law to the facts in the ordinary sense: as we have seen in earlier chapters, the Convention is so broad that it can plausibly be said to apply to a huge range of situations. Nor is it about squaring the right with parliamentary supremacy: that comes later, if and when s 3 is kick-started to life by a finding of presumptive incompatibility. Rather what matters here is the atmosphere of a case, the institutional/policy background against which the right under scrutiny comes to be analysed and applied. It might be helpful at this point to draw on a metaphor. Suppose we locate a case in a swimming pool with the shallow end marked 'legal principle' and the deep end marked 'public policy'. Are the judges hearing a case at the right end where they belong, that

---

[12] M Loughlin, 'Rights Discourse and Public Law Thought in the United Kingdom' in GW Anderson (ed), *Rights and Democracy . Essays in UK-Canadian Constitutionalism* (London: Blackstone Press, 1999) 193, 210.

of legal principle, and therefore in a position to thrash about with confidence, managing the issue before them with assurance and skill? Or does seeking to resolve the case cause them to drift across the pool until they are on their tip-toes, barely able to claim they are still where they belong, asserting an issue to be one of legal principle while all the time they are sliding into ever-deeper water? Or perhaps a case has forced them entirely out of their depth, into the deep end of politics or of pure public policy? A judge's view of where he or she is in this metaphorical pool will inform his or her approach to how robust the analysis of Convention rights should be in the case before the court. The issue is a difficult but not impossible one to resolve, with the Strasbourg case law providing quite a range of guidance on the matter, albeit not always as explicitly as might be desirable, and (inevitably) with the occasional wrong turning.[13] We look first at that case law before returning to the domestic jurisprudence on the point.

B. When should judges act: the lessons from Strasbourg

The first relevant pointer is as to whether any one of the principles discussed in chapters three to five of this book is involved in any given case. A fair general statement to make would be that the closer the issues before the court connect with one of the key underlying principles of the Convention, then the more likely it is that the judges can be assertive and intrusive in their application of the disputed right to the facts before them; in other words the case is right in the shallow end of legal principle. If a decision directly involves the principle of the protection of civil liberties, or an issue of legality or a clear matter of human dignity, then the more confident can a judge inclined to activism be that he or she is on the right lines. It follows from this that where none of these principles is directly engaged, then it is likely to be the case that a restrained, or at least less aggressive, application of the Human Rights Act is called for. In this way, the work done earlier in this book provides a guide not only to what the European Convention and the Human Rights Act are about, but (equally importantly) what they are *not* about. In broad terms an approach based on prioritizing principle has been evident in the case law of the European Court of Human Rights since it first began to build up a head of steam in the 1970s. Factual situations in line with the court's perspective on what the Convention is primarily about have received more robust protection than those further away from the centre of the jurisprudential action. The mechanism deployed in Strasbourg for fine-tuning the application of the Convention in any particular case so as to reflect the underlying importance of principle in this way has been the attractively protean margin of appreciation.

---

[13] See *Hatton v United Kingdom*, n 52 below. But for the later decision of the Grand Chamber see *Hatton v United Kingdom (No 2)*, n 66 below.

This is a much discussed and intensely analysed topic upon which it will not be necessary to dwell at any great length here.[14] An early leading case reflective of much that follows in the Strasbourg case law is *Handyside v United Kingdom*.[15] The issue was whether the applicant's conviction under the UK's obscenity law for having published a book aimed at schoolchildren containing (among much else) some sexual material was a breach of his rights under the Convention and in particular his freedom of expression under Article 10. The court held by a huge majority (13 votes to one) that it was not, and in so doing outlined an understanding of the judicial function that, though rooted in an analysis of Article 10(2), was reflective of a more general approach to the whole question of its appropriate role:

The Court points out that the machinery of protection established by the Convention is subsidiary to the national systems safeguarding human rights. The Convention leaves to each Contracting State, in the first place, the task of securing the rights and freedoms it enshrines. The institutions created by it make their own contribution to this task but they become involved only through contentious proceedings and once all domestic remedies have been exhausted (Art 26).

These observations apply, notably, to Article 10(2).... By reason of their direct and continuous contact with the vital forces of their countries, State authorities are in principle in a better position than the international judge to give an opinion on the exact contact of these requirements as well as on the 'necessity' of a 'restriction' or 'penalty' intended to meet them. The Court notes at this juncture that, whilst the adjective 'necessary', within the meaning of Article 10(2), is not synonymous with 'indispensable', neither has it the flexibility of such expressions as 'admissible', 'ordinary', 'useful', 'reasonable' or 'desirable'. Nevertheless, it is for the national authorities to make the initial assessment of the reality of the pressing social need implied by the notion of 'necessity' in this context.

Consequently, Article 10(2) leaves to the Contracting States a margin of appreciation. This margin is given both to the domestic legislator ('prescribed by law') and to the bodies, judicial amongst others, that are called upon to interpret and apply the laws in force.

Nevertheless, Article 10(2) does not give the Contracting States an unlimited power of appreciation. The Court ... is empowered to give the final ruling on whether a 'restriction' or 'penalty' is reconcilable with freedom of expression as protected by Article 10. The domestic margin of appreciation thus goes hand in hand with a European supervision. Such supervision concerns both the aim of the measure challenged and its 'necessity'; it covers not only the basic legislation but also the decision applying it, even one given by an independent court.[16]

The final paragraph of this long extract is at least as important as the opening sections. The court uses the margin of appreciation as a kind of constitutional weather-vane, an ever present guide to the appropriateness of Strasbourg intervention. Sometimes the wind is blowing hardly at all and little judicial energy can be mustered; on other occasions the gales are severe and the judges are propelled

---

[14] See Y Arai-Takahashi, *The Margin of Appreciation Doctrine and the Principle of Proportionality in the Jurisprudence of the ECHR* (Antwerp: Intersentia, 2002).

[15] (1976) 1 EHRR 737.

[16] Ibid paras [48]–[49] (footnotes omitted).

into determined action. Thus, in the very next paragraph after the section quoted above, the court goes on to assert that it is required 'to pay the utmost attention to the principles characterising a "democratic society," '[17] and we have already noted in chapter three how robust Strasbourg has been in defence of political speech. In the same chapter we saw evidence of equally high levels of determination in the court's analysis of the other civil-liberties-based rights in the Convention (Article 11 and Article 3 of the first protocol in particular), especially in cases where the exercise of the right in a broadly political way was the central issue. Similar activism has been on display in our discussion of the Strasbourg cases on legality and human dignity.[18]

The theory of judicial activism propounded in this book has in large measure grown out of this coherent and principled Strasbourg jurisprudence, which in turn has been based upon interpreting rights in a way sensitive to the question of whether an issue of principle is involved in any given case. The latter point is made clearer if we consider the operation of the Convention rights where no issue of principle is directly engaged. Sometimes, where the right itself is only tangentially connected to principle (as I have argued is the case with the right to property in the first protocol), the guarantee set out in the Convention is itself highly diluted and attenuated, with the case law that then follows being also lack-lustre, and (viewed from the perspective of the judicial activist) tediously anaemic. Thus the Westminster estate's challenge to the leasehold enfranchisement laws passed by the Labour government of Harold Wilson in 1967 was heavily defeated,[19] as were the applications to Strasbourg of those adversely affected by the nationalization achieved by the Aircraft and Shipbuilding Industries Act 1977.[20] In *Allgemeine Gold-und Silberscheideanstalt v United Kingdom*,[21] the applicant company found that 1,500 Krügerrands which it had agreed to sell to two persons (but the ownership of which it had retained) had been seized by British customs and, after judicial proceedings, declared forfeit. Though victorious before the Commission on these harsh facts, the company nevertheless lost before the court, with the judges finding by a majority of six to one that the authorities had been within their 'wide margin of appreciation' both as regards how they chose to enforce the relevant law and also as to whether the consequences of such enforcement were 'in the general interest for the purpose of achieving the object of the law in question'.[22]

An even more extreme example of the same point was the court's acceptance in a later case, albeit only by a majority of five to four, that a commercial aircraft valued at over £60 m but on which was found a consignment of cannabis resin could be seized and rendered liable to forfeiture, notwithstanding the blameless-

---

[17] (1976) 1 EHRR 737, para [49].   [18] See chapters four and five above.
[19] *James v United Kingdom* (1986) 8 EHRR 123.
[20] *Lithgow and others v United Kingdom* (1986) 8 EHRR 329.
[21] (1986) 9 EHRR 1.
[22] Ibid para [52].

ness of the aircraft's owner.[23] In vain did two of the dissenting judges try to turn the case into one of principle, arguing that:

[t]here is no room for a margin of appreciation here. Confiscating property as a sanction to some breach of the law—however important that breach may be and, consequently, however weighty may be the general interest in preventing it by severely penalizing the offence—without their being any 'relationship between the behaviour of the owner or the person responsible for the goods and the breach of the law' *is* definitely incompatible both with the rule of law and with the right guaranteed in Article 1 of Protocol No 1.[24]

This attempt to link the case to the principle of the rule of law (or as I would call it legality) did not persuade enough of the judges to transform the case into one involving a core Convention principle, which perspective—had it been adopted by the majority—might well have produced a different result.

The property right is already some way from the core principles of the Convention. Other rights are more directly connected to principle, and consequently wider in their potential reach. Where a Convention right is broad enough to encompass both areas of immediate concern to principle and more peripheral matters, then the margin of appreciation operates to prioritize the court's protective energies as between those issues which demand full attention and those which matter less. Article 10 is a good case in point here. The guarantee clearly extends far beyond political speech, the provision baldly stating that 'everyone has the right to freedom of expression'. Yet as Michael Smyth has correctly observed, the 'European Convention jurisprudence fails to confer upon commercial speech the same measure of protection that it confers upon political speech'.[25] This is because in the court's view 'there is not the same nexus between the need for commercial speech in a functioning democracy that there is for political speech'.[26] Smyth is right when he observes that applicants who have sought to use Strasbourg's commitment to free speech to promote or to protect their business interests have usually left empty-handed. This was not always certain to be the case, with an early decision of the court appearing to suggest an opening for commercial speech.[27] A turning point was *Markt Intern and Beerman v Germany*,[28] in which it was only by the casting vote of its president (the bench having tied nine to nine) that the court was able to reject the assertion that it 'is just as important to guarantee the freedom of expression in relation to the practices of a commercial undertaking as it is in relation to the conduct of a head of government'.[29]

---

[23] *Air Canada v United Kingdom* (1995) 20 EHRR 150.
[24] Ibid 183 *per* Judge Martens joined by Judge Russo (footnotes omitted) (emphasis in the original).
[25] *Business and the Human Rights Act* (Bristol: Jordan Publishing, 2000), 238.
[26] Ibid 239.
[27] *Barthold v Germany* (1985) 7 EHRR 383.
[28] (1989) 12 EHRR 161.
[29] Ibid 177 (joint dissenting opinion of Judges Gölcüklü, Pettit, Russo, Spielmann, De Meyer, Carrillo Salcedo and Valticos).

By 1994, the case law had stabilized in the direction indicated by Smyth. It was during that year that the applicant lawyer in *Casada Coca v Spain*[30] failed in his argument that the Bar Council's ban on his advertising his professional services violated his right to freedom of expression. It was true that the right to freedom of expression was engaged, with Article 10 making '[n]o distinction . . . according to whether the type of aim pursued is profit-making or not.'[31] However when it came to applying the 'necessary in a democratic society' criterion in Article 10(2), the 'complex and fluctuating area of unfair competition' and of advertising meant that a 'margin of appreciation [was] particularly essential' and that therefore in 'the instant case, the Court's task [was] confined to ascertaining whether the measures taken at national level [were] justifiable in principle and proportionate'.[32] This essentially adopted the reasoning of the winning side in the drawn *Markt Intern* litigation. But as seven of the dissenting judges had remarked in that case, deploying the margin of appreciation in this way had 'the effect in practice of considerably restricting the freedom of expression in commercial matters' with the court 'in fact eschewing the task, which falls to it under the Convention, of carrying out "European supervision", as to the conformity of the contested "measures" "with the requirements" of that instrument'.[33] Whether this was true or not, there is no doubt that the passive approach adopted by the narrowest of conceivable majorities in the *Markt Intern* case is now the dominant thread in the court's approach to commercial speech.[34]

The key to success remains the ability to connect an application before the court directly with principle, something that, as we have just seen, two of the dissenting judges tried and failed to do in *Air Canada*. As far as Article 10 is concerned, Strasbourg's deference to state regulation of free speech and artistic expression on grounds of morality and public decency has been controversial precisely because such speech, broadly defined, would seem to require protection from an instrument whose version of democracy so clearly encompasses a strong commitment to tolerance and pluralism.[35] In contrast, where speech can be said to relate to politics in general, even if not in the narrower party political sense, the judges have found themselves capable of being stimulated into activism. In *Hertel v Switzerland*, the European Court observed that it was 'necessary to reduce the extent of the margin of appreciation when what is at stake is not a given individual's purely "commercial" statements, but his participation in a debate affecting the general interest, for example, over public health'.[36] As a

---

[30] (1994) 18 EHRR 1.   [31] Ibid para [35].   [32] Ibid para [50] (footnotes omitted).
[33] n 28 above, 177 (footnotes omitted).
[34] See eg *Jacobowski v Germany* (1994) 19 EHRR 64.
[35] See the conservative decisions in *Müller v Switzerland* (1988) 13 EHRR 212; *Otto-Preminger Institute v Austria* (1994) 19 EHRR 34; and *Wingrove v United Kingdom* (1996) 24 EHRR 1. In an English case in 2003, a prisoner predictably failed in his attempt to have the prohibition of receipt of hard core pornography declared a breach of his Art 10 rights: *R (Morton) v Governor of Long Larton Prison* [2003] EWCA Crim 644. To similar effect is *R (Nilger) v Governor of Full Sutton Prison*, Administration Court, 19 December 2003 (refusal to return prisoner's anutobiographical writings did not involve a breach of Art. 10).
[36] (1998) 28 EHRR 534, para [47].

result, the Swiss attempt to silence the applicant's concerns about the health risk of microwave ovens was found to have infringed his Article 10 rights. The outcome and the reasoning behind it seem perfectly in accord with the principle of civil liberties set out in chapter three of this book, albeit one expanded beyond the remit of party politics to reach political activism more broadly defined.

Hertel's anxieties about microwaves appeared in a journal which ran his article with a front cover picture of the Reaper holding out one hand towards a microwave oven. As the editor proudly claimed on page two, 'To say that our journal is fearless is almost to state the obvious'.[37] No doubt such a statement was aimed at hooking potential new readers, or, more to the present point, buyers. There is no necessary disconnection between human rights principle and profit, and it does not follow from any of what I have been saying here that mere legal persons, and in particular companies, *necessarily* enjoy a lower level of protection than do 'real' persons under the European Convention. The success of many newspapers in Strasbourg is testament to the fact that it is possible to make money and promote political expression at the same time.[38] The vital question in every case involving corporations is whether one or other of our three central principles is engaged. This will not be easy for artificial entities where human dignity is concerned,[39] but it is entirely possible in relation to the principle of legality, as we saw in the extract from the dissenting opinions in the aircraft confiscation case where the judges strived to turn the facts before them into an example of an infringement of the rule of law. It is not in the least surprising that the most activist protection of corporations has been in the sphere of due process. The court has not generally been bothered whether it is a limited company or an individual that is claiming before it the protection of Article 6(1) in relation to the determination of a civil right[40] and of course as far as criminal safeguards are concerned it is quite irrelevant whether the defendant stands accused of a crime committed in his or her corporate as opposed to personal capacity.[41] The point in each case is that the principle of legality requires fair play, and any litigant is entitled to this, whether he, she or it be natural or legal, or the claimant or defendant in any particular action.

Our second guideline from Strasbourg as to when judges should act under the Convention, and by extension the Human Rights Act, flows from our first, and is really nothing more than a positive expression of the negative propositions that I have outlined above. The point is well put in the course of the court's unanimous judgment in the Duke of Westminster's case, which as I have already noted involved a direct challenge to primary legislation aimed at lease-hold enfranchisement. The issue before the judges related to what was in the

---

[37] Ibid para [11].

[38] There are of course many such cases: see eg *Sunday Times v United Kingdom (No 2)* (1991) 14 EHRR 229.

[39] But see now *Stés Colas Est v France*, European Court of Human Rights, 16 April 2002, confirming the availability to corporations of the right to respect for privacy.

[40] See for eg *Bielectric SRL v Italy* (2000) 34 EHRR 784.

[41] *Saunders v United Kingdom* (1996) 23 EHRR 313.

public interest, a matter upon which as we have seen article one of the first protocol explicitly demands an opinion, but the answer that the court gave was of general application:

[T]he notion of 'public interest' is necessarily extensive. In particular... the decision to enact laws expropriating property will commonly involve consideration of political, economic and social issues on which opinions within a democratic society may reasonably differ widely. The Court, finding it natural that the margin of appreciation available to the legislature in implementing social and economic policies should be a wide one, will respect the legislature's judgment as to what is 'in the public interest' unless that judgment be manifestly without reasonable foundation.[42]

Summarizing the case law, two distinguished commentators have observed that under the property guarantee as interpreted by the Strasbourg court, it 'is primarily for the state to identify the objective of a deprivation and determine whether it is in the "public interest"'.[43]

The point goes beyond Article 1 of the first protocol. In *Immobiliare Saffi v Italy* it was in the context of an Article 8 case that the court accepted that in 'spheres such as housing, which plays a central role in the welfare and economic policies of modern societies, the court will respect the legislative's judgment as to what is in the general interest unless that judgment is manifestly without reasonable foundation'.[44] As the court remarked in the course of a number of gypsy cases in 2001, the Convention 'does not in terms give a right to be provided with a home' and that the question whether the State 'provides funds to enable everyone to have a home is a matter for political not judicial decision'.[45] Such remarks reflect a limitation on the judicial role which is accepted by even such strong proponents of judicial activism as the leading barrister and writer on human rights Rabinder Singh QC:

The court should adopt a stance of relative deference to the judgment of the political organs of the state when they make decisions in the arena of social and economic policy affecting such civil rights as the right to property. One reason for doing this is that Parliament may be trying to implement social and economic rights when, for example, it taxes those who can afford to pay so as to train young people for employment. Just as the theories of Herbert Spencer are not part of the US Constitution, so the merits of redistributive taxation are hardly the province of the judiciary.[46]

---

[42] *James v United Kingdom*, n 19 above, para [46].

[43] R Clayton and H Tomlinson, *The Law of Human Rights* (Oxford: Oxford University Press, 2000), 1315, citing *Lithgow v United Kingdom* n 20 above, and dealing with other related authorities in the same paragraph.

[44] (1999) 7 BHRC 256, para [49]. See also *Botta v Italy* (1998) 26 EHRR 241. Cf *Chassagnou v France* (1999) 7 BHRC 151.

[45] See *Lee v United Kingdom* (2001) 33 EHRR 677, para [101].

[46] R Singh, *The Future of Human Rights in the United Kingdom. Essays on Law and Practice* (Oxford: Hart Publishing, 1997), 57, citing *Svenska Managementgruppen AB v Sweden* (1985) 45 DR 211, 223.

This restrained approach has been thought especially important where the court has been invited to read positive obligations into particular Convention rights. The idea of a positive (as opposed to a negative) obligation is that it imposes a duty on the state to act rather than to refrain from acting. This distinction recalls our discussion in an earlier chapter about the different approach taken to rights by liberals and socialists, with the former seeing the subject as an essentially negative one, requiring the state merely to refrain from interfering with the liberty of the individual, and the latter viewing the language of rights as an ideal opportunity through which to compel the state to do good. The European Court of Human Rights has sat on the fence as best it can, not being overly keen to develop positive obligations but at the same time recognizing that, for example, a right to life that merely stopped the authorities from deliberately killing would not have much scope for development. The moment a court tries to articulate the extent of such a duty, however, even one as seemingly simple as the 'positive obligation on the authorities to take preventive operational measures to protect an individual whose life is at risk from the criminal acts of another individual,'[47] various structural deficiencies in judicial law-making come inevitably to the fore: which 'operational measures' are to be put in place? From which budget? How many officers should be assigned to such duties? and so on. The further the positive obligation drifts from the traditional central concerns of the courts, life, liberty, due process and such like, the more acute these problems become, the deeper the water in our metaphorical swimming pool seems to be.

A very important provision, on account of its expansionary potential, is the right to respect for privacy in Article 8. In *Lopez Ostra v Spain*,[48] the European Court took a very robust view of the obligation on the respondent state to deal with a serious pollution problem from a waste treatment plant which was badly affecting the lives of the applicant and others in its vicinity. The Convention right upon which the case was hung was the right to respect for private and family life, with the fact that the polluter was a limited company not absolving the state from responsibility. The plant was operating without the appropriate licences, so in that case the state was at least indirectly tied to the pollution that it was failing to prevent. In *Guerra v Italy*, decided four years later,[49] the facts revealed a quite shocking case of dangerous atmospheric pollution and governmental neglect which duly produced a unanimous judgment from the court that Article 8 had been infringed. Once again, the actual polluters were not the government itself, but this was not allowed to restrict the court's freedom of manoeuvre. While recognizing that 'Italy [could] not be said to have "interfered" with the applicants' private or family life', the court thought it clear that, 'although the object of Article 8 [was] essentially that of protecting the individual against arbitrary

---

[47] *Osman v United Kingdom* (1998) 29 EHRR 245, para [115].
[48] (1994) 20 EHRR 277. See generally M de Merieux, 'Deriving Environmental Rights from the European Convention for the Protection of Human Rights and Fundamental Freedoms' (2001) 21 *OJLS* 521.
[49] (1998) 26 EHRR 357.

interference by the public authorities', the provision did 'not merely compel the State to abstain from such interference: in addition to this primarily negative undertaking, there may be positive obligations inherent in effective respect for private or family life.'[50] It was a variety of these positive obligations that combined to produce the unanimous decision in the case. The *Lopez Ostra* decision contains an important indication of the court's preferred theoretical basis for this new, robustly expansionist, approach to Article 8:

> Whether the question is analysed in terms of a positive duty on the State—to take reasonable and appropriate measures to secure the applicant's rights under paragraph 1 of Article 8, as the applicant wishes in her case, or in terms of an 'interference by a public authority' to be justified in accordance with paragraph 2, the applicable principles are broadly similar. In both contexts regard must be had to the fair balance that has to be struck between the competing interests of the individual and of the community as a whole, and in any case the State enjoys a certain margin of appreciation. Furthermore, even in relation to the positive obligations flowing from the first paragraph of Article 8, in striking the required balance the aims mentioned in the second paragraph may be of a certain relevance.[51]

In Autumn 2001, the *Lopas Ostra* and *Guerra* cases combined to produce the remarkable (but as it turned out merely interim) ruling in *Hatton v United Kingdom*,[52] a case in which—to put it at its mildest—a positive obligation has been imposed in a factual situation which pushed the court beyond the limits of its judicial competence. The application concerned a challenge from a number of persons living in the vicinity of Heathrow airport to the impact on them and their families of the noise caused by the movement of aircraft into and out of that airport during the extreme early morning. The court recognized that neither the airport nor the aircraft which use it were 'owned, controlled or operated by the Government or by any agency of the Government', but that nevertheless, citing the *Guerra* case,[53] the applicants' complaints fell 'to be analysed in terms of a positive duty on the State to take reasonable and appropriate measures to secure the applicants' rights under Article 8(1) of the Convention'.[54] Then, having quoted almost verbatim the extract from the *Lopez Ostra* case that I have set out above, the court asserted that 'in striking the required balance, States must have regard to the whole range of material considerations',[55] and that the question therefore was whether, quoting once more from the *Lopez Ostra* case, 'the national authorities [had taken] the measures necessary for protecting the applicant's right to respect for her home and for her private and family life'.[56]

---

[50] (1998) 26 EHRR 357, para [58] (footnote omitted).

[51] n 48 above, para [51] (footnote omitted).

[52] (2001) 34 EHRR 1. The decision was released on 2 October 2001, the first anniversary of the full implementation of the Human Rights Act.

[53] And an earlier case, *Powell and Rayner v United Kingdom* (1990) 12 EHRR 355.

[54] n 52 above, para [95].

[55] Ibid para [97].

[56] Ibid with the extract from *Lopez Ostra*, n 48 above, being at para [55] of the court's judgment in that case.

Given this approach to the issue, it was inevitable that the court would find itself drawn into detailed analysis of a number of complex matters such as the various governmental initiatives on the problem already in place, the independent analysis that had appeared in 1999 dealing with the economic effect of night flights, and the content of and responses to a number of government consultation papers that had been published on the topic.[57] The court also conducted a brief assessment of the measures that the authorities had already put in place to mitigate the problem of night noise nuisance.[58] By a majority of five to two, and on the basis of its analysis of all this data, the court decided that it could 'not accept that [the] modest steps at improving the night noise climate' which the authorities had admittedly taken were 'capable of constituting "the measures necessary" to protect the applicants' position'.[59] In particular, 'in the absence of any serious attempt to evaluate the extent or impact of the interferences with the applicants' sleep patterns, and generally in the absence of a prior specific and complete study with the aim of finding the least onerous solution as regards human rights', it was 'not possible to agree that in weighing the interferences against the economic interest of the country—which itself had not been quantified—the Government [had] struck the right balance'.[60] It followed that, 'despite the margin of appreciation', the state had 'failed to strike a fair balance between the United Kingdom's economic well-being and the applicants' effective enjoyment of their right to respect for their homes and their private and family lives'.[61]

It was certainly quite a coup for the applicants to have persuaded the five European Court judges that formed the majority in this case (Judges Costa from France, Loucaides from Cyprus, Kuris from Lithuania, Tulkens from Belgium and Jungwiert from the Czech Republic) that the UK government's management of the noise problem at Heathrow violated their Convention rights. The dissenting UK judge Sir Brian Kerr thought that the record showed that the government had clearly not been 'unwarrantably inactive' in the field, with the many measures that had been taken being indicative of 'a concern that the right to a private life should not be unduly interfered with rather than a failure to accord that right the requisite respect'.[62] He drew attention to the 'importance to the national economy of the aircraft industry as a whole, and of Heathrow airport in particular' and suggested that the 'preponderance of the evidence available to the Court strongly favour[ed] the conclusion that there [would] be considerable adverse effect to the economy if night flights [were to be] curtailed'.[63] But Sir Brian's main criticism was of the inappropriateness of judicial engagement in this issue:

A further point to be considered in striking the balance between the various interests is that the applicants are challenging not a specific decision which affected them, but a macro-economic policy. It is open to the Court to consider the effect of general policies or laws on individuals, but it must be aware that to make an assessment

[57] Ibid paras [98]–[104]. [58] Ibid para [105]. [59] Ibid para [106]. [60] Ibid.
[61] Ibid para [107]. [62] *Hatton v United Kingdom*, n 52 above, 36–37. [63] Ibid 37.

of a general policy on the basis of a specific case is an exercise that is fraught with difficulty....

If Convention standards are not met in an individual case, it is the role of the Court to say so, regardless of how many others are in the same position. But when, as here, a substantial proportion of the population of south London is in a similar position to the applicants, the Court must consider whether the proper place for a discussion of the particular policy is in Strasbourg, or whether the issue should not be left to the domestic political sphere.[64]

The applicants' victory was a short-lived one, with the Grand Chamber later overturning the first ruling by a majority of 12 to five.[65] The critique by Sir Brian Kerr was largely accepted by the enlarged court of judges which reheard the case. The national authorities had 'direct democratic legitimation and [were], as the Court ha[d] held on many occasions, in principle better placed than an international court to evaluate local needs and conditions'.[66] Furthermore, in 'matters of general policy, on which opinions within a democratic society may reasonably differ widely, the role of the domestic policy maker should be given special weight'.[67] The dissenting judges could merely assert in response that '... the close connection between human-rights protection and the urgent need for a decontamination of the environment leads us to perceive health as the most basic human need and as pre-eminent'. And then with even greater rhetorical energy, '[a]fter all, as in this case, what do human rights pertaining to the privacy of the home mean if day and night, constantly or intermittently, it reverberates with the roar of aircraft engines?'[68] It is hard not to sympathize with the spirit of these remarks, even if acting on them would produce unwarranted judicial activism. In some ways, and counter-intuitively, the majority seem to be saying that the more people that are affected by a governmental action (or inaction), the less easy it is to characterize that conduct as a breach of individual human rights. We shall encounter this paradox again later in this chapter, in the context of an interesting decision from Scotland, *Napier v Scottish Ministers*.[69] It is to the domestic case law, of which that decision forms a part, that we now turn.

---

[64] *Hatton v United Kingdom*, n 52 above, 36–37, 39–40. The case quickly attracted unfavourable comment from within the United Kingdom, with even the normally activist Lord Steyn having admitted extra-judicially to being 'troubled' by its 'creativity': see the John Maurice Kelly Memorial Lecture 'Perspectives of Corrective and Distributive Justice in Tort Law' delivered at UCD on 1 November 2001 published by the Law Faculty of UCD. (It might be however that Lord Steyn was merely concerned about the decision being taken by the European rather than the UK judges, rather than with any issue of constitutional principle relating to the separation of powers.)
[65] *Hatton v United Kingdom* [Grand Chamber] (2003) 37 EHRR 611.
[66] Ibid para [97].
[67] Ibid.
[68] Judges Costa, Ress, Türmen, Zupancic, and Steiner.
[69] See n 104 below.

C. Judicial restraint under the Human Rights Act[70]

The UK cases so far decided reveal a British judiciary apparently well versed in the need to discriminate between principled intervention under the Human Rights Act on the one hand and naive frolics into public policy on the other. The themes and argument of this chapter are, I can say with reasonable confidence, exemplified in the case law. In *R (K) v Camden and Islington Health Authority*,[71] for example, an attempt to use the Convention to transform a qualified duty on the part of the defendant into an absolute obligation was unsuccessful. The case raised a question about the after-care of restricted patients under the Mental Health Act who are discharged by order of a review tribunal into the community. On the facts before it, the Court of Appeal found that the health authority was certainly required to do what it could to provide after care services for such persons, but an interpretation of the relevant law which would have 'imposed on Health Authorities absolute duties which they would not necessarily be able to perform would [have been] manifestly unreasonable'.[72] It was clear that '[n]either Article 5 nor [the] Strasbourg jurisprudence [laid] down any criteria as to the extent to which member States must provide facilities for the care of those of unsound mind in the community, thereby avoiding the necessity for them to be detained for treatment in hospital,'[73] and since this was the case it followed that if a health authority was 'unable, despite the exercise of all reasonable endeavours, to procure for a patient the level of care and treatment in the community that a Tribunal considers to be a prerequisite to the discharge of the patient from hospital ... the continued detention of the patient in hospital [would not] violate the right to liberty conferred by Article 5'.[74]

Even clearer on this point is *Lee v Leeds City Council*,[75] in which what was before the court was the question whether the Convention had made any difference to the statutory position in relation to 'the familiar issue [of] whether a local authority is under any, and if so what, obligation to a tenant or occupier of a dwelling house let as part of its housing stock in circumstances where the dwelling house is or has become unsuitable for occupation by reason of condensation, damp and mould caused by some defect in design'.[76] Rejecting the applicant's argument that the Human Rights Act had radically transformed the duties of the authority, the Court of Appeal considered it important 'to keep in mind Lord Hoffmann's observations ... as to the need "to show a proper sensitivity to the limits of permissible judicial creativity" in the field of social housing

---

[70] For an excellent study see F Klug, 'Judicial Deference under the Human Rights Act' [2003] *EHRLR* 125. A study which is very useful for the way in which it draws on relevant Canadian jurisprudence is RA Edwards, 'Judicial Deference under the Human Rights Act' (2002) 65 *MLR* 859.
[71] [2001] EWCA Civ 240, [2002] QB 198.
[72] Ibid para [30] *per* Lord Phillips MR.
[73] Ibid para [33].   [74] Ibid para [34].
[75] Decided with *Ratcliffe v Sandwell Metropolitan Borough Council* [2002] EWCA Civ 06, [2002] 1 WLR 1488.
[76] Ibid para [1] *per* Chadwick LJ.

responsibilities; a field which is "very much a matter for the allocation of resources in accordance with democratically determined priorities." '[77] There was 'no support in the Strasbourg jurisprudence—or in the jurisprudence which has been developing in these courts since the advent of the 1998 Act—for the proposition that section 6, in conjunction with Article 8, impose[d] some general and unqualified obligation on local authorities in relation to the condition of their housing stock.'[78] In *Wilson v Secretary of State for Trade and Industry*, Lord Nicholls remarked that '[t]he more the legislation [under review] concerns matters of broad social policy, the less ready will be a court to intervene.'[79] Arising in an entirely different context, though producing a not dissimilar result from the perspective of institutional competence was the decision in *R (Professional Contractors Group Ltd and others) v The Commissioners of Inland Revenue*.[80] In that case, reliance on a 'fall-back argument'[81] on human rights, developed as part of a complex challenge to taxation legislation, was comprehensively rejected, with Burton J quoting dicta from *Svenska Managementgruppen AB v Sweden* which we have already encountered in this chapter,[82] referring to the need for a measure of discretion to be accorded national authorities in relation to 'political, economic and social questions'.[83]

What is important to note about these cases is that they are identifying a zone of judicial restraint which derives more from an awareness of the limitations on the judicial function than it does from respect for parliamentary sovereignty as such. It is what the Convention requires—and more to the point does not require—that is directly in issue, rather than the need to defer to the legislature on account of its democratic legitimacy. However, as I have already noted earlier in this chapter, the two will frequently arise on the same set of facts. Thus in a case I have already referred to a number of times, *re S*, Lord Nicholls of Birkenhead quoted the 'wise words' of Cooke P in a New Zealand case that a proposed interpretation of a measure was unacceptable because it:

would amount to amending the Act by judicial legislation. In a sensitive and controversial field which the New Zealand Parliament may be said to have taken to itself, we do not consider that this court would be justified in such a course. If the Act is to be

---

[77] *Lee v Leeds City Council* decided with *Ratcliffe v Sandwell Metropolitan Borough Council* [2002] EWCA Civ 06, [2002] 1 WLR 1488, para [24]. The reference to Lord Hoffmann is from *Southwark London Borough Council v Tanner* [2001] 1 AC 1, 8 and 9–10. See also *Anufrijeva v Southwark London Borough Council* [2003] EWCA Civ 1406; *Royal Borough of Kensington and Chelsea v O'Sullivan* [2003] EWCA Civ 371; cf *Stonebridge Housing Action Trust v Gabbidon*, Queen's Bench Division, 22 October 2002, where an important issue of human dignity was centrally involved.

[78] n 75 above, para [49].

[79] [2003] UKHL 40, [2003] 3 WLR 568, para [70]. To similar effect are the remarks of Laws LJ in *R (Carson and Reynolds) v Secretary of State for Work and Pensions* [2003] EWCA Civ 797, [2003] 3 All E. R. 577, para [73]: 'In the field of what may be called macro-economic policy...the decision-making power of the elected arms of government is all but at its greatest, and the constraining role of the courts, absent a florid violation by government of established legal principles, is correspondingly modest.'

[80] [2001] EWHC 236 (Admin), [2001] EWCA Civ 1945.

[81] [2001] EWHC 236 (Admin), para [38].   [82] n 46 above.   [83] n 81 above, para [42].

amended it should be done by Parliament after full consideration of the arguments of policy.[84]

Areas which the judges are ill-equipped to enter will often be exactly those that the legislative branch has in any event 'taken to itself', and it is very easy to see in such circumstances how arguments against judicial intervention based both on competence and on respect for democracy can become intertwined. But I can perhaps be forgiven for stressing again that the two are not the same, with the former applying far more than the latter to demarcation disputes that involve the judicial and executive (rather than the judicial and the legislative) branches, particularly in relation to those areas of executive power which exist independently of Parliament, such as the royal prerogative. Thus, the restraint shown by the House of Lords in the *Rehman* decision, on the proper role of the courts in relation to the oversight of executive judgments about international terrorism, had more to do with the limits of judicial activism in the sphere of national security than it had with the (in any event rather precarious) democratic basis for such vital decisions.[85]

D. Shallow or deep end: engaging principle under the Human Rights Act

Without a successful connection to a central Convention principle of the sort I have discussed in chapters three to five of this book, litigants seeking to rely on the Convention before the UK courts have generally been unsuccessful, whether it has been a direct piece of legislation or an executive act under legislative powers that they have been challenging. Thus in *Goldsmith v Commissioners for Custom and Excise*,[86] an Article 6 based attack on the power of the defendants to forfeit goods where there was a failure to pay an appropriate amount of duty was unsuccessful, notwithstanding that the statutory scheme before the court envisaged a shift in the burden of proof onto the defendant in certain situations. The burden placed on members of the public was not, in the view of the Lord Chief Justice, 'excessive or unreasonable'.[87] However, Lord Woolf went on to make clear that he was not saying that 'if a criminal offence was being charged, the Commissioners should depart from their present practice of accepting that so far as an offence involves mens rea it is one where the onus must be on the Crown in the usual way to satisfy the tribunal of the person's guilt to the usual standard of proof'.[88] Such a case would have engaged a central Convention principle and (it is implied) led to a different result. The *Goldsmith*

---

[84] n 9 above, para [44]. The quotation is from *R v Stack* n 11 above, 261–262.

[85] *Secretary of State for the Home Department v Rehman* [2001] UKHL 47, [2002] 1 AC 153. See A Tomkins, 'Defining and Delimiting National Security' (2002) 118 *LQR* 200.

[86] [2001] EWHC Admin 285, [2001] 1 WLR 1673.

[87] Ibid para [24].

[88] Ibid para [25]. See *Gora v Commissioners of Customs and Excise* [2003] EWCA Civ 525, [2003] 3 WLR 160.

case could be decided the way it was because the judges saw it as *not* directly
involving a key Convention principle. In *Lindsay v Commissioner for Customs
and Excise*, in contrast, a general policy of condemnation of vehicles in which
contraband has been found was held by the Court of Appeal to have infringed
Convention rights because it had not properly distinguished between the import-
ation of goods for personal use on the one hand and commercial trafficking on
the other.[89] Since the effect of the general policy was to prevent the customs
officer from applying his or her judgment on proportionality on a case-by-case
basis, it was an unlawful fettering of the discretion reposed in such officials under
the relevant legislation. As we saw in chapter five, this decision can be characterized as one in which a central principle (the dignity of the possessive individual) has been successfully invoked (albeit perhaps controversially) and as one,
therefore, in which no undue restraint from the judiciary was judged to be
required.[90]

   It would be right to conclude from these decisions that the route to success in
business and commercial cases, or in those which seem to require remedies that
involve the expenditure of large sums of money or the discharge of a set of
positive obligations by the state, lies in *effectively* characterizing the factual
matrix before the court as one in which an issue of principle is centrally rather
than merely peripherally involved. In the commercial sector, the relevant
principle will usually be that of legality,[91] and it is a tribute of sorts to the
pervasiveness as well as the depth of this idea that so many of the leading cases
under the Human Rights Act have involved corporate and other business entities
attempting to invoke the principle to override any judicial diffidence that there
might otherwise have been about the Act not being intended for their litigious
consumption. The efforts of pawnbrokers,[92] road haulage companies[93] and
persons convicted of corporate crime[94] under the Human Rights Act have all
been by reference to variations of this general principle. Sometimes it does not
quite come off, as in *R (Morgan Grenfell & Co Ltd) v Special Commissioner of
Income Tax*,[95] in which not even the eloquence of Michael Beloff QC could
persuade the Court of Appeal that a revenue power to compel the handing over
of otherwise legally privileged material engaged an issue of central constitutional

[89] [2002] EWCA Civ 267, [2002] 1 WLR 1766. See further *Gascoyne v Commissioners of Customs
and Excise* [2003] EWHC 257 (Ch), [2003] Ch 292.
   [90] To similar effect are *Fox v HM Customs and Excise* [2002] EWHC 1244 (Admin), [2003] 1 WLR
1331 and *Commissioners of Customs and Excise v Newbury* [2003] EWHC 702 (Admin) [2002]
1 WLR 2131; but cf *R (HM Customs and Excise) v Helman* [2002] EWHC 2254 (Admin).
   [91] But see C Munro, 'The Value of Commercial Speech' (2003) 62 *CLJ* 134.
   [92] *Wilson v First County Trust (No 2)* [2001] EWCA Civ 633, [2002] QB 74; *Wilson v Secretary of
State for Trade and Industry* [2003] UKHL 40, [2003] 3 WLR 568.
   [93] *International Transport Roth GmbH v Secretary of State for the Home Department* [2002]
EWCA Civ 158, [2002] 3 WLR 344.
   [94] Cf *R v C (CL)* [2001] EWCA Crim 2845.
   [95] [2001] EWCA Civ 329, [2002] 2 WLR 255. For the decision in the House of Lords see [2002]
UKHL 21, [2003] 1 AC 563.

principle.[96] But the claimants enjoyed more success in *Han and another v Commissioners of Customs and Excise*[97] in which a majority of the Court of Appeal held that the imposition of penalties on taxpayers for dishonest evasion of VAT amounted to a 'criminal charge' to which therefore the full protection of Article 6 applied.[98]

The power of the principle of legality is what makes the issue of legal aid such a difficult one for the courts and for those who promote the Human Rights Act as a source of justice for all. On the one hand the provision of a 'right of access'[99] to the courts without the financial means to make that access worthwhile seems to make a mockery of the Convention's commitment to legality in general and equality of arms in particular. On the other hand, decisions on the financial resources that should be made available by the taxpayer to facilitate such litigation seem intuitively to be pre-eminently political in character. Both the Strasbourg court and now the domestic judges have wrestled with the issue in a not entirely satisfactory way.[100] The 'human right' to legal aid must be regarded as one of those frontier points at which the rhetoric of enforceable human rights is confronted with its own limitations in a society committed to the retention of unequal levels of resources as between its members.

Similar difficulties arise where a clear matter of human dignity is only capable of resolution at a high cost to the state. In *R (Noorkoiv) v Secretary of State for the Home Department*,[101] the Court of Appeal was emphatic in its assertion of support for the right to liberty in the prison context and clear that the government could not excuse what were otherwise breaches of Article 5 'simply by pointing to a lack of resources that are provided by other arms of government'.[102] As we have already noted, the courts have, in contrast, been more indulgent of resource problems in the area of discharge from detention under the Mental Health Act, where the proposed release is of a person who is still

---

[96] Ibid paras [43]–[46] dealing with the 'powerful submission' of Mr Beloff on the point. Note that in this case, in line with a number of such decisions, the notion of legality is used in a very broad way to refer to a judicial assumption about the human rights compatibility of legislation under challenge before it. This line of decisions, sowing it might be thought an unnecessary seed of confusion in the field of post-Human Rights Act litigation, principally derives from the highly influential but pre-implementation decision of *R (Simms) v Secretary of State for the Home Department* [2000] 2 AC 115 (see esp at p 131 *per* Lord Hoffmann).

[97] [2001] EWCA Civ 1040; [2001] 1 WLR 2253.

[98] See also *King v Walden* [2001] STC 822.

[99] Implied into Art 6(1): *Golder v United Kingdom* (1975) 1 EHRR 524.

[100] As far as the European Court of Human Rights is concerned, the frequently cited *Airey v Ireland* (1979) 2 EHRR 305 (with its ringing assertion that the Convention was 'intended to guarantee not rights that are theoretical or illusory but rights that are practical and effective' (para [24])) has not produced the long line of authorities that might have been expected. In the UK, the issue which was skirted around and half tackled before implementation (*R (Witham) v Lord Chancellor* [1998] QB 575; *R (Lightfoot) v Lord Chancellor* [2000] QB 597) has yet to catch fire: see *McLean v Buchanan* [2001] UKPD 3, [2001] 1 WLR 2425; *re K (children)* [2002] EWCA Civ 1559; *R v Oates* [2002] EWCA Crim 1071, [2002] 1 WLR 2833 cf *R (Khan) v Secretary of State for Health* [2003] EWCA Civ 1129, [2003] 4 All ER 1239.

[101] [2002] EWCA Civ 770, [2002] 1 WLR 3284.   [102] Ibid para [31] *per* Buxton LJ.

mentally unwell.[103] The resources versus rights dilemma arose in a most interesting way in a Scottish decision to which I have already referred in passing, *Napier v Scottish Ministers*.[104] The petitioner was a remand prisoner who complained that he was being held in conditions which amounted to a violation of his Article 3 rights. He made three points in particular, (i) that the cell in which he was being detained was 'grossly inadequate in living space, lighting and ventilation, particularly since he [was] require[d] to share the cell with another prisoner'; (ii) that the sanitary arrangements, which involved 'the process known as "slopping out", that is, urination and defecation in vessels which are kept in the cell and emptied two or three times a day,' were 'grossly inadequate'; and (iii) that the extent to which he was confined in his cell was 'excessive, and the periods of exercise and recreation outside the cell [were] inadequate'.[105]

Lord MacFadyen, hearing the case as an interim application for relief, agreed that the petitioner's Convention rights under Article 3 were being infringed. In considering what kind of remedial order to make, the problem with which the judge had then to wrestle was that Napier's treatment was no different from that meted out to all those who were being held in this particular location within the Scottish system. Barlinnie prison in general and C wing (where Napier was) in particular had been the subject of critical reports from the European Committee for the Prevention of Torture and Inhumane or Degrading Treatment or Punishment and from Her Majesty's Inspector of Prisons. Counsel for the prison authorities pointed to the various improvements that were being undertaken at the prison and argued that 'the balance of convenience was against making an *interim* order in favour of the petitioner that could not be implemented in respect of the other prisoners who were in the same position as the petitioner'.[106]

Lord MacFayden accepted that '[i]f it were right to take into account the impracticability of implementing a similar order in respect of all of the prisoners in C Hall in determining where the balance of convenience lies in the petitioner's case, . . . the balance would be tilted' against granting relief,[107] but he went on to emphasize that what was before him was merely a single case: 'the fact that the respondents [did] not seek to argue that it would be impracticable to implement an *interim* order in respect of the petitioner. . . entitled [him] to have his case determined according to its own merits.'[108] Just because 'there were other remand prisoners who might be in as strong a position as the petitioner to seek a similar order, and that it would be difficult or impracticable for the respondents to relocate all of those other remand prisoners' did not mean that there was 'a good reason for refusing the petitioner an *interim* order to which he was *prima facie* entitled and which would, by itself, involve no impracticability or incon-

---

[103] *R (K) v Camden and Islington Health Authority* n 71 above. Cf *R (K) v Mental Health Review Board* [2002] EWHC 639 (Admin).
[104] Outer House, Court of Session, 26 June 2001 (Lord MacFadyen).
[105] Ibid para [6].
[106] Ibid para [13] of the judgment.
[107] Ibid para [15] of the judgment.
[108] Ibid.

venience for the respondents'.[109] The judge ordered that the petitioner be moved to an Article 3 compliant situation within the Scottish prison service within 72 hours. The 'broader consequences of treating all the prisoners in C Hall'[110] in the same way as the petitioner were not matters of direct concern to the court.[111]

It may be that Lord MacFayden was confident that his ruling would have a general effect with the authorities acting immediately to prevent similar cases in the future. But on its face, the *Napier* decision seems to rely on the disconcerting assumption that only those persons whose human rights' plights are directly before a court deserve protection, while victims without the resources or the enterprising temperament for litigation can properly be left unnoticed. Such an idea runs counter to one of the central ambitions of the Human Rights Act, which was to create a culture of rights which would reach past the law courts into civil society, binding all government departments without the need for litigation to give it reality in each and every case. Of course it is true that Lord MacFayden ignored all the other prisoners in order to dodge the resource implications of his decision, something that would not have been possible if the action had been a class one to which all prisoners in C Hall had been joined. Indeed he mentions in his judgment that had he had to take all the prisoners into account he would come down against the grant of relief, a curious admission by a judge that the worse the human rights violations before him the more secure would have been the position of the responsible authorities.

The *Napier* ruling could indulge in the luxury of being unequivocal because it had so narrowed the issues before it that no resource implications arising from it could be said to have arisen. As we have already observed when analysing the case law on human dignity,[112] the closer a case can be made to resemble a one-off assertion of legal rights, the more likely it is that the courts will be brave in their assertion of principle. In chapter five I saw how the principle of human dignity frequently manifests itself in a demand not necessarily for a substantive improvement in the situation of the claimant, but rather in a requirement that his or her wishes be more carefully heard by the authorities. A decision like that in the case of *P and Q*, involving the removal of babies from imprisoned mothers, is an example of such a ruling.[113] Viewed from the perspective of this chapter, the Court of Appeal's insistence in that case on the right of a mother to be heard—rather than on her entitlement to keep her baby with her—meant that the financial implications of the ruling were less stark than would otherwise have been the case.[114] It is certainly true that where resource issues are not directly in

---

[109] Ibid para [14].   [110] Ibid para [15].

[111] For the sequel to the case, see R Mackenzie, 'Bringing Human Rights to the Prison Population' (2003) 48 *Journal of the Law Society of Scotland*, no 1, 26. The article takes the form of an interview with the lawyer Tony Kelly who has been a driving force behind the *Napier* case, and other Scottish prison cases.

[112] See pp 101–103 above.

[113] See pp 105–106 above.

[114] The cost of providing due process is difficult to gauge and in any event is an expense that judges will invariably deem to be worthwhile.

point, a bold assertion of principle should not be at all problematic. In particular, if the facts before the court directly and unambiguously raises a point of core principle, there should be no need to invoke any self-denying judicial restraint over and above that already to be found in the scheme of the Human Rights Act itself. This is what made the *Pearson and Martinez* decision, discussed in chapter three, so disappointing.[115] Once it was clear that a key Convention right was involved in that case (the entitlement to vote), and that there were no significant resource implications to balance against the denial to prisoners of the right before the court, nor any other reason why the matter was inappropriate for judicial scrutiny, an infringement of the relevant provision (Article 3 of the first protocol) should have been found. This being the case, there should then have been no room for any extra deference to Parliament as such, over and above that already to be found in the Human Rights Act, ss 3 and 4. The Court of Appeal however allowed its deference to Parliament to manifest itself in a finding of no violation of the Convention. As I suggested in chapter three, this was a case in which a declaration of incompatibility should have been made.

The risk in rolling the question of Convention compatibility into the ss 3 and 4 issue of parliamentary sovereignty is that the Convention rights get unnecessarily diluted so as to produce a false consistency with Convention rights. *Hirst and Martinez* is one such case. Another was the Court of Appeal decision in *Bellinger v Bellinger*[116] in which the court, by a majority, refused the applicant a declaration that her marriage was valid, giving as the reason that she had been born a man and that the law as it stood did not accept that her gender had changed, despite the successful completion of gender reassignment surgery some years before. The legislation on the subject from the early 1970s provided a clear framework for the court which the majority was not inclined to disturb. The question as to at 'what point [it would] be consistent with public policy to recognise that a person should be treated for all purposes, including marriage, as a person of the opposite sex to that to which he/she was correctly assigned at birth' could not 'properly be decided by the court'.[117] When 'considering social issues in particular judges must not substitute their own views to fill gaps' in the law.[118] The matter was for Parliament, despite the majority's view that 'there [was] no doubt that the profoundly unsatisfactory nature of the present position and the plight of transsexuals require[d] careful consideration' and that the 'problems [would] not go away and may well come again before the European Court sooner rather than later'.[119]

---

[115] See pp 58–59 above.

[116] [2001] EWCA Civ 1140, [2002] Fam 150.

[117] Ibid para [105] of the judgment of Butler-Sloss P and Robert Walker LJ.

[118] Ibid para [106].

[119] Ibid para [109]. The subject had been frequently before the European Court of Human Rights with no applicant having been successful when the *Bellinger* case fell to be decided by the Court of Appeal: see what was then the most recent case: *Sheffield and Horsham v United Kingdom* (1998) 27 EHRR 163. After the *Bellinger* case in the Court of Appeal but before the Lords hearing came *Goodwin v United Kingdom* (2002) 35 EHRR 447.

All this is entirely defensible, but why did it not lead to a declaration of incompatibility? In a powerful dissent, Thorp LJ accepted that, '[o]f course judges must not usurp the function of parliament'[120] but that with implementation of the Human Rights Act, the majority should have been more willing to appreciate its new role in the protection of the person:

The [European] Convention is founded upon the concepts of human dignity and human freedom. Human dignity and human freedom are not properly recognised unless the individual is free to shape himself and his life in accordance with his personality, providing that his choice does not interfere with the public interest. . . .

. . . The range of rights claimed by transsexuals falls across the divisions of our justice systems. The present claim lies most evidently in the territory of the family justice system. That system must always be sufficiently flexible to accommodate social change. It must also be humane and swift to recognise the right to human dignity and to freedom of choice in the individual's private life. One of the objectives of statute law reform in this field must be to ensure that the law reacts to and reflects social change. That must also be an objective of the judges in this field in the construction of existing statutory provisions. I am strongly of the opinion that there are not sufficiently compelling reasons, having regard to the interests of others affected or, more relevantly, the interests of society as a whole, to deny this appellant legal recognition of her marriage.[121]

What is interesting about these two extracts from Thorp LJ's dissent is the way in which he sought to characterize the case as directly concerned with human dignity and therefore comprising a set of facts which demanded a more engaged judicial function than the majority were prepared to provide. Though the situation was complicated in the Court of Appeal by the then reluctance of the European Court of Human Rights to recognise the plight of transsexuals as one that warrants protection under Article 8,[122] Thorp LJ was surely right that the issue in the case was transparently one of human dignity, and that therefore there was no basis for the deferential approach that the majority had chosen to adopt. This was exactly the line taken by the House of Lords when the matter came before it in early 2003, with their lordships seeing the case as an appropriate one for a declaration, in other words as one requiring judicial deference rather than judicial restraint.[123]

E. Conclusion

The argument that has gradually unfolded here can now be usefully summarized. A distinction has been made between *judicial deference* on the one hand and *judicial restraint* on the other. In a situation in which the Convention is presumptively breached by a statutory provision as ordinarily understood, the interpretive duty under s 3 the Human Rights Act, is engaged, and every effort is then

---

[120] Ibid para [148].   [121] Ibid paras [156(ii)] and [160].
[122] *Sheffield and Horsham v United Kingdom* n 119 above; *Goodwin v United Kingdom*, n 119 above.
[123] [2003] UKHL 21, [2003] 2 AC 467.

required to be made (within the limits of the possible) to manipulate the provision so as to achieve compatibility. There are limits to the judicial creativity that is permitted under s 3(1), and we saw in chapter three how the Human Rights Act, through its protection of certain statutes and its provision for non-binding declarations of incompatibility in relation to such measures, explicitly sets out to protect the sovereignty of the legislative body. To this extent, therefore, it is clear that *judicial deference* to Parliament is built into the very structure of the Human Rights Act itself. The statutory command to the courts to defer to the legislative will which is explicit in the Human Rights Act also covers executive action necessary to give effect to that will (s 6(2)), and extends not only to matters which are peripheral to human rights but also to parliamentary action that attacks the very core of the subject; in theory any provision no matter how heinous from a human rights perspective can be enacted, and then safely enforced.

This issue of *judicial deference* has been mainly discussed in chapter three. In this chapter, my interest has lain in the prior question, arising before s 3 is brought into the fray, of the circumstances in which it can be said that the Convention is in fact infringed, and what has been argued here is that this issue is informed by the overlapping but autonomous notion of *judicial restraint*. Of course the matter of an alleged breach of the Convention is easily dealt with where the violation is obvious, and such cases have not particularly concerned me here, there being no restraint to be shown. Rather it has been in setting boundaries to the Convention's potential impact on the administrative process that my interest has lain. The Convention's explosive breadth is such that it has the capacity, if untamed, to fill practically every nook and cranny in our law, and indeed in our political process. Its circumscription is less a matter of what it says (since in the hands of a creative lawyer it can be made to say practically anything) than it is a question of what its interpreters can be trusted properly to do. The institutional competence of the judicial branch becomes then, on this argument, an important guide to the breadth of the Convention rights. My concept of judicial restraint flows from the judges' own appreciation of the limitations of the adjudicative process, and from their mature appreciation that certain matters are beyond the capacity of any court to resolve. This explains why Convention arguments intruding into economic, social, and policy areas invariably produce a finding of no breach, thereby not even getting to the point where the s 3 interpretive duty needs to be brought into the picture. Judicial restraint being required, the question of judicial deference does not arise. On the other hand, where a central principle of the Convention is engaged, and there are no countervailing resource issues, then there is no reason why a presumptive Convention breach should not be found, with it then being up to ss 3 and 4 to resolve the question of whether this is a case in which it is appropriate to defer to the wishes of the legislature in relation to the measure under scrutiny.

There is therefore not one stage in which judicial self-control must operate in relation to the Human Rights Act, but two. First there is the issue of institutional competence, addressed when asking whether the Convention is presumptively infringed, and second, arising only if this first hurdle is negotiated, there is the issue of whether Parliament's supremacy is required to be acknowledged under ss 3 and 4. In this early phase of the Human Rights Act's life, it is not surprising that the courts have not always separated out these two stages in their interpretation of the measure. Instead there has been a general feeling that both issues are required by the Act to be taken very seriously. An important dictum from the pre-implementation period was Lord Hope's in *R (Kebilene) v Director of Public Prosecutions* that in 'some circumstances it will be appropriate for the courts to recognize that there is an area of judgment within which the judiciary will defer, on democratic grounds, to the considered opinion of the elected body or person whose act or decision is said to be incompatible with the Convention'.[124] This sounds very much like judicial deference. Then later in the same paragraph, referring to the 'discretionary area of judgment' afforded the other branches of the state, Lord Hope describes this concept as more easily 'recognized where the issues involve questions of social or economic policy,' but 'much less so where the rights are of high constitutional importance or are of a kind where the courts are especially well placed to assess the need for protection'.[125] This is closer to our understanding of judicial restraint than it is to judicial deference. In *R v Lambert*[126] in the Court of Appeal, the Lord Chief Justice Lord Woolf put the point in the following way:

It is ... important to have in mind that legislation is passed by a democratically elected Parliament and therefore the courts under the Convention are entitled to and should, as a matter of constitutional principle, pay a degree of deference to the view of Parliament as to what is in the interest of the public generally when upholding the rights of the individual under the Convention. The courts are required to balance the competing interests involved.[127]

This is a strong statement of judicial deference, to be contrasted with Lord Woolf's later remark on competence in the *Poplar* housing case that the 'economic and other implications of any policy in this area are extremely complex and far-reaching' and that this was as a result 'an area where, in our judgment, the courts must treat the decisions of Parliament as to what is in the public interest with particular deference'.[128] This is a different kind of judicial restraint, applying when a court is 'deciding whether there has been a breach of the Convention',[129] than the one rooted in respect for parliamentary sovereignty.

The most stimulating and original attempt thus far to deal with these various issues in a structured and methodical way is to be found in the dissenting judgment of Lord Justice Laws in the Court of Appeal decision in *International Transport Roth gmbh v Secretary of State for the Home Department*.[130] My

---

[124] [2000] 2 AC 326, 381.   [125] Ibid.   [126] [2002] QB 1112.   [127] Ibid para [16].
[128] *Poplar Housing and Regeneration Community Association Limited v Donoghue* [2001] EWCA Civ 595, [2002] QB 48, para [69].
[129] Ibid.   [130] n 93 above.

interest lies in the structure of the Lord Justice's argument rather than with the exact facts in, or the outcome of, the case. According to Laws LJ, the protective attention of the courts in relation to 'constitutional rights' under the Human Rights Act 'is engaged where a statute admittedly travels in the field of a constitutional right, and the issue is whether the right is violated, or if it is whether the extent of the statute's intrusion is acceptable or justified'.[131] If the word 'and' were substituted for the penultimate 'or', this would be a near perfect formulation, capturing the three-stage nature of the judicial inquiry, an investigation which as we have seen asks first if the Convention is engaged (is the statute one which 'travels in the field of a constitutional right'?), then whether the right is violated (the issue of judicial restraint operating at this stage) and finally thirdly, if it is, whether nevertheless the extent of the statute's intrusion is to be permitted (the judicial deference point).

In his judgment Laws LJ then goes on to develop four principles of interpretation which fit this structure very well. The first, 'that greater deference is to be paid to an Act of Parliament than to a decision of the executive or subordinate measure'[132] is as I have argued in this chapter implicit in ss 3, 4, and 6 of the Act itself. The second, that 'there is more scope for deference "where the Convention itself requires a balance to be struck, much less so where the right is stated in terms which are unqualified"'[133] reflects the Convention's own hierarchical structure, with certain rights being more central to the basic principles in the Convention than are others—another theme that I have explored in this chapter. The third and fourth of Laws LJ's principles, 'that greater deference will be due to the democratic powers where the subject-matter in hand is peculiarly within their constitutional responsibility, and less when it lies more particularly within the constitutional responsibility of the courts'[134] and that 'greater or lesser deference will be due according to whether the subject-matter lies more readily within the actual or potential expertise of the democratic powers or the courts'[135] are clear versions of what I have called here judicial restraint. As Laws LJ recognizes, everything depends on how the issue before a court is characterized. As long as the matter is accepted to be primarily a governmental one, judicial restraint will invariably follow: '[t]here are no tanks on the wrong lawns.'[136] But if the case is perceived to be primarily about a legal matter, then the outcome will be different. It was exactly a difference of this kind as to how the issues in the *Roth* case were to be characterized that led to Laws LJ dissenting from the result in that case. He saw the facts before him as primarily about state security (and therefore a case in which judicial restraint was appropriate) while his colleagues on the bench saw it primarily as a criminal or quasi criminal matter deserving of the closest judicial scrutiny.[137] If there are to be

---

[131] n 93 above, para [74].   [132] Ibid para [83].
[133] Ibid para [84] citing Lord Hope in *ex parte Kebilene*, n 124 above.
[134] Ibid para [85].   [135] Ibid para [87].   [136] Ibid para [86].
[137] Cf Laws LJ at para [97] with Simon Brown LJ at paras [47] and [53] and Jonathan Parker LJ at para [139].

disputes about the application of the Act, then it is exactly on such key questions that they should turn, since they make clear the key issue, that of judicial competence, which is all too often obscured by the thicket of authority and blind reliance on dicta designed for a different era. This is an aspiration which is desirable and, given the judicial record so far under the Human Rights Act, entirely realizable.

7

The Aspiration of Proportionate Intrusion

A. A modest proposal?

The drafters of the Human Rights Act did not intend it as an alien growth on UK domestic law, flattening all before it with a new and radically different guide to rights' adjudication. Even distinguished proponents of the measure in its strongest form, such as Lord Lester of Herne Hill, never thought that the reform should do other than locate itself carefully in the prevailing legal culture.[1] In the judicial training that occurred after enactment but prior to implementation, much emphasis was placed on the need to interpret the Act in a way that respected the prevailing status quo.[2] To use one of the Convention's own favourite phrases, the intrusion into the law of the Human Rights Act was intended by its drafters and sponsors to be 'proportionate'. This chapter is concerned with how this humble aspiration has manifested itself in the case law. I start by considering the reception of the Act in areas already covered by legislation for which it was not obvious the Human Rights Act was designed. This takes me into a discussion of the impact of the measure on judicial review of administrative action. Then I explore a topic I have touched on earlier, namely the question of how the common law has coped with this dramatic legislative challenge to its culture. Finally I consider the knotty problem of retrospectivity, an issue which has, rather unexpectedly, provided the first major crisis for the judicial branch in its interpretation of the Act. In all of these areas, the Human Rights Act has had to be managed so as to enable its best features to be revealed while preventing the measure from spinning out of control, damaging whole branches of law at which it was not primarily aimed.

Before we embark on our discussion of these various themes, it is worth mentioning three general points that will help to frame what follows. First, we should recall that even prior to 2 October 2000, the mild presumption that UK legislation was compatible with the nation's international law obligations (of which adherence to the Convention was one) meant that pre-existing laws already had a slight presumption of compatibility operative in their favour,

---

[1] See eg his 'The Art of the Possible—Interpreting Statutes under the Human Rights Act' [1998] *EHRLR* 665. And for an interesting review of the thinking behind the Act, see Lord Irvine of Lairg, 'The Impact of the Human Rights Act: Parliament, the Courts and the Executive' [2003] *PL* 308.

[2] For a very useful appraisal of this training see S Sedley, 'Learning Human Rights' in F Butler (ed), *Human Rights Protection: Methods and Effectiveness* (London: Kluwer Law International, 2002), ch 4.

even before any visitation from s 3(1).[3] This was especially the case with regard to the Convention since the obligation in issue was concerned with a matter—respect for human rights—that the judiciary had for some years claimed to take very seriously.[4] Secondly, it is clear that the Human Rights Act was not designed to be in any way the last word on the protection of human rights.[5] The Convention itself alerts those tempted to rely upon it to the fact that the member states may provide more effective protection,[6] and the theme is carried though into the substantive provisions of the Human Rights Act, with s 11 asserting that a 'person's reliance on a Convention right does not restrict—(a) any other right or freedom conferred on him by or under any law having effect in any part of the United Kingdom; or (b) his right to make any claim or bring any proceedings which he could make or bring apart from sections 7 to 9.' Thirdly there is the perhaps obvious point that the rights set out in the Convention by no means cover the full range of commitments that the UK has made in the international human rights law arena, the international covenants on civil and political rights and on economic, social, and cultural rights—both agreed in 1966—being two clear examples.

It follows, therefore, that the Human Rights Act was never intended to supersede existing civil libertarian protection, to reinvent established law, to dispense with the need for better law, to dismantle all that went before, or dramatically to fix that which was not broken in the first place. At the same time, and this is a tension in the Act with which we are by now very familiar, if the modesty of the Act's impact were too readily accepted, its proper remit might shrink to practically nothing, and if this were to happen, its revolutionary potential—rooted in the radical and moral claims made by its title—would risk being drained of life. In the period prior to implementation, enthusiasts for the measure found themselves occasionally in the quandary of simultaneously saying the Act would change everything and at the same time that it would alter nothing.[7] Since October 2000, a more balanced picture has emerged,

---

[3] M Hunt, *Using Human Rights Law in English Courts* (Oxford: Hart Publishing, 1997), ch 1 covers this ground very well.

[4] See *R (Smith) v Ministry of Defence* [1996] QB 517; *R (Simms) v Secretary of State for the Home Department* [2000] 2 AC 115, esp 131 *per* Lord Hoffmann. This is not to say that the Convention inevitably trumps other international obligations: see *Al-Adsani v United Kingdom* (2001) 34 EHRR 273; *Fogarty v United Kingdom* (2001) 34 EHRR 302; *McElhinney v Ireland* (2001) 34 EHRR 322; and *Holland v Lampen-Wolfe* [2000] 1 WLR 1573; see generally M Kloth, 'Immunities and the Right of Access to Court under the European Convention on Human Rights' (2002) 27 *European Law Review Human Rights Survey* 33.

[5] See K Starmer, *European Human Rights Law. The Human Rights Act 1998 and the European Convention on Human Rights* (London: Legal Action Group, 1999), 33–34.

[6] See Art 53: 'Nothing in this Convention shall be construed as limiting or derogating from any of the human rights and fundamental freedoms which may be ensured under the laws of any High Contracting Party or under any other agreement to which it is a Party.'

[7] For a neat solution to this conundrum, offered by the senior law lord in the course of some extra judicial remarks, see T Bingham, *The Business of Judging. Selected Essays and Speeches* (Oxford: Oxford University Press, 2000), 140. Also of interest is the way the Lord Chancellor in his review of the operation of the Act, n 1 above, approached this point.

with the new legislation being strongly deployed in the areas of principle identified and discussed in chapters three to six of this book, even where this involves sharp changes to the inherited status quo, but being rather less to the fore where these principles are not so frontally engaged, and where the legislative and/or common law landscape is already well-settled. As Lord Nicholls remarked in a recent case, citing a Strasbourg authority, there has to be some willingness on the part of the judges to take a 'pragmatic approach to the practicalities of government'.[8]

B. The impact on mainstream statute law

A great deal of legislation neither directly engages the principles that are at the core of the Human Rights Act nor so obviously involves matters outside the judicial remit that its provisions are beyond the reach of the courts. To recover an analogy from chapter six, many statutes are in the middle of the swimming pool, equidistant from the shallow end of principle and the deep end of policy and public expenditure. The judges can just about reach these measures if they try, and impose the Human Rights Act upon them if they are determined. Should they do so? The answer—right in principle and also true as a matter of practice since 2 October 2000—is that in general they should leave well enough alone. Such Acts of Parliament reflect Parliament's specific solution to particular problems. Frequently they will have been very recently enacted. They are often extremely detailed documents, the result of a complex legislative process in which various groups will have been deeply involved. Such statutes invariably need to be read as a whole, and they will often contain various safeguards and concessions for interested parties that might seem otherwise to be unduly affected by certain provisions when viewed in isolation. Unless an issue of human rights principle is directly engaged, it would be quite wrong for the short and rather general Human Rights Act to be permitted blithely to wreak destabilizing havoc on such legislation. The bull would be in the wrong china shop, or (recalling Laws LJ in the *International Roth GmbH* case)[9] the judicial tanks would be on the wrong lawns.

A good case in point is the Police and Criminal Evidence Act 1984 (known as PACE). Here is a core document, setting out the nature of the relationship between the police and the individual where a crime is suspected. Though amended as judged necessary by Parliament over the years, the statute has achieved a quasi-constitutional status in the English system, with numerous statutory instruments, codes of practices and cases having grown up around

---

[8] *Bellinger v Bellinger* [2003] UKHL 21, [2003] 2 AC 467, para [53] referring to *Walden v Liechenstein*, European Court of Human Rights, 16 March 2000.
[9] *International Transport Roth gmb v Secretary of State for the Home Department* [2002] EWCA Civ 158, [2002] 3 WLR 344; see above p 144.

it.[10] The measure deals with areas which are manifestly of concern to the European Convention (in particular the right to liberty in Article 5 and the due process guarantees in Article 6), but it does so in a way that seems designed more to concretize than to subvert those rights. It is clearly a complex and wide-ranging piece of law that it is necessary to consider as a whole, and the human rights challenges to specific sections that have inevitably arisen since 2 October 2000 have not, on the whole, been successful.[11] In *R (S and Marper) v Chief Constable of South Yorkshire*,[12] the focus was on an amendment to PACE which retrospectively permitted the retention of fingerprints and DNA samples taken from suspects notwithstanding that the person from whom they were obtained had been cleared of the offence of which they had been suspected.[13] The Convention rights relied upon were Articles 8 and 14.

At first instance, the Administrative Court had difficulty in characterizing the retention of such samples (as opposed to their acquisition) as involving an issue of respect for privacy under Article 8(1), but even if this were the case the court was clear that the provision was a legitimate and proportionate response by Parliament to an issue on which it was entitled to legislate. As far as Article 14 was concerned, the treatment of persons sanctioned by the Act was not discriminatory but, if it was, the discrimination had a 'legitimate aim and [an] objective and reasonable justification'.[14] Giving a judgment with which Lord Justice Rose agreed, Mr Justice Leveson took into account the whole statutory scheme, noting that:

not only do the new powers contained within this provision comply with Convention obligations but also the system of retention is not open to abuse, because a crime scene forensic sample is an essential pre-requisite to any search against the data base and, without a match, the data of any one person will remain untouched. Save for anyone whose material does match (in which event, the investigation of crime is legitimately furthered), the only possible effect, if there is one, will be to exclude from investigation others on the data base. Furthermore, section 78 of PACE exists to provide additional safeguard should that be necessary.[15]

The Court of Appeal saw the retention of the evidence as clearly engaging Article 8 but nevertheless as an invasion of privacy that was justified under Article 8(2).[16] The three members of the court also agreed that Article 14 was

---

[10] Scotland and Northern Ireland have their own systems of criminal procedure and police law, though that of the latter now draws heavily on PACE: see respectively the Criminal Procedure (Scotland) Act 1995 and the Police and Criminal Evidence (Northern Ireland) Order 1989 (SI 1989 1341).

[11] Cf *R v Z* [2003] EWCA Crim 191, [2003] 1 WLR 1489, in which the Court of Appeal correctly notes the need to reconsider the meaning of a confession in PACE, s 76 so as to ensure consistency with Art 6.

[12] [2002] EWHC 478 (Admin).

[13] Criminal Justice and Police Act 2001, s 82 adding a new subsection to PACE, s 64.

[14] Ibid para [41] *per* Leveson J.

[15] Ibid para [50]. Section 78 allows for the exclusion from criminal proceedings of unlawfully obtained evidence.   [16] [2002] EWCA Civ 1275, [2002] 1 WLR 3223.

not violated, albeit with Lord Woolf CJ and Walker LJ taking a different approach to the guarantee from that of Sedley LJ. As with the judges in the court below, the appellate bench regarded 'the scheme of the legislation and the history of how it ha[d] been amended' as 'important when determining the issues which [had been] raised by this appeal'.[17] This was because 'PACE was intended to play a central role in achieving greater fairness within the criminal justice system and it has undoubtedly made a significant contribution towards achieving that objective'.[18] In an important passage from the perspective of our present discussion, the Lord Chief Justice went on to say:

> Whether or not the statutory provisions comply with the articles of the Convention, they undoubtedly represent an attempt by Parliament to achieve a fair balance between the interests of the law-abiding public as a whole and the individual citizen. Where this is the situation, it is important that the courts show appropriate deference to the body whose decision has the advantage of being able to rely on unimpeachable democratic credentials. Any judge, or for that matter any member of the public, will have his or her own opinion as to how the balance should be drawn. However, their individual opinions will lack any democratic support. In considering each of the submissions [of counsel for the claimants] I regard it as being fundamental that the court keeps at the forefront of its consideration its lack of any democratic credentials.[19]

Where there has been no statutory guidance, the courts have felt able to be intrusive, as was the case in relation to the Essex police offender naming scheme for example.[20] But where statutes have been to the fore, other cases have echoed the reluctance of the judges in the *S and Marper* case to allow the Human Rights Act to eat too deeply into criminal law, police powers and the rules of criminal evidence. As far as the first of these is concerned, in *Barnfather v Islington London Borough Council*, a frontal assault on Parliament's power to create strict liability offences, rooted in Article 6.2 of the Convention, was seen off by Kay and Elias JJ in the Administrative Court.[21] As regards police powers, in *Kennedy v Crown Prosecution Service*,[22] the entitlement to insist on a breath specimen in a case of suspected drunk driving, even where a legal adviser for the individual concerned had not yet arrived, was held not to involve any breach of Article 6. In relation to criminal procedure, *R v Pearce*[23] is of interest in this context. The issue was whether requiring the partner of an accused to testify against him at his trial was a breach of the right to respect for family life set out in Article 8 of the Convention. Despite the fact that a spouse enjoyed protection from compellability, the Court of Appeal was unpersuaded:

> The relevant words are to be found in section 80(1) of the Police and Criminal Evidence Act 1984. Those words were reconsidered by Parliament as recently as 1999, when the section was re-enacted in an amended form by the Youth Justice and Criminal Evidence Act of that year. They speak of the 'wife or husband of a person charged'

---

[17] [2002] EWCA Civ 1275, [2002] 1 WLR 3223, [15] *per* Lord Woolf CJ.
[18] Ibid.   [19] Ibid para [16].
[20] *R (Ellis) v Chief Constable of Essex Police* [2003] EWHC 1321 (Admin).
[21] [2003] EWHC 418 (Admin), [2003] 1 WLR 2318.
[22] [2002] EWHC 2297 (Admin).   [23] [2001] EWCA Crim 2834, [2002] 1 WLR 1553.

being compellable only in certain circumstances. They do not speak of a person in the position of a wife, and [the partner of the accused] was not the wife of the appellant. [Counsel's] primary submission is that we should read down the words of section 80(1) so as to make them compliant with his interpretation of the Convention, but the words are clear and are not capable of being expanded so as to embrace a relationship to which they plainly do not apply. In any event we do not accept the proposition which underlies [counsel's] submissions in relation to this aspect of the case, namely that proper respect for family life as envisaged by Article 8 requires that a co-habitee of a defendant, whether or not married to him, should not be required to give evidence or to answer questions about a statement which he has already made. This is plainly ... an area where the interests of the family must be weighed against those of the community at large, and it is precisely the sort of area in which the European Court defers to the judgment of states in relation to their domestic courts.[24]

The most well-known of these PACE cases have been those concerned with the question whether the pre-existing rules on the admissibility of evidence contained in that Act, particularly in s 78, have been affected by the new legislation. The big question has been whether evidence obtained in breach of the Act has now to be excluded from subsequent legal proceedings, something that neither the common law nor PACE had ever insisted upon, but which the apparently highly charged finding of a breach of human rights might seem to suggest should occur. In a succession of decisions since October 2000, however, the courts have restated the PACE approach and firmly accommodated the requirements of human rights within the pre-existing framework of law,[25] a line that is not discouraged by the Strasbourg authorities on the subject.[26] In one of the s 78 cases to reach the House of Lords, on the issue of police entrapment, Lord Nicholls observed that he could 'not discern any appreciable difference between the requirements of art 6, or the Strasbourg jurisprudence on art 6, and English law as it has developed in recent years'.[27] In the same case Lord Scott described the article as a provision which 'restates what was already English law' with the 'court's discretion under section 78 of the 1984 Act to exclude evidence [providing] the remedy in domestic law and ... [enabling] the domestic law to accord with what is required for compliance in this area with art 6'.[28] As Lord Hobhouse remarked in another House of Lords case on the subject, the case law on Articles 6 and 8 does not 'alter the vital role of section 78 as the means by which questions of the use of evidence obtained in breach of article 8 are to be resolved at a criminal trial'.[29]

---

[24] Ibid para [12] *per* Kennedy LJ giving the judgment of the court.
[25] See in particular *R v Loveridge, Lee and Loveridge* [2001] EWCA Crim 973, [2001] 2 Cr App R 591 and *R v Mason, Wood, McClelland and Tierney* [2002] EWCA Crim 385, [2002] 2 Cr App R 628.
[26] See in particular from the United Kingdom *Khan v United Kingdom* (2000) 31 EHRR 1016 and *Chalkley v United Kingdom* (2003) 37 EHRR 680.
[27] *R v Looseley; Attorney General's Reference (No 3 of 2000)* [2001] UKHL 53, [2001] 1 WLR 2060, para [30].
[28] Ibid para [122].
[29] *R v P* [2002] 1 AC 146, 162.

If the courts have been reluctant to get too deeply immersed in a human rights based re-evaluation of PACE, it will be immediately appreciated that their perspective on legislation even further from the core of the Convention rights than PACE is likely to have been even more restrained, and this is indeed the case. The protection for journalist sources in the Contempt of Court Act 1981, s 10 has accommodated both Article 10 of the Convention and the Strasbourg case law within its remit.[30] The statutory ban on disclosure of jury deliberations has survived scrutiny under Article 6[31] as have judicial warrants under the Competition Act by reference to Articles 6 and 8.[32] Likewise the approach to the levels of sentencing currently taken by the English courts is unaffected by Article 7 of the Convention.[33] Nor does the indefinite disqualification from working with children permitted under the Criminal Justice and Court Services Act 2000 amount to a penalty under Article 7 so as to be incapable of being imposed in respect of convictions arising prior to that Act coming into force.[34] The giving of evidence via live video links, provided for by recent legislation, has been deemed not incompatible with Article 6.[35] The parenting order regime under Crime and Disorder Act 1998, s 8 has likewise been held not to violate Articles 6 or 8.[36] The court rules on vexatious litigants have been found not to be incompatible with Article 6.[37] The principles underpinning the pleading of the defence of justification in libel in cases where the issue relates to the reasonable suspicion that a crime has been committed have also been found to be unaffected by the Human Rights Act.[38] So too have the powers of the Law Society in relation to intervention in solicitors' practices where breaches of the rules have occurred, with the Court of Appeal holding that the matter was more than adequately governed by the relevant domestic legislation.[39]

A similar pattern of restraint has been evident in copyright law where an attempt to widen various defences to infringement of copyright by reference to the guarantee of freedom of expression in Article 10 of the Convention has proved unsuccessful.[40] The relevant legislation, the Copyright, Designs and Patents Act 1988, was extensive and the Court of Appeal considered that while 'rare circumstances [could] arise where the right to freedom of expression

[30] *Ashworth Hospital Authority v MGN Ltd* [2001] 1 WLR 515, [2002] UKHL 29, [2002] 1 WLR 2033. See also *R v MacLeod*, Court of Appeal, 29 November 2000.
[31] *Attorney General v Scotcher* [2003] EWHC 1380 (Admin).
[32] *Office of Fair Trading v X* [2003] EWHC 1042 (Comm), [2003] 2 All ER (Comm) 183.
[33] *R v Alden and Wright* [2001] EWCA Crim 296, esp para [54] *per* Henriques J.
[34] *R v Field* [2002] EWCA Crim 2913, [2003] 1 WLR 882. See also on Art 7 *R v Muhamad* [2002] EWCA Crim 1856, [2003] QB 1031.
[35] *R (D and N) v Camberwell Green Youth Court; R (R) v Balham Youth Court; R (DPP) v Camberwell Green Youth Court* [2003] EWHC 227 (Admin).
[36] *R (M) v Inner London Crown Court* [2003] EWHC 301 (Admin).
[37] *Attorney General v Ebert* [2001] EWHC 695 (Admin), [2002] 2 All ER 789, para [36] *per* Brooke LJ giving the judgment of the court. See also *Ebert v Official Receiver* [2001] EWCA Civ 340, [2002] 1 WLR 320; *Attorney General v Covey*, Court of Appeal 19 February 2001.
[38] See *Chase v News Group Newspapers* [2002] EWCA Civ 1772.
[39] *Holder v Law Society* [2003] EWCA Crim 39, [2003] 1 WLR 1059.
[40] *Ashdown v Telegraph Group Ltd* [2001] EWCA Civ 1142, [2002] Ch 149.

[would] come into conflict with the protection afforded by the 1988 Act', it did 'not foresee this leading to a flood of litigation'.[41] Even where the result comes out in favour of the litigant relying on the Convention in cases in which the issue of human rights is somewhat peripheral, there is no guarantee that the Convention argument will have been the reason for his or her success. Thus in an important case on the extent to which family proceedings should be heard in public, the judgments in the Court of Appeal were firmly rooted in the domestic law with the President of the Family Division Dame Elizabeth Butler-Sloss describing the references to open hearings in Article 6(1) as doing no more than serving to 'underline our own long-established principles of open justice which are entirely in conformity with the convention and which our exceptions [to those principles] do not . . . breach'.[42] The same was true of the arguments put before the court based on Articles 8 and 10.[43]

Of course it is sometimes difficult to assess whether a key human rights principle is engaged to such a degree as to require a reordering of the domestic law notwithstanding the clarity of pre-existing legislation. As we saw at the end of the last chapter, there are bound to be many hard cases in which the battle is as much over whether to regard the facts as engaging a core principle as it is over what the implications of any such characterization might be. In the language of this chapter, the test of the proportionality of a judicial response to a particular human rights argument does depend on how centrally engaged with human rights the judges see the point to be. Thus in *R (Smith) v Barking LBC*,[44] the fact that gypsies did not enjoy tenure in council caravan sites provided under the Caravan Sites Act 1968 did not involve a breach of either Article 8 or Article 14 of the Convention. Giving judgment, Mr Justice Burton was clear that he did not feel that any principle in the Convention was fully in point, and therefore he felt able to assert in general terms that, 'following on from the principle well established by the European Court of Human Rights of the "*margin of appreciation*" left to the legislatures of the Convention signatories, the domestic courts, now that the Convention has been "imported", [would] give both respect and leeway to policy established by Parliament; particularly in an area of policy with competing social and economic considerations such as housing'.[45] In his eyes this was a housing rather than a human dignity case. In another line of cases, the courts have not allowed each and every county court repossession hearing under the relevant housing legislation to become a platform for fresh analysis of Convention compliance (principally by reference to Article 8); the statute itself

[41] Ibid para [45] *per* Lord Phillips MR giving the judgment of the court.
[42] *Clibbery v Allan* [2002] EWCA Civ 45, [2002] Fam 261, para [81]. Compare Keene LJ at para [121].
[43] Ibid paras [82]–[83] *per* Dame Butler-Sloss P. See also *in re B (A Minor) (Adoption: Natural Parent)* [2001] UKHL 70, [2002] 1 WLR 258, para [30] where Lord Nicholls of Birkenhead observed that there was 'no discordance between the statute and article 8' on the point before the Lords.
[44] [2002] EWHC 2400 (Admin).
[45] Ibid para [8]. See also *R (Mitchell) v Horsham District Council* [2003] EWHC 234 (Admin), paras [47]–[48].

has been held to have engaged in the appropriate balancing exercise for Convention purposes, and it has not been thought right for this legislative judgment to be capable of being perpetually reopened in each proceedings occurring under its aegis.[46]

C. Judicial review of administrative action

The problem of proper characterization arises with particular acuity in relation to the principle of legality, and especially when the broad requirements of Article 6(1) are in issue. This is the widest and potentially most invasive of the three core principles I have identified in this book. As will by now be appreciated, that provision declares that in 'the determination of his civil rights and obligations' everyone should be 'entitled to a fair and public hearing within a reasonable time by an independent and impartial tribunal established by law'. These procedural requirements have over time been extended by the European Court of Human Rights in such a way that they now reach many disputes over a great variety of administrative (as opposed to judicial) decisions.[47] Clearly such actions by local authorities, licensing bodies, planning committees, government inspectors and the like will frequently infringe the due process requirements of Article 6 since they will often (one might even say invariably) involve decision-making by a body which has an interest in the result: are these determinations all to be brought cascading down in a welter of legality as a result? The European Court of Human Rights has managed to avoid such an outcome by allowing procedures that are flawed in this way at the primary decision-making stage to be cured by the availability of a properly constituted forum in which appeals against such decisions can be heard. This has meant that many of Europe's administrative procedures have survived challenge. To work this redeeming trick, however, such an appellate body (and in practice it will invariably be a court) has to have 'full jurisdiction' over not only the law but also the facts of the case before it.[48]

The problem with this from the British perspective is that judicial review of administrative action has traditionally made a clear point of *not* being concerned with the factual issues.[49] As a result, the early Strasbourg case law saw a more robust oversight of domestic law than might otherwise have been expected, with the European Court insisting that judicial review which was indifferent to merits

---

[46] *R (Gangera) v Hounslow London Borough Council* [2003] EWHC 794 (Admin); *Harrow London Borough Council v Qazi (FC)* [2003] UKHL 43, [2003] 3 WLR 792; *Bradney v Birmingham City Council* [2003] EWCA 1783; *Newham London Borough Council v Kibota* [2003] EWCA Civ 1785. For an excellent study of the proper role of the Human Rights Act in local government, see P Leyland, 'The Human Rights Act and Local Government: Keeping the Courts at Bay' (2003) 54 *NILQ* 136.

[47] For the historical development of the jurisprudence, see CA Gearty, 'Unravelling Osman' (2001) 64 *MLR* 159.   [48] See *Albert and Le Compte v Belgium* (1983) 5 EHRR 533.

[49] The best known case is *Associated Provincial Picture Houses Ltd v Wednesbury Corporation* [1948] 1 KB 223.

was *not* capable of redeeming Article 6 type flaws that had gone before.[50] Even as recently as November 2000, the restricted nature of the judicial review available in the context of the oversight of decisions by the gaming board proved decisive in proceedings brought against the United Kingdom government.[51] If this requirement for some kind of factual as well as legal review were enthusiastically embraced by the British courts in the aftermath of implementation, the nature of judicial review would be fundamentally altered, with the courts being inevitably drawn into a role involving much more elaborate fact-finding than is the case at present. This is not in fact what has happened, with the domestic courts having confronted such an explosive possibility on a number of occasions but having managed so far gingerly to skirt around its more incendiary aspects.

Where a case involves a Convention right to which exceptions which are 'necessary in a democratic society' are permitted (such as the right to respect for privacy or the right to freedom of expression), then it is clear from *R (Daly) v Secretary of State for the Home Department*[52] that some factual oversight is bound to be required when the review court is applying the test of proportionality that these provisions of the Convention now require of it. Equally, as we saw in chapter five, where a core right such as the right to life or to be protected from torture is engaged, the courts will not regard themselves as required by the principles of judicial review to grant the executive a substantial leeway on disputed issues of fact.[53] But what of situations where all that is alleged is that the 'civil right' of the claimant (as opposed to his or her Convention right) is being 'determined' in a non-Article 6 compatible way? An early Scottish case threatened an unexpected, human-rights-based unravelling of planning law[54] but there were enough special features to the planning system for the House of Lords unanimously to rule in a later case that the traditional judicial review jurisdiction of the High Court was generally sufficient in this area.[55] The ramifications of this line of decisions are still echoing through the law reports, an unsurprising fact in an area in which the sums of money involved are substantial.[56] At the opposite end of the legal market, Article 6 has also caused some early confusion in housing law, with a ruling on the compatibility with Article 6 of the procedure for the review of decisions on applications for housing assistance having been explicitly resiled from by a differently constituted Court of

---

[50] The best example is *W v United Kingdom* (1987) 10 EHRR 29, especially paras [81] and [82] of the court's judgment.

[51] *Kingsley v United Kingdom* (2000) 33 EHRR 288.

[52] [2001] UKHL 26, [2001] 2 AC 532.

[53] See above pp 92–99. For the role (if any) of proportionality in non-Convention cases, see *R (Association of British Civilian Internees: Far East Region) v Secretary of State for Defence* [2003] EWCA Civ 473, [2003] QB 1397.

[54] *County Properties Ltd v Scottish Ministers* 2000, SLT 965.

[55] *R (Alconbury Developments Ltd) v Secretary of State for the Environment, Transport and the Regions and other cases* [2001] UKHL 23, [2003] 2 AC 295. An important Strasbourg decision in the area is *Bryan v United Kingdom* (1995) 21 EHRR 342.

[56] *R (Friends Provident Life Office) v Secretary of State for the Environment and the Regions and others* [2001] EWHC 820 (Admin), [2002] 1 WLR 1450; *R (Burkett) v London Borough of Hammersmith and Fulham* [2002] UKHL 23; [2002] 1 WLR 1593.

Appeal bench less than three months later.[57] Another area of continuing uncertainty is the extent to which, if at all, Article 6(1) bites on the school exclusion process, a subject around which litigation is also gathering at a rapid rate.[58]

It is clear that the issue at the heart of these cases, whether to apply Article 6(1) as a fresh and autonomous requirement of administrative law or to regard it as a manifestation of traditional principle to be carefully embedded in pre-existing law, has yet to be conclusively resolved. On the one hand, it would surely be ludicrous if the first sentence of Article 6(1) were permitted uncompromisingly to impose itself as a new code of administrative justice, for which role it was not intended and in consequence of which the courts would surely (and quite quickly) find themselves drowning in a sea of deep factual waters from which the rules of judicial review have up to now protected them. On the other hand, it must be the case that there are aspects of the current framework of judicial review that do not deliver the basic idea that underpins not just Article 6(1) but the Convention as a whole, namely the requirement that government be conducted under and in accordance with the law (a part of which is what I have called here the principle of legality). Legislative clauses which exclude the possibility of judicial review altogether immediately come to mind in this regard,[59] and there are bound to be other, albeit less extreme, examples of gaps in procedural protection which Article 6(1) should now properly be deployed to fill.

By careful attention both to the underlying rationale of Article 6(1) and to the full statutory context of the cases coming before them, the courts should be able to steer a path between the excessive legalism and factual review that threatens on one side and the undue quiescence that is to be found on the other.[60] If they can do this successfully, then they will be well on the way to a successful translation of the demands of the Convention, in the area of procedural protection, into sensible additions to the country's already reasonably effective system of administrative justice. As Lord Justice Laws remarked in the context of a speculative Article 8 challenge to straightforward possession order proceedings, what the courts should not do is 'take a position which disrupts the day-to-day

---

[57] *Runa Begum v Tower Hamlets London Borough Council* [2002] EWCA Civ 239, [2002] 1 WLR 2491 disapproving dicta of Brooke, Hale LJJ and David Steel J in *Adan v Newnham London Borough Council* [2001] EWCA Civ 1916, 1 WLR 2120. The composite procedure under the Housing Act 1996, Part VII, involving the review of homelessness decisions by a council housing officer and appeal to the county court on a question of law, has now been found by the House of Lords to be compatible with Art 6: *Begum v Tower Hamlets LBC* [2003] UKHL 5, [2003] 2 AC 430. I Loveland, 'Does Homelessness Decision-making engage Article 6(1) of the European Convention on Human Rights?' [2003] *EHRLR* 177 is a very good study.

[58] See *S T and P v London Borough of Brent and others, Oxfordshire County Council, Head Teacher of Elliott School and Others* [2002] EWCA Civ 693; *R (A) v Kingsmead School Governors* [2002] EWCA Civ 1822.

[59] But see *Matthews v Ministry of Defence* [2003] UKHL 4, [2003] 1 AC 116.

[60] As in *Runa Begum v Tower Hamlets LBC*, n 57 above.

operation of the scheme provided by Parliament'.[61] It was important, 'in all this odyssey of jurisprudence' for the judges and practitioners alike 'not [to] lose sight of the fact that the courts are not primary decision-makers in areas such as housing policy'.[62] Such sentiments should properly inform a judicial assessment of the appropriately proportionate response to legislation which does not directly engage human rights principles in just the same way as they should inform a judge's approach to a law which appears to require from him or her a degree of deference or of restraint. To this extent, therefore, it is true to say that what I have been discussing here could fairly be described as an adjunct to the aspiration of institutional competence considered in chapter six.

D. The common law

The issue of proportionate intrusion takes a different form when it comes to wholly judge-made law. Here neither judicial deference nor judicial restraint is to the fore, and the courts must decide for themselves how far to allow this legislative newcomer loose on its own patch. The initial instinct of the common law has been to claim the Human Rights Act as its own. At first glance this may seem an unlikely assertion on the part of a system of law that never permitted the European Convention on Human Rights a proper place prior to 1998, and might well have gone on largely ignoring it had not Parliament stepped in during that year with the Human Rights Act.[63] On the other hand it is true that the substantive rights in the document were to some extent modelled upon the common law system that its drafters (many of them British) found operating in the United Kingdom in the aftermath of the Second World War.[64] The emphasis on civil and political rights reflects this fact. With the emergence into the legal mainstream of the rights movement in the 1990s, many judges and other influential advocates of incorporation showed themselves willing (albeit the judges invariably extrajudicially) to locate the Convention within the common law tradition, and to draw strength for their argument for change from these Anglo-Saxon roots.[65]

Even so, what has been surprising after incorporation has been the way in which the courts have speedily identified with the Convention, welcoming it as a long lost friend rather than running from it as an alien intruder. This has been

[61] *Sheffield City Council v Smart: Central Sunderland Housing Company v Wilson* [2002] EWCA Civ 04, [2002] LGR 467, para [40].

[62] Ibid para [42].

[63] For the background see generally F Klug, *Values for a Godless Age. The Story of the United Kingdom's New Bill of Rights* (London: Penguin Books Ltd, 2000), ch 1; CA Gearty, 'The United Kingdom' in CA Gearty (ed), *European Civil Liberties and the European Convention on Human Rights. A Comparative Study* (The Hague: Martinus Nijhoff, 1997), ch 2.

[64] AWB Simpson, *Human Rights and the End of Empire. Britain and the Genesis of the European Convention* (Oxford: Oxford University Press, 2001) is the leading study; see esp ch 1.

[65] The details are in J Rosenberg, *The Search for Justice* (London: Hodder and Stoughton, 1994), 213–217.

particularly marked in the criminal sphere. While the courts have generally been passive in the way described in the first part of this chapter, the judges have been prepared on a number of significant occasions to deploy the Convention as a defensive weapon against parliamentary incursion into the criminal justice system. In these cases, the Human Rights Act has come to be regarded as an important ally in the ongoing jurisdictional disputes between the judiciary and the other branches of government over which parts of the legal system are rightfully the responsibility of the judges exclusively to manage. The issue has been particularly to the fore in the field of criminal justice because that is the border territory most hotly disputed between the rival forces of the state.

Three early cases under the Human Rights Act illustrate the point. In the first, *R v Offen*,[66] Parliament's attempt to introduce mandatory life sentences on persons previously convicted of serious offences was found by the Court of Appeal to be inconsistent with the right to liberty in Article 5 of the Convention. The relevant provision in the Crime (Sentences) Act 1997[67] permitted a departure from the rule in 'exceptional circumstances' and Lord Woolf and his colleagues felt able to interpret this phrase expansively so as to reach all situations in which continuing incarceration would breach Article 5. The advantage of such an approach was that the Court of Appeal was thereby able to avoid a declaration of incompatibility: the provision continued to function, albeit as a shadow of its former self. A similar trick is evident in *R v Lambert*[68] where the House of Lords used the Convention as a means through which to restore the traditional burden of proof on the prosecution in a statute in which Parliament had thought it had made clear that the burden was being shifted to the accused. The context was the sensitive one of anti-drugs legislation, though the provision under scrutiny was just one of very many similar clauses covering a wide range of criminal areas. Article 6(2) of the Convention stated that '[e]veryone charged with a criminal offence shall be presumed innocent until proved guilty according to law' and while the right could not be viewed as 'absolute and unqualified, the test to be applied [was] whether the modification or limitation of that right pursue[d] a legitimate aim and whether it satisfie[d] the principle of proportionality'.[69] These were matters for the judicial rather than the legislative branch, and the effect of the *Lambert* case is to require all the statutory interventions on the burden of proof to be reassessed for their compatibility with Article 6(2) on a case-by-case basis.[70] As in the *Offen* case this is unlikely to involve any

[66] [2001] 1 WLR 253.
[67] s 2, re-enacted as the Powers of Criminal Courts (Sentencing) Act 2000, s 109.
[68] [2001] UKHL 37, [2002] 2 AC 545.
[69] Ibid para [88] *per* Lord Hope of Craighead. To similar effect are Lord Slynn of Hadley, para [17], Lord Steyn, para [34] and Lord Clyde paras [150]–[152].
[70] Among the many post-*Lambert* cases see *Sliney v Havering LBC* [2002] EWCA Crim 2558; *L v Director of Public Prosecution* [2001] EWHC 882 (Admin), [2003] QB 137; *Davis v Health and Safety Executive* [2002] EWCA Crim 2949; *Director of Public Prosecutions v Charlebois* [2003] EWHC 54 (Admin); and *Coca-Cola Ltd v Aytacli*, Chancery Division, 30 January 2003; *Attorney General's Reference (No 4 of 2002)* [2003] EWCA Crim 762, [2003] 3 WLR 1153; *R v Matthews* [2003] EWCA Crim 813, [2003] 3 WLR 693. The whole question of the burden of proof may be back before their lordships: see *Sheldrake v Director of Public Prosecutions* [2003] EWHC 273 (Admin), [2003] 2 WLR 1629.

declarations of incompatibility since their lordships in the *Lambert* case felt able to regard themselves as empowered by the Human Rights Act, s 3 to transform the meaning of the provision before them. It is hard to characterize such activism as other than the 'judicial legislation' that the judges unanimously say they deplore, but the important point is that it is perceived by the judges to be merely the recasting of rules that properly belonged to them in the first place. They are shifting tanks off their lawn, not moving to fresh pastures.

By far the most controversial of these early cases reasserting common law principles was the third, *R v A (No 2)*.[71] The issue before the Lords was the compatibility with Article 6(1) of a 'rape shield' law which had only been recently enacted by Parliament and the effect of which was greatly to restrict the questions that could be put to complainants in cross-examination.[72] These statutory restrictions applied to questioning about alleged sexual activity by the complainant not only with third parties but also with the defendant in the case of which such cross-examination would ordinarily have been a part. This was too much for their lordships who unanimously transformed the section (once again using their s 3 power) so as to allow questions on alleged prior sexual experience between an accused and a complainant where, with 'due regard always being paid to the importance of seeking to protect the complainant from indignity and from humiliating questions... the evidence (and questioning in relation to it) [was] nevertheless so relevant to the issue of consent that to exclude it would endanger the fairness of the trial under article 6 of the convention'.[73] The common law courts have long regarded with suspicion attempts by the legislative branch to fix in advance the deployment of evidence in a criminal trial, and the issue has frequently been controversial in the field of sexual offences.[74] But it is not impossible to view the statutory provision under scrutiny in *R v A* as reflecting a deliberate choice by the legislature that in a situation which is bound to be unfair to one side, the burden of unfairness should be placed upon the defendant. Now, under the guise of the Human Rights Act, s 3(1) and emboldened by the traditional concerns of the common law of both criminal procedure and of evidence, the House of Lords has placed that disadvantage squarely back on the complainant.

The origins of the Convention, the confidence with which the UK judges have located it in the common law tradition, and the evidence of these three cases combine to suggest a Human Rights Act that is the servant rather than the master of the common law. Like all generalizations in contemporary human rights law, however, this one is apt to mislead if left unqualified. It is of course the case that many of the Convention's substantive provisions replicate existing common law protection. Neither the state nor your neighbour could kill, torture, enslave,

---

[71] [2001] UKHL 25, [2002] 1 AC 45.

[72] Youth Justice and Criminal Evidence Act 1999, s 41.

[73] n 71 above, *per* Lord Steyn, para [46], whose formulation was explicitly supported by Lord Slynn of Hadley, para [15], Lord Hope of Craighead, para [110], Lord Clyde, para [140], and Lord Hutton, para [163].

[74] See *Director of Public Prosecutions v Morgan* [1976] AC 182, followed by Sexual Offences (Amendment) Act 1976.

falsely imprison, libel you, or seize your assets at will, before 2 October 2000. The traditional range of remedies in tort to a large extent anticipated the Convention rights that became available on that date. Indeed the common law is wider than the Human Rights Act in the sense that its remedies are explicitly designed to be available against all while the Convention's rights are capable of being asserted only against what are characterized (in s 6 of the Act) as 'public authorities'. But the European Convention on Human Rights does go beyond the common law in a number of important respects. The duty to protect life in Article 2 is potentially wider than the mainstream English law. The unqualified right to 'security of the person' in Article 5(1) has no obvious analogue in UK law. The guarantee of the 'right to respect for [one's] private and family life, [one's] home and [one's] correspondence' in Article 8(1) perhaps reflects but is certainly wider than the torts of nuisance and *Rylands v Fletcher*[75] and the equitable remedy for breach of confidence that in the past have covered, or partly covered, the subject matter at which the general thrust of this provision is aimed. The discrimination prohibition in Article 14 is not obviously rooted in any ordinary remedy, and the same is even more clearly true of the right to marry in Article 12 and the right to education in Article 2 of the first protocol.

After 2 October 2000, these rights are all capable of being asserted against public authorities: this much is clear from s 6(1). The interesting question from the perspective of the common law is whether or not they also reach or affect in any way the duties that that code of judge-made law imposes on private parties. I have already briefly considered this issue in the course of my discussion of the principle of legality and the common law in chapter four, but I need now to return to it. The point is of fundamental importance to the structure of the Human Rights Act, and therefore to its ideological architecture. The way that the European Convention is itself designed suggests that it has in mind only the conduct of state organs, although the European Court of Human Rights has modified the effect of this by construing state responsibility very broadly on a number of occasions.[76] The construction of the body of the Human Rights Act also suggests that it is exclusively concerned with the protection of individual rights from unwarranted interferences by public authorities. It is with the actions of public authorities that the procedure set out for guaranteeing human rights in s 7 are concerned and it is only 'any act (or proposed act) of a public authority' that engages the attention of the remedies identified in s 8. A public authority will still be bound by the Act notwithstanding that it derives its power from the common law or the prerogative rather than from statute, but without this characterization as a 'public authority' the whole scheme of the Act suggests

---

[75] (1868) LR 3 HL 330.
[76] *A v UK* (1998) 27 EHRR 611; *X and Y v Netherlands* (1985) 8 EHRR 235; *Nerva v United Kingdom* (2002) 36 EHRR 31. This point seems to have been missed in *Aston Cantlow and Wilmcote with Billesley Warwickshire v Wallbank and Another* [2003] UKHL 37, [2003] 3 WLR 283, where a narrow reading of state responsibility under the Convention was a vital part of the reasoning that led to a very restricted interpretation of s 6(1): see below pp 186–187.

that a body or an individual litigant need not worry that the Act affects them in any way. On this approach to the Act, the only concessions that are made in the direction of protection against private power lie first in the expansion of the notion of a public authority in s 6(3)(b) to encompass private bodies engaged in public functions, and secondly in s 3(1), which as we have seen requires that all statutes be interpreted compatibly with the Convention rights '[s]o far as it is possible to do so', with there being no restriction here to proceedings in which the defendant happens to be a public authority.[77]

But these ameliorations of the sharp state-individual divide still leave out in the cold the simple common law action between private parties. The Convention rights would seem, on the construction of the Act set out above, to have no role to play in the resolution of such disputes. To those of a liberal frame of mind this is not a lacuna in the Act at all, merely the consequence of a clear philosophy that rights should be engaged only against the state.[78] Indeed on this view, it is the breadth of ss 3 and 6(3)(b) that are to be criticized as going further than they should when they reach private proceedings and/or impose duties on private bodies engaged in 'public functions'. To others, however, and in particular to those who hoped that the implementation of the Human Rights Act would usher in a new 'culture of rights',[79] the gap looks like a huge and potentially subversive one. Those anxious about the abuse of private power are firmly in this camp; these intuitive sceptics about the market and the power of capital are not concerned with governmental power (which on the whole they often rather like) so much as with the misuse of private—and in particular corporate—power.[80] On this apparently small point, therefore, an ideological gulf has opened, with traditional liberals on one side and more socialist-minded rights' advocates on the other.

Being the complex, ambiguous document that it is, the Human Rights Act manages to complicate its otherwise clear commitment to the liberal version, as set out in ss 6–8 and discussed above, with a single potentially devastating nod in the direction of a far fuller engagement with the whole of law, the common law included. This is in s 6(3)(a) where it is specifically stated that the term 'public authority' includes 'a court or tribunal'. It is around the meaning of this sentence that the debate about the extent of the reach of the Act into the common law has centred.[81] The important point for present purposes is that the courts have neither ruled the Convention rights out completely when dealing with common law actions between private parties, but nor have they allowed such actions to be entirely dominated by these new rights. Instead we have seen proportionate

---

[77] A good example is *Wilson v First County Trust Limited (No 2)*, n 102 below.

[78] D Oliver, 'The Frontiers of the State: Public Authorities and Public Functions under the Human Rights Act' [2000] *PL* 476 is an excellent study.

[79] There is a refreshing analysis of the concept of a human rights culture in A Ashworth, *Human Rights, Serious Crime and Criminal Procedure* (London: Sweet and Maxwell, 2002), 119–124.

[80] See K Starmer, 'Positive Obligations Under the Convention' in J Jowell and J Cooper (eds), *Understanding Human Rights Principles* (Oxford: Hart Publishing, 2001), 139–159.

[81] See pp 81–83 above.

intrusion in action. Building on a timely article by Murray Hunt which I have already mentioned when I was discussing this issue in chapter four,[82] the judges have gone about infiltrating the Convention into the common law in a way which has allowed it slowly to assert an influential place within that law. This has been begun in a way which suggests that many of the wider goals of the proponents of the Act's remit will over time be achieved, but without the destabilizing consequences of moving immediately to an extreme position on automatic applicability.

An important early authority pointing in this direction was *Douglas v Hello! Ltd.*[83] This was the well known case in which a couple of internationally famous film stars sought to prevent pictures of their marriage appearing in a journal which was a bitter rival of the magazine to which they had sold exclusive rights to the event. The matter reached the Court of Appeal on an interlocutory basis and was dealt with primarily as a decision involving application of the well-established equitable law on confidentiality. But the possibility of a new human-rights-inspired tort of privacy was never far from the judges' minds. To Brooke LJ whether the courts develop such a tort 'by an extension of the existing frontiers of the law of confidence, or by recognising the existence of new relationships which give rise to enforceable legal rights (as has happened in relation to the law of negligence ever since the 3–2 decision of the House of Lords in *Donoghue v Stevenson*) [was] not for this court, on this occasion, to predict' but his lordship was clear that it was possible, praising 'the versatility of the common law to adapt to new situations'.[84] Keene LJ recognized that the obligation on the courts to act compatibly with Convention rights 'arguably include[d] their activity in interpreting and developing the common law, even where no public authority is a party to the litigation'. However, '[w]hether this extend[ed] to creating a new cause of action between private persons and bodies [was] more controversial' but this question was 'unnecessary to determine . . . in these proceedings, where reliance is placed on breach of confidence, an established cause of action, the scope of which may now need to be approached in the light of the obligation on this court arising under section 6(1) of the Act'.[85] Most ambitiously of all, Sedley LJ thought that the courts had 'reached a point at which it can be said with confidence that the law recognises and will appropriately protect a right of personal privacy'.[86]

This first *Douglas* decision stimulated a large number of cases in which celebrities and other persons sought to deploy the Convention's guarantee of respect for privacy to limit the scope of action of other private parties, invariably newspapers intent on exercising their freedom of expression for commercial gain. The issue has frequently come before the courts as one involving an

---

[82] M Hunt, 'The "Horizontal Effect" of the Human Rights Act' [1998] *PL* 423. See also J Morgan, 'Questioning the "true effect" of the Human Rights Act' (2002) 22 *LS* 259.
[83] [2001] QB 967.
[84] Ibid para [88]. *Donoghue v Stevenson* is reported at [1932] AC 562.
[85] Ibid para [166].   [86] Ibid para [110].

application for an *ex parte* or an interim injunction.[87] In *A v B plc and another*[88] a Court of Appeal composed of the Lord Chief Justice Lord Woolf, Lord Justice Laws, and Lord Justice Dyson laid down guidelines as to the principled basis upon which such litigation was to be approached. Articles 8 and 10 of the Convention did not underpin totally novel kinds of legal proceedings. Rather they:

have provided new parameters within which the court will decide, in an action for breach of confidence, whether a person is entitled to have his privacy protected by the court or whether the restriction of freedom of expression which such protection involves cannot be justified. The court's approach to the issues which the applications raise has been modified because under s 6 of the 1998 Act, the court, as a public authority, is required not to act 'in a way which is incompatible with a Convention right'. The court is able to achieve this by absorbing the rights which arts 8 and 10 protect into the long-established action for breach of confidence. This involves giving a new strength and breadth to the action so that it accommodates the requirements of those articles.[89]

It was 'most unlikely that any purpose [would] be served by a judge seeking to decide whether there exists a new cause of action in tort which protects privacy. In the great majority of situations, if not all situations, where the protection of privacy is justified, relating to events after the Human Rights Act came into force, an action for breach of confidence now will, where this is appropriate, provide the necessary protection'.[90]

The courts seem to have embraced the spirit of s 6(3)(a) without permitting themselves to be driven by pedantry into a common law revolution.[91] This is surely right in principle even if it is not precisely correct as a (narrow) reading of the Act and even if it leaves the obvious loose end of working out when a Convention right can attach itself to a pre-existing common law remedy and when it cannot. No doubt this matter will be gradually resolved through litigation. It is worth reminding ourselves at this stage why the issue we are discussing has arisen so often in the context of Article 8 and so little in relation to other of the Convention rights. The privacy right lies midway between two kinds of rights. On the one hand there are those rights (such as the right to marry and to an education) which cannot easily be packaged in any kind of common law action at all and which therefore it is hard to imagine being central features of

---

[87] See eg *Theakston v MGN* [2002] EWHC 137 (QB).

[88] [2002] EWCA Civ 337, [2003] QB 195.

[89] Ibid para [4] *per* Lord Woolf CJ giving the judgment of the court.

[90] Ibid para 11(vi). This was the position eventually adopted in the *Douglas* case when the matter went to trial: *Douglas v Hello! (No 3)* [2003] EWHC 786 (Ch), [2003] 3 All ER 996. See *Campbell v Mirror Group Newspapers* [2002] EWCA Civ 1373, [2003] 1 All ER 224. In *Wainwright v Home Office* [2001] EWCA Civ 2081, [2002] QB 1334 the Court of Appeal was critical of the county court's finding of an invasion of privacy with alternative remedies being more appropriate (if any were appropriate at all), in that case rooted in trespass to the person rather than breach of confidence. The House of Lords also did not take an enthusiastic approach to privacy when the case came before it: [2003] UKHL 53, [2003] 3 WLR 1137.

[91] For a good discussion see AL Young, 'Remedial and Substantive Horizontality: the Common Law and *Douglas v Hello! Ltd*' [2002] PL 232.

any kind of proceedings between private parties. On the other hand there are those Convention rights of a more traditional sort, such as to liberty and to the non-subjection to torture, in relation to which the common law already offers fairly decent protection for claimants as against both public and private bodies.[92] The right to respect for privacy looks like but is not quite the same as a number of common law actions, not just breach of confidence but nuisance and *Rylands v Fletcher* as well.[93] It is therefore with some optimism that it hangs around the law courts seeking the chance to ride on the back of the different kinds of actions that are passing through, closing gaps in the old rules by reference to the substance of Article 8. Inevitably its hitch-hiking is occasionally successful, particularly if it can credibly show that another Convention right is also engaged, as happened in the well-known *Venables* case where in wholly exceptional factual circumstances it was the right to life in Article 2 that was able to come to the fore in the context of breach of confidence proceedings against a number of national newspapers.[94]

E. Retrospectivity

In no area is the potential for disproportionate impact greater than that of retrospectivity. The Human Rights Act was somewhat Delphic on the key question of its backward reach. From the moment that the whole measure came into force, on 2 October 2000, it was clear that all primary and subordinate legislation 'whenever enacted'[95] was required to be 'read and given effect'[96] in a way that was compatible with the Convention rights. From that day onwards, it was also obligatory for all public authorities to refrain from acting in any way which was 'incompatible with a Convention right'.[97] The statutory framework was not without its complexities. Where a public authority had acted or proposed to act in an unlawful way, then any victim or potential victim of such conduct was specifically empowered, under s 7(1), either '(a) [to] bring proceedings against the authority under this Act in the appropriate court or tribunal, or (b) [to] rely on the Convention right or rights concerned in any legal proceedings'. The phrase 'any legal proceedings' in the second of these formulations was specifically said in s 7(6) to include both 'proceedings brought by or at the instigation of a public authority' and 'an appeal against the decision of a

---

[92] Gaps are still possible of course, especially when it is remembered that the Art 3 prohibition of torture includes also a prohibition of inhuman or degrading treatment or punishment: see *A v United Kingdom*, n 76 above.

[93] See *Pemberton v Southwark London Borough Council* [2000] 1 WLR 1672; *Marcic v Thames Water Utilities Limited* [2002] EWCA Civ 64, [2002] QB 929, [2003] UKHL 66; *Dennis v Ministry of Defence* [2003] EWHC 793 (QB), *Jones v University of Warwick* [2003] EWCA Civ 151, [2003] 1 WLR 954. For a good study see A Garwood-Gowers, 'Improving Protection Against Indirect Interference with the Use and Enjoyment of Home: Challenging the Legacy of Hunter v Canary Wharf using the European Convention on Human Rights and Human Rights Act 1998' (2002) 11 *Nottingham LJ* 1.

[94] *Venables v News Group Newspapers Ltd* [2001] Fam 430.

[95] See s 3(2)(a).   [96] s 3(1).   [97] s 6(1).

court or tribunal'. It was in relation to such proceedings, that is, those covered by s 7(1)(b) as further explained (but not exhaustively) by s 7(6), that the Act provided its one pointer on retrospectivity. Under s 22(4):

Paragraph (b) of subsection (1) of section 7 applies to proceedings brought by or at the instigation of a public authority whenever the act in question took place; but otherwise that subsection does not apply to an act taking place before the coming into force of that section.

As a general rule, legislation is invariably presumed not to be retrospective in effect unless it is specifically stated to be so. By a 'retrospective' law is meant one that changes the consequences in law of a fact situation which was concluded prior to that law coming into force. It is not hard to find reasons to explain why the legal process should be set against backward-reaching laws. Why should parties that have behaved perfectly properly in light of the law as it was when they acted find that their legal relations have been profoundly altered, merely on account of some subsequent legislative intervention that was at the relevant time entirely unknown to them? Clearly this would be a rank injustice, and it would also be offensive to the principle of legality, a concept which, as we have seen in chapter four, is fundamental to our legal system.[98] Related to the concept of legality is the important issue of legal certainty: if every action were vulnerable to subsequent legal re-characterization at the behest of future parliaments, then the law would quickly decline into an anarchic state, capable of offering only tentative contingent judgments rather than definitive statements. So the bias against retrospectivity is strong, and rightly so.[99] On the other hand, the demands of 'human rights' are intense as well. After all, the very phrase suggests absolutism, universality and an imperative need for legal protection. Confronted with its moral power, the arguments against retrospectivity rehearsed above seem mealy-mouthed, pedantic even, a trivial way of avoiding moral responsibility. But, as I have perhaps sought over-exhaustively to demonstrate, the legal conception of human rights in the Human Rights Act is more technical, more complicated and less morally unambiguous than the wide nature of the phrase would seem to suggest.

Parliament's solution to this clash of values, between human rights on the one hand and certainty on the other, with the demands of justice ambiguously straddling the two, is to be found in s 22(4). In the absence of any further guidance in the Act (and there is none), it is surely correct in principle to assume that participants in fact situations completed in advance of 2 October 2000 cannot demand to have the legal implications of their conduct assessed by reference to a measure that was not then in force. Equally, and on this the Act is explicit, actions cannot be taken against public authorities on the basis

[98] See above pp 79–81 for a discussion of the problem of squaring a developing common law with this prohibition on imposing new rules on litigants.
[99] FAR Bennion, *Statutory Interpretation. A Code* 3rd edn (London: Butterworths, 1997) contains a valuable discussion, 235–243.

of s 7(1)(a) where the authority's disputed conduct occurred prior to 2 October 2000. However as we have seen, and exceptionally, there is s 22(4). We should not lose sight of the fact that on its face this is a remarkable provision, imposing on public authorities that have initiated proceedings an apparent duty to adhere to legislation which, at the time of the relevant, now disputed actions of that (or another) authority, was certainly not in force and might not even have existed. The subsection had grabbed the attention of the House of Lords as early as 1999, when five of their lordships found themselves in the unusual position of having to wrestle with the retrospective effects of a prospective law.[100] When the first major case in which the issue of retrospectivity arose after implementation, in May 2001, the Court of Appeal was beguiled into a wrong turning by a solution to the problem that should have been seen to be, and was, too simple to be true.

In *Wilson v First County Trust Limited (No 2)*,[101] a loan agreement between the parties was concluded well in advance of implementation of the Human Rights Act. When a dispute arose, the agreement was found by Judge Hull QC in the county court to have been properly executed: this happened on 24 September 1999. The borrower appealed, and on 23 November 2000—just after implementation of the Human Rights Act—the Court of Appeal found that in fact the agreement had not been properly executed.[102] The importance of this victory for the appellant was that it therefore followed, as a result of the operation of certain provisions of the Consumer Credit Act 1974,[103] that the loan company was now absolutely disabled from going to court to enforce either the agreement or the security that had been offered on foot of it. The borrower was home free, the beneficiary of a technical defect the effect of which was to exonerate her from any responsibility for the debt that she had incurred. Faced with this unexpected turn of events, the pawnbroker respondent raised a new argument, that the denial of its access to a court under the 1974 Act was a breach of its Convention right to just such a tribunal under Article 6(1). That there was such an implied, albeit qualified, right within Article 6(1) was clear,[104] and it might well have been breached in this case (the Court of Appeal held that it was). But did the right bite, given that the fact situation engaging it had occurred prior to implementation of the Act?

Giving the judgment of the court, the Vice Chancellor Sir Andrew Morritt VC found that it did. But this was not on account of the operation of the Act's retrospectivity provisions:

The effect of section 22(4) is not in doubt. It provides (by the second limb of the section) that, in general, section 7(1) does not apply to an act taking place before 2 October 2000. So, for example, a person who claims that a public authority has acted in a way which is incompatible with a Convention right (contrary to section 6(1) of the Act) cannot bring

[100] *R (Kebilene) v Director of Public Prosecutions* [2000] 2 AC 326.
[101] [2001] EWCA Civ 633, [2002] QB 74.
[102] The details are at ibid.
[103] In particular ss 113 and 127.
[104] *Golder v United Kingdom* (1975) 1 EHRR 524.

proceedings against the authority under the Act (pursuant to section 7(1)(a)) if the unlawful act took place before 2 October 2000.... If the act which is said to be unlawful under section 6(1) has taken place before 2 October 2000, it is only where the person who claims to be the victim of that act is party to proceedings brought by or at the instigation of a public authority that he can rely on that section.[105]

The effect of this analysis was to destroy the power of the pawnbroker's submission so far as s 22(4) was concerned. But Sir Andrew's search for a relevant act against which to test compatibility with the Convention also led him to an appraisal of the present, and in particular to the conduct of the court over which he was presiding. The Vice-Chancellor noted that under s 6(3)(a), the public authorities that have to act compatibly with the Convention after 2 October 2000 included the courts themselves. This being the case:

the relevant question, in the present case, is not whether some Convention right of First County Trust was infringed when it made a loan to [the borrower] upon the terms of the agreement dated 22 January 1999; nor whether, before 2 October 2000, there was any domestic remedy in respect of any such infringement. The relevant question is whether in allowing an appeal from the order made by Judge Hull QC—or, more precisely, in making an order after 2 October 2000 which gives effect to a decision to allow the appeal—this court would be acting in a way which is incompatible with an existing Convention right. That is a question which has to be answered on the basis of the facts as they are at the time when the order is made in this court.[106]

On this analysis, the case was not one involving any element of retrospectivity at all. The action of the court was what mattered, and the Convention would therefore—indeed inevitably—be taken into account.

The argument is sustainable on a reading of s 6(1) and (3) viewed in isolation, but its overall effect is to impose a dramatic retrospectivity, stretching back into the distant past. For it is only in a most unreal and constitutionally incoherent sense that the action of the court in a case like *Wilson* can be described as that of a public authority. We have already made this point in the context of the application of the Human Rights Act to the common law. As Lord Hobhouse remarked when this case reached the House of Lords:

[t]he inclusion of provisions relating to the Executive and to the Judiciary all under the heading 'Public authorities' and the unqualified inclusion of the courts in the definition of the term 'public authority' do not assist the reader in making the necessary distinction between the Executive and the Judiciary and their different constitutional functions.[107]

A public authority is usually thought of as part of the executive branch of the state. A court in contrast belongs to the adjudicative wing of organized society. Sometimes courts do engage in executive acts, managing their court room, prescribing rules under relevant legislation and the like, but in this instance the

[105] *Wilson v First County Trust Limited (No 2)*, n 101 above, para [20].
[106] Ibid para [18].
[107] In *Wilson v Secretary of State for Trade and Industry*, n 108 below, para [133].

Court of Appeal was clearly wearing its adjudicative hat. If the Vice Chancellor's reasoning had been correct, any fact situation no matter how ancient could achieve a retesting for human rights compatibility merely by securing a hearing before a court or for that matter, since they are also covered by subsection 3(a), before any tribunal. The retrospectivity restriction in s 22(4) would be largely undermined, since it could so easily be obviated by the simple denial of its relevance to any current situation before a court, and an assertion instead of the court's contemporary duty to act compatibly with the Convention today, whatever might have been the position with regard to other public authorities in the past.

Not surprisingly this part of the Court of Appeal's reasoning in the *Wilson* case was widely criticized and did not survive scrutiny in the House of Lords.[108] But it was not the fault of Sir Andrew and his colleagues that Parliament had chosen through its enactment of s 6(3)(a) so cavalierly to collapse the distinction between the branches of the state: there was no avoiding the fact that the courts were a 'public authority' for the purposes of s 6(1). What was missed, however, were the presumption against retrospectivity in the common law tradition and—more precisely for present purposes—the application of the Human Rights Act, s 6(2) Under this latter provision, subsection (1) is specifically stated not to apply to an act of a public authority if 'as the result of one or more provisions of primary legislation, the authority could not have acted differently' (subsection 1(a)) or 'in the case of one or more provisions of, or made under, primary legislation which cannot be read or given effect in a way which is compatible with the Convention rights, the authority was acting so as to give effect to or enforce those provisions' (subsection 1(b)). So even if the provision under scrutiny (the relevant bit of the Consumer Credit Act blocking access to the courts) did infringe the Convention—and their lordships held that it did not—it could not be 'read or given effect' to compatibly with the Convention because, as a matter of general law (the presumption against retrospectivity, not rebutted here), the court was bound to apply the pre-Human Rights Act legal position to it. It was a public authority, therefore, which could not act in any other way. Both subsections 1(a) and 1(b) would seem to apply.[109]

The limits of this exception under s 6(2) should be carefully understood. Any fresh action by an 'ordinary' public authority after 2 October 2000 needs to be in accordance with the law as it is when that action occurs, including that law insofar as it might have been modified by the Human Rights Act, and regardless of when the general fact situation from which it emerged had occurred. But a court, as an adjudicative body is in a special position, different from other public bodies: it is not a player engaged in a new move against a private party but is rather the referee, adjudicating above the fray. The 'action' of a court involving

---

[108] *Wilson v Secretary of State for Trade and Industry* [2003] UKHL 40, [2003] 3 WLR 568.
[109] Ibid para [25] (Lord Nicholls of Birkenhead, referring to s 6(2)(a) only); para [92] (Lord Hope of Craighead); para [133] (Lord Hobhouse of Woodborough).

the application of a law to a fact situation predating October 2000, and in relation to which no fresh action by an 'ordinary' public authority has supervened, is an action which in its adjudicative capacity that court cannot avoid taking and to which therefore, both as a matter of statutory interpretation and in the interests of legal certainty, s 6(2)(a) and/or (b) should apply.[110] It may be that the law is gradually moving in this direction, but with several wrong turnings along the way. A measure of the complexity of the subject is that in the next important Court of Appeal decision on the point, *Aston Cantlow and Wilmcote with Billesley Warwickshire v Wallbank*,[111] it was not even clear whether there has been any relevant Convention-infringing act of a public authority at all, much less one that has occurred so long before the case as to require the concession on retrospectivity that was made by the respondents.[112]

An important issue of retrospectivity in connection with criminal appeals arose in *R v Lambert*.[113] There the relevant act of a public authority alleged to have infringed the Convention was the direction of the trial judge in a criminal trial which, it was said, amounted to a violation of the accused's Article 6 rights in relation to the burden of proof. The trial with its impugned ruling had occurred before 2 October 2000, but both appeals, first to the Court of Appeal and afterwards to the House of Lords, took place after that date. On the assumption that the Convention had indeed been infringed (and the Lords held by a majority of four to one when the case reached them that it had),[114] was this a proper ground of appeal? All the trial judge had done was apply the law as it stood when the matter came to him for judicial action. Was he now to be found wanting on the basis of a test not then known to be required of him? In the Lords, only Lord Steyn dodged this question by concentrating, like Sir Andrew Morritt in *Wilson v First County Trust* before him, on the contemporaneous duty upon the appeal court as the relevant public authority to act compatibly with the Convention: '[s]o interpreted, no true retrospectivity is involved. Section 6(1) regulates the conduct of appellate courts *de futuro*'.[115] Anxieties about the opening of the litigious floodgates were misplaced: 'A healthy scepticism ought

---

[110] Note however that the *Wilson* case leaves the door ajar for further challenges on a case-by-case basis, rooted in fairness, thereby providing a flexibility for the judges that may cause s 6(2) to become disengaged in the right set of circumstances: ibid para [21] (Lord Nicholls of Birkenhead); para [98] (Lord Hope of Craighead); para [153] (Lord Scott of Foscote); para [201] (Lord Rodger of Earlsferry); compare Lord Hobhouse of Woodborough, paras [131]–[135].

[111] [2001] EWCA Civ 713, [2002] Ch 51.

[112] Ibid para [7]. The church council wanted to make the Wallbanks pay for their church repairs, and this desire was found to be beyond the powers of the relevant legislation, viewed in light of the Convention and the Human Rights Act, s 3(1). But though various nasty notices had been served, the money had not yet been taken. As Sir Andrew Morritt recognized in the judgment of the court which he handed down, 'the critical issue [was] whether the common law liability upon which the claim [was] based [was] one which the PCC [was] *debarred from enforcing* because it [was] incompatible with the defendants' Convention rights': para [25] (emphasis added). For the House of Lords decision see n 76 above, esp paras [31]–[32] (Lord Hope of Craighead).

[113] n 68 above.

[114] Lords Slynn of Hadley, Steyn, Hope of Craighead, Clyde; Lord Hutton dissenting on this point.

[115] Ibid para [28].

to be observed about practised predictions of an avalanche of dire consequences likely to flow from any new development.'[116]

None of Lord Steyn's judicial colleagues shared his confidence that the matter could be so easily and so unproblematically resolved. The interests of legal certainty surely required that the (at the moment of its delivery) impeccable direction of the trial judge be left undisturbed. As Lord Slynn observed, it was 'plain . . . that the effect of opening up an examination of convictions prior to the coming into force of the Act . . . could [be to] lead to great confusion and uncertainty'.[117] The difficulty lay in surmounting the plain words of ss 6(1) and 6(3). A majority of their lordships—Lords Slynn, Hope, and Hutton— achieved the outcome they desired by dint of a complex analysis of the interrelationship of ss 7(1)(a), 7(1)(b), 7(6), 9, and 22(4), with the full details of which we need not concern ourselves here, but which produced the result that appeals from convictions arising out of trials held prior to 2 October 2000 were not required to take the Convention into account.[118] Embarrassingly, within six months, a nearly identical committee of law lords in the subsequent appeal of *R v Kansal (No 2)* was forced to admit that this analysis had been fundamentally flawed, while insisting nevertheless that, in the interests of a higher level commitment to legal certainty, it had to be followed in both that case and in the future.[119] So appeals from trials held prior to 2 October remain Convention free zones. The impact of the Human Rights Act had to be curtailed to this extent, whatever about the defects in the reasoning that produced this outcome.

Refusing to rectify human rights violations against accused persons on the basis of, as one law lord put it, 'plainly erroneous' reasoning[120] was not what the Human Rights Act was supposed to be about, but the outcome is capable of being justified by disregarding the reasoning of the majority (on which I have not concentrated here) and returning to the points I have made earlier about s 6(2). The speech of Lord Hope in the case of *Kansal (No 2)* is of interest in this regard. He had taken a narrower line than the majority in the *Lambert* case while concurring in the outcome of that case. Now he sought to put the end-result of both the *Lambert* and the *Kansal* decisions on a sounder analytical footing:

---

[116] *R v Lambert*, n 68 above, para [30].

[117] Ibid para [10].

[118] Essentially the argument was that because s 7(6), when explaining what 'any legal proceedings' meant, distinguished between appeals and proceedings initiated by public authorities, the reference in s 22(4) to 'proceedings brought by or at the instigation of a public authority' could only refer to the latter of these kinds of proceedings and not to the former: see ibid paras [138]–[147] *per* Lord Clyde; paras [7]–[9] *per* Lord Slynn of Hadley; paras [169]–[176] *per* Lord Hutton.

[119] *R v Kansal (No 2)* [2001] UKHL 62, [2002] 2 AC 69. The Law Lords who heard this appeal were: Lord Slynn of Hadley, Lord Steyn, Lord Hope of Craighead, Lord Hutton, and (in the only change from the *Lambert* case) Lord Lloyd of Berwick instead of Lord Clyde. Lord Hope thought that the decision should have been overturned. For the effect of the *Kansal* case see *R v Benjafield* [2002] UKHL 2, [2003] 1 AC 1099; *R v Rezvi* [2002] UKHL 1, [2002] 2 WLR 235. For a strong critique see D Beyleveld, R Kirkham and D Townend, 'Which Presumption? A Critique of the House of Lords' Reasoning on Retrospectivity and the Human Rights Act' (2002) 22 *LS* 185.

[120] *R v Kansal*, ibid para [17] *per* Lord Lloyd of Berwick.

I would hold that the interpretative obligation in section 3(1) cannot be applied so as to change retrospectively the meaning which was previously given to a provision in primary legislation. It does not make unlawful acts of courts or tribunals or other public authorities which, as a result of provisions in primary legislation, could not at the time when the acts were done have been done differently: see section 6(2)(a).[121]

The key phrase here is 'at the time when the acts were done'. To allow s 3(1) a role in redefining pre-implementation judicial decisions 'would not be consistent with the general principle on which primary legislation depends, which is legal certainty'.[122] The public authorities to which Lord Hope is referring in this extract clearly are courts and tribunals. However his lordship also developed a similar analysis, this time rooted in subsection 2(b), that could be applied to prosecutors whose initial actions had precipitated the need for such a judicial decision in the first place. Insofar as these officials were engaged in actions which were broadly permitted by the law as it stood at the time when they acted, then to this extent they were merely 'acting so as to give effect to' provisions which could not *at that time* 'be read or given effect in a way which [was] compatible with the Convention right'. This being the case, they also had a defence under s 6(2).

The point being made by Lord Hope here is the same one as I made earlier in general terms in relation to the potential of s 6(2) in this field, and it can be made clearer by turning to the facts of the *Kansal* case itself. This was a case on self-incrimination and the right to a fair trial. On Lord Hope's reasoning, the authorities could ask questions of the suspect under compulsory powers and then use his answers at his subsequent trial notwithstanding any breach of the Convention that might be involved because this interrogation and the act of leading evidence all occurred prior to 2 October 2000 and '[a]ccording to the traditional rules of construction by reference to which at the time that provision was to be interpreted, [the prosecutor was] authorised . . . to lead and to rely on that evidence. He was entitled also to give effect to [the provision] by asking the judge to hold that in terms of that section the evidence was admissible'.[123] In Lord Hope's opinion, s 6(2)(b) did not depend on the narrow question of whether the prosecutor had had any discretion to forbear from leading such evidence (of course he had); rather the application of the subparagraph depended on assessing whether 'having decided to use the answers and invite the judge to hold them to be admissible, [the prosecutor] was doing what he was authorised to do' by the section.[124] To this question 'there could be only one answer':[125] s 6(2)(b) therefore applied.

This approach deals more than adequately with the problems raised by the application of s 3(1) to fact situations prior to 2 October 2000 where the legal issues to which they give rise are rooted in statute law.[126] The impact of the

---

[121] Ibid para [83].   [122] Ibid para [84].   [123] Ibid para [88].
[124] Ibid.   [125] Ibid.
[126] See further *R v Lyons, Parnes, Ronson and Saunders* [2001] EWCA Crim 2860, [2002] UKHL 44, [2002] 3 WLR 1562 (HL).

Human Rights Act is rendered proportionate and is all the more effective as a result. Different questions inevitably come to the fore where the common law is the basis for a legal claim. Here no element of retrospectivity can be said to arise, because one of judge-made law's enduring myths (and a necessary one if the democratic deficit in such rule-making is not to be noticed) is its timelessness. Since this law is never made afresh but merely rediscovered from time to time, there is no room for the notion of retrospectivity to operate. In *Wainwright v Home Office*[127] the claimants, a mother and son, sued for compensation for the manner in which they were strip-searched by prison officers when they went to Armley prison in Leeds in order to visit another of the family's sons who was being held there. The disputed event occurred on 2 January 1997, but the matter came up for decision on 23 April 2001, well after the Human Rights Act had been implemented. Sitting at Leeds County Court, Judge McGonigal awarded basic and aggravated damages for trespass to the person which the judge ruled had been committed through infringement of the victims' right to privacy and also via a breach of their legal right to personal safety (the latter of these being justified by reference to the common law rule in *Wilkinson v Downton*).[128] Before the Court of Appeal, the focus was on the extent to which the prison rules permitted the prison authorities to act as they did in 1997, and, if the rules were in their favour, then whether the Human Rights Act could (now) make any difference to that fact. Since the rules were themselves based on primary legislation, the court found this part of the case governed by the *Lambert* and *Kansal* cases. Though neither case had been concerned directly with the retrospective effect of s 3, as this one was, they were both 'consistent with the general presumption that legislation should not be treated as changing the substantive law in relation to events taking place prior to legislation coming into force'.[129] The Act could not reach backwards in this way to effect a reinterpretation of the prison rules insofar as they had impacted on the claimants at the relevant time.[130] The Court of Appeal decision in *Wilson v First County Trust* was cited to the court but its reasoning on the s 6(3) point, which would of course have led to a different result, was not directly addressed by any of the judges.[131]

The more interesting aspect of the case had to do with how the judges dealt with the common law part of the claimants' arguments. Because of the way the county court judge had addressed the matter, rooting the claimants' case in the infringement of their right to privacy, the question arose as to whether any such right had existed when it had purportedly been violated, namely on 2 January

---

[127] n 90 above.   [128] [1897] 2 QB 57.

[129] n 90 above, para [27] *per* Lord Woolf MR. Cf *Pearce v Governing Body of Mayfield School* [2001] EWCA Civ 1347 which takes a similarly restrictive line where an appellant in civil proceedings seeks to rely on s 3 in an appeal arising out of proceedings that occurred prior to 2 October 2000. The decision in the House of Lords appeal in that case is decided with *Macdonald v Advocate General for Scotland*: [2003] UKHL 34, [2003] ICR 937.

[130] n 90 above, paras [27]–[39] *per* Lord Woolf MR; para [61] *per* Mummery LJ; para [122] *per* Buxton LJ.

[131] On which see pp 166–7 above.

1997. Had the facts arisen after 2 October 2000, the case would have been a relatively simple one of an action under s 7(1)(a) for breach of the claimants' Article 8 rights. But the Act not being in force, the claimants were forced to fall back on an allegedly indigenous common law action. The Court of Appeal rejected the judge's assertion that a tort of breach of privacy 'described as an aspect of trespass to the person'[132] had existed at the time the incident occurred.[133] This being the case, the Human Rights Act 'certainly [could not] be relied on to change substantive law by introducing a retrospective right to privacy which did not exist at common law'.[134] The Appeal Court judges then dealt rather conservatively with the law on tort that did definitively apply at the time the facts of the case occurred, concluding that neither by reference to the rule in *Wilkinson v Downton*[135] nor the law on assault could the judge's conclusions favourable to the claimants be justified.[136]

At least two of the judges in the three-person Court of Appeal in the *Wainwright* case were distinctly unenthusiastic about a general right to privacy existing even in the post-Human Rights Act law of tort.[137] Were it now to be discovered that there is such a tort, the question would inevitably arise as to exactly how and when it had found its way into the common law. The kinds of questions about retrospectivity that have always been asked about statutes but have been obscured by the common law's mythic unchangeability would inevitably rise to the surface. The mask of timelessness worn by the common law would be blown away. As the very sceptical Buxton LJ put it in the course of his judgment in the *Wainwright* case, 'in being invited to recognise the existence of a tort of breach of privacy we are indeed being invited to make the law, and not merely to apply it'.[138] One of the effects of the Human Rights Act therefore might be to expose the legislative nature of common law adjudication, with the *Lambert/Kansal* questions having to be asked of judge-made law just as they have been of legislative enactments.

---

[132] Ibid para [65] *per* Buxton LJ. [133] See esp ibid para [102].
[134] Ibid para [40] *per* Lord Woolf LCJ. See also Buxton LJ, para [89].
[135] n 128 above.
[136] n 90 above, paras [41]–[51] *per* Lord Woolf; paras [72] and [85] *per* Buxton LJ.
[137] Ibid paras [57]–[60] *per* Mummery LJ; paras [92]–[115] *per* Buxton LJ. Lord Woolf is more circumspect: see ibid para [40].
[138] Ibid para [112].

8

The Aspiration of Analytical Coherence

A. The nature of legal reasoning

Our final aspiration for the Human Rights Act may seem too self-evident to be worthy of note, much less a special chapter devoted to it. Its importance can be appreciated, however, once we have taken a moment to consider the nature of legal reasoning in the system into which the Human Rights Act has been introduced, and the potentially large effects that the Act may have on that system. If there is one thing that the adjudicative process should be able to boast of, take for granted even, particularly when it is the responsibility of a highly trained independent body of experienced professionals, it is that the results that it produces, and the reasoning that underpins those results, are intelligible, at least to the professional if not to the ordinary layperson. An important part of this central requirement for a coherent framework of law is a commitment to consistency, a goal that has been a cornerstone of the common law method of case-by-case adjudication since it first emerged as a separate source of law in the feudal period.[1] An elaborate system of precedent sets out to ensure not only that the law enjoys internal consistency in relation to each case but that it also benefits from an external consistency, with each case linked to relevant others in a pyramidic chain of decisions carrying different levels of authority.[2] The law's foundational commitment to coherence and consistency has been evident in the way in which judges have approached a second responsibility that has come over time to be placed upon them, that of the proper interpretation of statutes.

Of course the system has not always practised what it preaches. The aspirations to intelligibility and to consistency are not always fulfilled. Mistakes are made, with some decisions being deficient in their reasoning and others creating confusion by failing properly to adhere to the rules of precedent. The student of law sometimes finds that cases that he or she is required to examine fail to live up to expectations, and the early study of law is on this account occasionally a source of intellectual frustration. On the other hand, it is precisely in this gap between the theory and practice of judicial reasoning that practitioners find

---

[1] See generally JA Holland and JS Webb, *Learning Legal Rules* (London: Blackstone Press Ltd, 1991).

[2] There is a good account in any edition of G Williams's classic text *Learning the Law*, eg 11th edn (London: Stevens and Sons, 1982), ch 6.

opportunities for litigation and legal academics the chance to display their scholarly eruditon. If lack of intelligibility is one risk in the defective deployment of legal reasoning, then the chasing of argument by analogy down blind alleys is another. Whereas the first is a consequence of bad reasoning, the second flows from an excess of reasoning power, with initially minor faults being expanded by repetition into grievous errors. The common law is littered with wrong turnings which the transfixing power of precedent has turned into near permanent mistakes, capable of being redeemed only by legislative action or by re-examination at the highest appellate level—neither of which interventions is however at all easy to secure, even when the need for a corrective is manifest and grave. A characteristic of many of these branch lines to obscurity is that they preoccupy themselves with issues of form over substance, with the judges often being tempted by the nature of legal argument into a concentration on procedural peripherals at the expense of the core issues before them. The result can be whole networks of decisions devoted not to whether a litigant has or has not a good case but whether he or she should be allowed plead it in the first place.

A third challenge to the coherence and consistency of law is the seduction of the well-crafted lie. Since the emergence of the idea of expert adjudication, generations of judges have found themselves embracing various kinds of deception as an essential way of bridging the gap between what tradition demands they must assert the law requires and what legal practice in the name of justice requires. The biggest myth of all, made inevitable by the doctrine of precedent, is that the common law is an unchanging juristic entity which has governed all cases within its remit in the same way since time immemorial. I discussed this idea in chapter four, when I was considering the effect of the principle of legality on the common law, and at the end of chapter seven when I was reflecting on the problem of retrospectivity, and I look at it again at the conclusion of this chapter when I contrast Strasbourg and Anglo-Saxon approaches to judicial authority. But there are many other, albeit lesser, fabrications scattered across the legal process. Every student learns early of the lubricating power of these legal fictions, and their usefulness in allowing the rigidity of this or that common law rule to be glossed over pending its euthanasia at the hands of the legislature. An outstanding example of just such a devise was the way in which in the past the courts avoided Crown immunity by allowing suits in which the Crown furnished the name of a servant against whom an action could be brought but then stood behind that servant, paying any damages or costs that might be awarded against him or her. Where there was no servant available on whom fault could be imputed (eg where the alleged liability related to the duty of an owner of land towards licensees), the servant involved had a purely fictional culpability. The practice was eventually exposed by the courts for the sham that it was,[3] and legislation followed soon afterwards.[4] Not all lies are essential and

---

[3] *Adams v Naylor* [1946] AC 543; *Royster v Cavey* [1947] KB 204.
[4] Crown Proceedings Act 1947.

the legal process has constantly to guard itself against deceit that is all the more inopportune for being unnecessary as well as confusing.

This is the legal culture into which the Human Rights Act has had to nestle down and find its niche. The breadth and importance of the Act make these issues of coherence and consistency both harder than in other areas of law and yet more important properly to resolve. The challenge for the judges has been to maintain intelligibility and consistency in their case law while avoiding the various challenges to their coherence that have been identified above. It is with how these difficult tasks have been discharged in the first years of the Human Rights Act that this chapter is concerned. Of course it has not been easy with a piece of legislation as open-textured as this one is to preserve intelligibility while avoiding lapses into procedural aridity on the one hand and unnecessary deceit on the other. As we shall see, in this as in other areas of our subject, a firm grasp of principle is essential if an uncontrollable kind of legal anarchy is to be avoided. An understanding of principle allows practitioner and judge alike confidently to identify what the Human Rights Act is supposed to be about on any given set of facts, and then to steer a case reasonably competently to the safe port of an intellectually defensible conclusion.

B. The imperative of intelligibility

A full-throttled invitation to incoherence was successfully seen off in the decision of the House of Lords in *R v Weir*.[5] The accused had had his conviction for a serious offence quashed by the Court of Appeal on the basis of the interpretation of a particular statutory provision relating to the admissibility of evidence against him.[6] The appellate court's approach to the issue was shortly afterwards shown (as a result of an unrelated decision of the law lords on the same legal issue)[7] to have been misconceived. Had the Court of Appeal correctly interpreted the relevant provision, the accused's conviction would certainly have been upheld. But when the Director of Public Prosecutions sought to take the case on appeal to the Lords, he found that he was one day outside the 14-day period limited by statute for the receipt of such appeals,[8] and the judicial office accordingly rejected the application. Was this a denial of the DPP's right to a court as guaranteed (albeit impliedly) in Article 6(1) of the European Convention on Human Rights? Counsel for the DPP argued to this effect in proceedings before their lordships on the question whether the statutory time limits needed unwaveringly to be followed.

---

[5] [2001] 1 WLR 421.

[6] This was Police and Criminal Evidence Act 1984, s 64 (as amended) relating to the retention of DNA profiles in cases in which proceedings against the person from whom they have been obtained have been discontinued.

[7] *Attorney General's Reference (No 3 of 1999)* [2001] 2 AC 91.

[8] Criminal Appeal Act 1968, s 34(1).

The idea is however transparently nonsensical: while it is true that this was a submission that would have been open to the defendant, it did not therefore follow that the government's representative should be placed in exactly the same position. This was a false analogy, and it could be exposed as such by reaching past the words of the Human Rights Act to an understanding of what the statute had been intended to be about. Remarking in relation to Article 6(1) that the 'civil rights of the Director are not here in issue and he is not charged with a criminal offence',[9] the senior law lord Lord Bingham then went on to locate the issue before him in its wider context:

The convention was conceived in the aftermath of war as a bulwark to protect private citizens against the abuse of power by state and public authorities. This explains why certain important rights are guaranteed to criminal defendants. But it would stand the convention on its head to interpret it as strengthening the rights of prosecutors against private citizens. In truth, the present situation does not engage the human rights of the Director at all.[10]

Despite such a sharp put-down, counsel for the DPP had not been wrong to raise this point, spurious though it turned out to be, since he was doing no more than engaging in creative advocacy on behalf of his client. It is up to the court, assisted by counsel for the other side, to spot and expose such adversarial sleights-of-hand. But if such detective work is not forthcoming, these tricks of advocacy can quickly develop a life of their own.

The traps are not always so visible as they were in *Weir's* case. Intellectual incoherence threatens the Human Rights Act on a number of fronts. As the *Weir* case demonstrates, the Convention rights themselves have the potential to cause this kind of mischief if not carefully attended to, a point graphically demonstrated by another human rights argument that was rejected, this time by Mr Justice Lightman in *Royal Society for the Prevention of Cruelty to Animals v Attorney General and others*.[11] These were charity proceedings commenced by the claimant charity (better known by its acronym the RSPCA) with a view to establishing its entitlement to deny membership to persons who wanted to join the Society while nevertheless opposing one of its longest standing and most fundamental of policies, namely its opposition to hunting with dogs. The Society feared that its membership rolls would be swamped by supporters of fox hunting, who would be determined to act together when strong enough to force the organization to change its ways. In court it was argued against the RSPCA that the Human Rights Act required the Society 'in the exercise of its powers under the rules to respect the human rights of members and applicants for membership, and most particularly their freedom of speech and thought; and

---

[9] *R v Weir*, n 5 above, para [17].

[10] Ibid.

[11] [2002] 1 WLR 448. A similar case in the present context is *R (Giles) v Parole Board*, [2003] UKHL 42, [2003] 3 WLR 736, where a burdensome addition to the sentencing process, imposed by an incorrect reading of Art 5(4) of the Convention, was averted on appeal.

the rules [of the Society] must, accordingly, be read as prohibiting the adoption of the membership policy and the scheme [for administering the policy], since they contravene those rights.'[12]

This was a fallacious argument at a number of levels: the RSPCA was 'not a public authority and ha[d] no public functions within the meaning of s 6.'[13] Furthermore, the acts of the Society that were being impugned in court related to 'its regulation of membership' which was a 'private act' and therefore not something that fell to be regulated by the Human Rights Act.[14] But Mr Justice Lightman was clear about what was the fundamental objection to the point:

> What really is in question in this case is not the freedom of speech or thought of members or applicants for membership, but the freedom of association, under art 11 of the European Convention on Human Rights, of the Society itself: that freedom embraces the freedom to exclude from association those whose membership it honestly believes to be damaging to the interests of the Society.[15]

Any other result would have destroyed the integrity of the Article 11 right, and created a chaotic situation in which every association in the country would have been vulnerable to subversive entry-ism disguised as the assertion of fundamental rights.

If we leave the Convention rights to one side, we can see that a number of the substantive provisions of the Human Rights Act also have a tendency towards unintelligibility if not read carefully by the judges. The curious and as yet largely unlitigated ss 11 and 13 of the Act certainly have this potential,[16] and we have already seen in chapter seven the embarrassing chaos into which the Act's provisions on retrospectivity have thrown the senior judiciary. The interaction between ss 3 and 4 also has the potential to confuse, particularly if the judges continue to regard it as a sufficient explanation of the exercise of their power under these provisions that they are engaged in 'interpretation' rather than 'legislation', without feeling the need to say much more about what exactly these phrases mean in this context. However, as we saw in chapter three, there has been a recent improvement on this score, with Lords Nicholls of Birkenhead and Hope of Craighead in particular having made a start in the delineation of some kind of textually-based philosophy which can underpin and justify both judicial activism and judicial restraint in this area.[17] The same slow emergence of a coherent response to the peculiar sideways expansion of the Human Rights Act

---

[12] [2002] 1 WLR 448, 465, *per* Lightman J.
[13] Ibid.
[14] Ibid.
[15] Ibid, 466 citing *inter alia Cheall v United Kingdom* (1985) 42 DR 178, 185.
[16] On safeguards for, respectively, existing human rights and freedom of thought, conscience and religion respectively.
[17] In *in re S (Minors) (Care Order: Implementation of care plan)* [2002] UKHL 10, [2002] 2 AC 291 and *R v Kansal (No 2)* [2001] UKHL 62, [2002] 2 AC 69 respectively.

into the common law via s 6(3)(a) of the Act has also been evident in the decisions on the application of the measure to the private sphere, again a topic I have earlier discussed.[18] In some ways, this whole book could be seen as being about the aspiration of analytical coherence in that its ambition is to present an argument for a consistent and principled approach to the interpretation of domestic human rights law.

The biggest danger to the coherence of our subject comes neither from the terms of the Convention nor from the provisions in the substance of the Act itself, nor (so far) from the judgments of the British courts, but rather from the case law of the European Court of Human Rights. This may seem an eccentric, even an inflammatory statement, at least when laid out in this bald and unqualified form. The Strasbourg court is the primary guardian of the whole system of regional European human rights protection that is encapsulated in the Convention, and it has spent its entire institutional life fleshing out the provisions within that document so as better to protect the rights that have been placed within its protective remit. Much of the court's work is impressive both in terms of its grasp of principle and in the coherent and consistent way in which it has presented its reasoning: this has certainly been clear from my analysis of that case law in chapters three to five. But in the 40 or so years of the court's operation, the record is, perhaps inevitably, not entirely faultless: some of the first bites that the court has taken at certain of the Convention's provisions have been awkward, and subsequent mastication has merely served to exacerbate the problem that these initial cogitative chews have created. This has been particularly the case in relation to some of the more technical aspects of the Convention (those that require a great deal of preliminary legal analysis rather than a simple application of law to facts, for example).[19] Matters have not been helped by the court having on occasion taken a more relaxed approach to the challenge of internal consistency than would be normal in a British courtroom. Under the Human Rights Act, UK courts have to take all the Strasbourg cases into account when considering Convention rights, but they are not obliged in either the British or the continental sense to follow them.[20] So there is an important challenge for British judges here, namely to decide when Strasbourg should be followed, but also to determine when its jurisprudence should be jettisoned or (more politely) recast in the interests of analytical coherence.

The point can be made by considering how the Strasbourg court has approached the first sentence of Article 6(1), the two or three lines in the Convention which are both the most important in the whole document from a litigation perspective, and at the same time the least easy to unpick and understand:

[18] See above pp 78–83 and 157–164.

[19] I am not now referring to the court's approach to precedent which, though admittedly different from the rules operative in the British domestic courts, is nevertheless entirely coherent and reasonably easy to follow: for a discussion of this issue see below pp 196–202.

[20] See the Human Rights Act 1998, s 2(1).

In the determination of his civil rights and obligations or of any criminal charge against him, everyone is entitled to a fair and public hearing within a reasonable time by an independent and impartial tribunal established by law.

Much of the way the European court has gone about drawing out the meaning of this sentence has been a model of consistency. Although the safeguards that Article 6(1) guarantee have generated a huge case law, the principles that underpin the court's rulings in these areas have been reasonably transparent. An entirely coherent test for distinguishing between criminal and civil proceedings has been developed and applied on numerous occasions,[21] the difference between the two being important because the 'criminal charge' brings with it protections additional to those set out above, while persons facing the 'determination' of their civil rights and obligations are required to be content with the Article 6(1) guarantees alone. The British judges have reasonably effortlessly absorbed this line of cases into their jurisprudence on the Human Rights Act.[22]

Where there have been problems has been in distinguishing between civil disputes which attract Article 6(1) protection and other kinds of proceedings which do not. Here the court has produced layers of jurisprudence of a detailed, complex and sometimes contradictory sort. The notion of 'the determination of a civil right' is most clearly evocative of the settling of a dispute in the civil courts. The first set of judges to sit in the European Court were however not content to restrict the ambit of the provision in this way, particularly when they noticed that there was no right to fair administrative procedures in any other article in the Convention. Faced with this (as they saw it) lacuna, these judges (not without a great deal of initial division within the court) set about expanding the meaning of a 'determination of a civil right' so that it could encompass decisions taken by public authorities which impacted on a person's civil rights and in relation to which some dispute mechanism was in place (not necessarily of a judicial sort) whereby such a decision could be challenged.[23] The need for some kind of a dispute about such decisions was a residual necessity derived from the origins of the provision in true civil proceedings and from the court's view that the word 'determination' involved some kind of conflict between parties, *contestation* in the French.[24] But the court had little difficulty in finding such a *contestation* when it wanted to impose Article 6(1) safeguards on administrative action of which it disapproved.[25] The effect of this expansion of Article 6(1) was

---

[21] The leading case is *Engel v The Netherlands* (1976) 1 EHRR 647.

[22] See for a good example *R (McCann) v Manchester Crown Court* [2002] UKHL 39, [2003] 1 AC 787. Also of interest are *R (West) v Parole Board* [2002] EWCA Civ 1641, [2003] 1 WLR 705; *R (Mudie) v Kent Magistrates' Court* [2003] EWCA Civ 237, [2003] QB 1238; and *R (Mitchell) v Horsham District Council* [2003] EWHC 234 (Admin).

[23] Three important early authorities are *Ringeisen v Austria (No 1)* (1971) 1 EHRR 455; *König v Federal Republic of Germany* (1978) 2 EHRR 170, and *Le Compte, Van Leuven and De Meyere v Belgium* (1981) 4 EHRR 1. For a taste of the internal divisions on the court at this time, see *Benthem v The Netherlands* (1985) 8 EHRR 1; *Feldbrugge v The Netherlands* (1986) 8 EHRR 425 and *Deumeland v Federal Republic of Germany* (1986) 8 EHRR 448.

[24] See *Ringeisen v Austria*, n 23 above.

[25] As in *Sporrong and Lönnroth v Sweden* (1982) 5 EHRR 35, esp paras [79]–[83].

that vast areas of administrative law found themselves having to comply with the procedural requirements of Article 6(1). Now this was a potentially disastrous scenario, in that it threatened a full scale legalization of practically the entirety of Europe's administrative processes, a ludicrously intrusive assertion of power by an international body of jurists.

The court diluted the impact of its expansionism in three ways: first by allowing judicial review 'to cure the defects' in the administrative procedure that had occurred without the Article 6(1) safeguards; secondly by defining 'civil right' so as to omit certain public law matters; and thirdly by asserting that domestic limitations on access to the courts are outside Article 6(1) altogether if they are substantive (as opposed to procedural) in nature. The first of these has produced a complex set of cases in its own right,[26] and we have already encountered briefly in chapter seven the way in which the domestic courts have sought to translate this material into national law.[27] It is with the second and third lines of attenuation that I am now mainly concerned, since each raises a number of challenges to analytical coherence which are of the first importance to the overall integrity of the Human Rights Act. As far as the civil/public law distinction is concerned, the European Court of Human Rights early developed the view that while the notion of a civil right was to be given a wide meaning, decisions concerning pure public law issues were never to be included within the term. Thus disputes concerning employment in the public sector, arguments about tax liabilities and entitlement to fiscal benefits and much else besides have been held to fall entirely outside Article 6 because they have involved public matters.[28] In one well known case from France a dispute about the forfeiture of a national assembly seat on account of the applicant having exceeded the permitted level of election expenditure was held to be about a 'public right' and therefore outside Article 6(1).[29] In contrast, where there has been a financial interest at stake in which the action of the state has been directly decisive, the issue has been more likely to be viewed as one to which Article 6(1) applied, even if it has otherwise had some public character.[30] Not all the Strasbourg judges have been comfortable with the path that these decisions have taken; as a dissenting voice asked in the French election decision, are not civil rights 'essentially, in the most literal meaning of the term, the rights of the citizen (*civis*)?' so that 'political rights' should not be regarded as outside the protection of the Convention but as "'civil" rights *par excellence*?'[31]

---

[26] UK authorities in Strasbourg include *W v United Kingdom* (1987) 10 EHRR 29; *Bryan v United Kingdom* (1995) 21 EHRR 342; and *Kingsley v United Kingdom* (2000) 33 EHRR 288: see generally I Leigh, 'Taking Rights Proportionately: Judicial Review, the Human Rights Act and Strasbourg' [2002] *PL* 265.

[27] See pp 154–157 above and I Leigh, 'Bias, Necessity and the Convention' [2002] *PL* 407.

[28] There is an exhaustive list in R Clayton and H Tomlinson, *The Law of Human Rights* (Oxford: Oxford University Press, 2000), para 11.172.

[29] *Pierre-Bloch v France* (1997) 26 EHRR 202.

[30] See among many authorities *Editions Périscope v France* (1992) 14 EHRR 597.

[31] n 29 above, 237 *per* Judge De Meyer.

The most frequently recurring problem on this tendentious borderline of the court's own making has arisen in the context of disputes concerning the conditions of service of public servants. Does Article 6(1) apply to such matters or does it not? In *Pellegrin v France*[32] the court made a determined effort to clarify its earlier, somewhat confused authorities on the point, declaring that it was henceforward adopting a 'functional criterion based on the nature of the employee's duties and responsibilities' as a guide to determining when a dispute concerning a public servant, 'whether established or employed under contract' attracted the protection of Article 6(1) and when it did not.[33] The court ruled:

that the only disputes excluded ... are those which are raised by public servants whose duties typify the specific activities of the public service in so far as the latter is acting as the depositary of public authority responsible for protecting the general interests of the State or other public authorities. A manifest example of such activities is provided by the armed forces and the police. In practice, the Court will ascertain, in each case, whether the applicant's post entails—in the light of the nature of the duties and responsibilities appertaining to it—direct or indirect participation in the exercise of powers conferred by public law and duties designed to safeguard the general interests of the State or of other public authorities.[34]

One of the concurring judges in the case referred to the decision as a 'landmark judgment',[35] though as the English Court of Appeal was later wryly to remark when the authority came before it, it 'had some difficulty in distinguishing the precise nature of the landmark'.[36] The civil/public distinction is not one which has any resonance for the English lawyer, but the fact of its partial incorporation in UK law via the Human Rights Act, s 2(1) has meant that it has been lying about domestic law available for use since 2 October 2000.

Its chance came in *Matthews v Ministry of Defence*,[37] a case involving an action for damages against the ministry by a claimant who had served in the Royal Navy for a number of years, during which time it was alleged that he had contracted various asbestos-related illnesses in consequence of the negligence and breach of statutory duty of the defendant ministry. The matter came before first the High Court and then the Court of Appeal on the preliminary question of whether the immunity from suit that the Crown claimed in such circumstances (under the Crown Proceedings Act 1947, s 10) was consistent with the procedural safeguards set out in Article 6(1). Spotting the usefulness of the *Pellegrin* case in the common law system of argument in which so much depends on reasoning by analogy, counsel for the ministry asserted that it reached not only

---

[32] (1999) 31 EHRR 651.   [33] Ibid para [64].   [34] Ibid para [66].
[35] Ibid 666 *per* Judge Ferrari Bravo.
[36] *Matthews v Ministry of Defence* n 37 below, para [24] *per* Lord Phillips of Worth Matravers giving the judgment of the Court of Appeal in that case.
[37] *Matthews v Ministry of Defence* [2001] EWCA Civ 773, [2002] 1 WLR 2621. The case went to the House of Lords where however the issue being discussed at this point in the text was not raised: [2003] UKHL 4, [2003] 1 AC 116, para [120] *per* Lord Walker of Gestingthorpe. See further *Mangera v Ministry of Defence* [2003] EWCA Civ 801.

disputes relating to the claimant's conditions of service, but also that it applied, 'to any claim against the state by a person whose functions fell within the *Pellegrin* criterion. The armed forces were expressly identified in *Pellegrin* as an example of those who fell within that criterion. Thus the exclusion of article 6 applied to claims in tort.'[38]

Such an argument, had it succeeded, would have turned the *Pellegrin* case on its head, transforming it from a narrow set of exceptions related to employment disputes into an engine for state immunity in private law. Fortunately the wrong turning was spotted by the court, despite its confession that it was 'in unfamiliar territory when considering' the issue.[39] Its 'firm opinion' was that the judge below, Keith J, had been right to restrict the *Pellegrin* case to disputes relating to conditions of service, of which this dispute was manifestly not one.[40]

Even when exploring the familiar terrain of the common law, judges engaged in adjudication in the adversarial system face an unenviable challenge in plotting a straight and analytically coherent course for their decisions, often being invited into cul-de-sacs by expert professional counsel (who are as I earlier observed in relation to *R v Weir* merely doing their job as promoters of their clients' interests) and sometimes also (because other counsel have queered the pitch in the past) been forced into such dead-ends by prior authority. Having resisted one such siren call, the Court of Appeal in the *Matthews* case unfortunately succumbed to another, finding that Article 6(1) was not engaged by the limitation on access to the courts in the 1947 Act because the denial of access was of a 'substantive' rather than a 'procedural' nature. This mistake was not rectified when Matthews's appeal to the Lords was later dismissed. As I have noted already, the origins of this peculiar and obscure distinction lie in the European Court's uncertainty about how far to push its jurisdiction down the throat of member states. In its early, expansionist days, the court insisted not only that the concept of a 'civil right' was for it rather than member states to define, but also that if a domestic system of law were to deny a person access to the courts entirely, then that denial was itself to be tested for proportionality and objective necessity. In these early decisions, two of the most important of which involved the United Kingdom,[41] there was no suggestion of any kind of procedural/ substantive escape hatch for domestic exclusionary clauses. This distinction only came about as a reaction to a later veering of the court in entirely the opposite direction, towards allowing member states to remove altogether the right to a court under Article 6(1) by the brutal expedient of extinguishing the relevant 'civil right' by express legislation.

This lurch into judicial passivity had been precipitated by *James v United Kingdom*[42] in which Parliament had (to paraphrase the language of the

---

[38] Ibid para [27] of the judgment of the Court of Appeal.   [39] Ibid para [18].
[40] Ibid para [31].
[41] *Golder v United Kingdom* (1975) 1 EHRR 524; *Ashingdane v United Kingdom* (1985) 7 EHRR 528.
[42] (1986) 8 EHRR 123.

Strasbourg court during this period) 'derecognized' the right to property of the applicants by transferring ownership in their freeholds to their lessees when certain clear conditions were met. The move had then been consolidated in two further British cases, *Lithgow v United Kingdom*[43] and *Powell and Rayner v United Kingdom*.[44] But the effect of these cases was to leave countries pretty free to deprive applicants of Article 6(1) protection as and when they desired, a result hardly in line with the early cases or with the court's self-image of itself as a primary guardian of the rule of law in Europe. Hence, after yet further twists and turns,[45] the relatively recent emergence of the procedural/substantive distinction, with the court now generally insisting that Article 6(1) is to apply only to applicants who can show on arguable grounds that their civil right continues to be 'recognized' in domestic law. A denial of the recognition of that right which is 'substantive' in nature, in other words which goes to the very existence of the right itself, will be a denial of recognition of the right which, therefore, causes Article 6(1) to have no application. However a denial of recognition which is of a procedural nature only, and which does not go to the essence of the right, will mean that the right has not been 'derecognized,' and so, as a result, Article 6(1) will be engaged in such cases, with the validity of this exclusion of the courts therefore falling to be assessed by reference to the court's well-established tests of proportionality and objective necessity.

Fortunately it is not necessary to delve much further into these deep and murky waters for the purposes of this book. The Strasbourg court itself is not even sure whether the procedural/substantive distinction has any validity,[46] but even if it has, we can be quite sure that identifying exactly where the borderline is between the two will be no easy task. Regrettably the problem has now been imported into domestic law, in the decision in the *Matthews'* case where first the Court of Appeal and then the House of Lords has applied the distinction to find that the relevant limitation on access to the courts before it, being substantive in nature, was not one which attracted the attentions of Article 6(1) and was not one, therefore, which needed to justify itself in terms of proportionality. But like all legal distinctions which are based not on substance but on an accident of form, and a form moreover that cannot be precisely defined in advance, this particular linguistic dichotomy is likely to require a very slow process of judicial explication on a case by case basis.[47] To some extent of course the judges' hands were tied; the Human Rights Act, s 2 does require the Strasbourg case law to be taken into account and the European Court continues to exert supervisory authority over the application of the Convention in domestic law. Nevertheless

---

[43] (1986) 8 EHRR 329.   [44] (1990) 12 EHRR 355.

[45] Detailed in CA Gearty, 'Unravelling Osman' (2001) 64 MLR 159.

[46] See *Fayed v United Kingdom* (1994) 18 EHRR 393, para [65]. For a useful summary of the law in relation to state immunity and Art 6, see M Kloth, 'Immunities and the Right of Access to Court under the European Convention on Human Rights' (2002) 27 *European Law Review Human Rights Survey* 33.

[47] A process which had begun even before the case had been decided in the Lords: see *re Deep Vein Thrombosis and Air Travel Group Litigation* [2002] EWHC 2825 (QB), [2003] 3 WLR 956.

a less pedantic approach and one which promoted content over form was surely possible. The key question in relation to all denials of access to the court is not whether the affected 'civil right' has been limited in form or in substance (a pretty meaningless inquiry however it might be phrased), but rather whether the denial is in all the circumstances a legitimate one. Sometimes it will be, as in the *Ashingdane* case itself,[48] sometimes it will not. But at least this is a real issue, where the public interest can be clearly identified, the relevant human right set out and a coherent assessment of the balance between the two duly made.

C. The priority of substance over form

Lord Nicholls has remarked that, 'Human rights conventions are concerned with substance, not form, with practicalities and realities, not linguistic niceties.'[49] The journey through some of the Article 6 case law that we have just completed is a reminder of how easily legal reasoning can take on a life of its own: once in a poorly constructed hole, the law finds it almost impossible to stop digging. The same is true in those many cases that spin off into consideration of collateral matters at a cost to speedy and beneficial consideration of the real issues. The procedural/substantive distinction we have just discussed is of this type, offending against the demands of intelligibility and also promoting a preoccupation with what is essentially a peripheral matter, with little if any connection to the human rights substance of the case. The distinction between public and private bodies in the Human Rights Act, s 6 also throws up various diversions into obscurity of a similar nature, but this time on an issue that goes right to the core of the human rights project. We have encountered the terms of s 6 on many occasions in the course of this book, and now is the time directly to confront its complexities. It will be remembered that the obligation to act compatibly with Convention rights in s 6(1) is imposed upon all 'public authorities'. This phrase is explicitly said to include 'any person certain of whose functions are functions of a public nature' (s 6(3)(b)), but the Act then provides that in 'relation to any particular act a person is not a public authority by virtue only of subsection (3)(b) if the nature of the act is private' (s 6(5)). Once it is appreciated that the Human Rights Act does not automatically impose on all of us a duty to respect each other's Convention rights,[50] the significance of the distinction being made here becomes apparent. The Act offers this enormously important fork in the road to those seeking to order their conduct in accordance with the law; public authorities are required to take the route marked Convention-compliance (backed up with all sorts of procedural and remedial provisions such as those to be found in ss 7 and 8 and indeed in judicial review proceedings generally),

---

[48] n 41 above. See also *Stubbings v United Kingdom* (1996) 23 EHRR 213.

[49] *Wilson v Secretary of State for Trade and Industry* [2003] UKHL 40, [2003] 3 WLR 568, para [35].

[50] In other words that the measure does not have direct horizontal effect, on which see above pp 157–164.

while the rest of us are left alone to continue our gambol through life along a Convention-free route.[51] The Act creates a strong structural incentive, therefore, for a defendant in a case to argue a preliminary point about its own status so as to avoid consequential human rights-based duties inimical to its interests.

The issue has already received close attention from the House of Lords, in the highly unusual case of *Aston Cantlow and Wilmcote with Billesley, Warwickshire v Wallbank*.[52] The parish council had sought to recover the cost of the repairs to the chancel of their church from the person legally responsible for such matters, designated the lay rector. It was not surprising that problems arose given that the sum involved was enormous (£95,260.84 in 1995) and that the position of lay rector was filled not by some church functionary or benefactor but by the joint owners of a nearby property (Glebe Farm) whose connections with the church appear to have been minimal and whose liability flowed out of an historical association between the land and the church that had long been broken (other than, significantly, in the form of an overriding interest registered under the Law of Property Act 1925, s 70). To the owners of Glebe Farm, the European Convention on Human Rights must have seemed like a Nirvana of justice in an otherwise barren legal landscape, giving formal voice to their sense of having been treated as landowners in a wholly disproportionate and discriminatory manner. But first they had to negotiate s 6: was the parish church council a 'public authority' in any of the senses required by the Human Rights Act? Their lordships were clear, by a majority of four to one, that it was not. All five considered that it was not a 'public authority' simpliciter under s 6(1) and only Lord Scott thought the function a public one under s 6(3).[53] So even if the action of the council had infringed the Convention (which their lordships went on unanimously to hold was not the case here), there was nothing the property owners could have done about this, short of finding a common law right with which to defend themselves or an Act of Parliament upon which to work some interpretative magic, though neither escape route was available on this set of facts.

The case takes a restrictive view of the breadth of s 6. To Lords Hope, Scott, and Rodger the phrase 'public authority' is the key: it is the nature of the person, not the function, that matters under s 6(1); it follows that an 'authority' may have regulatory and coercive powers and still be 'private' (ie not 'public') for Human Rights Act purposes.[54] Lord Hobhouse thought the council to be 'clearly not' a core public authority, since it was no more than a domestic body with no public responsibilities or functions.[55] Observing that it was the purpose of the

---

[51] Slightly overstated here of course, because the pre-existing law may itself be affected by the Convention, through its reinterpretation via s 3 of the Act or through the development of the common law to reflect Convention principle.

[52] [2003] UKHL 37, [2003] 3 WLR 283.

[53] The majority judges were Lord Hope of Craighead, Lord Nicholls of Birkenhead, Lord Hobhouse of Woodborough, and Lord Rodger of Earlsferry.

[54] n 52 above, para [41] *per* Lord Hope; para [129] *per* Lord Scott of Foscote; para [166] *per* Lord Rodger.

[55] Ibid para [86].

Human Rights Act that 'those bodies for whose acts the State [was] answerable before the European Court of Human Rights [should] in future be subject to a domestic law obligation not to act incompatibly with Convention rights,'[56] all their lordships put a great emphasis on the need to restrict the range of such bodies by reference to who could be a victim under Convention jurisprudence, a line of authorities that provided an 'important guide' to what was meant by public authority.[57] The argument adopted seems to have been that any body which could present itself as a 'victim' under the relevant article of the Convention[58] must therefore not be a body capable of being characterized as a public authority under s 6(1), since it was 'difficult to see how a core public authority could ever claim to be a victim of a Convention right'.[59]

This is a novel use of the Convention's case law on what constitutes a victim to hack away at the range of bodies that are properly to be regarded as 'public authorities' for the purposes of this part of English public law. It is not obvious why an issue of standing in a hypothetical case should determine when a real case should be allowed to proceed. The European Court itself has taken an increasingly relaxed view on the central issue before the House of Lords, the extent of state action required to attract responsibility for Convention breaches;[60] if the Strasbourg approach matters so much why ignore its consistently expansive line on the key matter while concentrating with unusual intensity on a question (who is a victim?) that was not merely peripheral but, on the facts, wholly irrelevant? But having taken this line on s 6(1), the House then went on also to rule out s 6(3), the actions of the parish council having nothing to do with the state and being merely the enforcement of a private power.[61] So overall, the case signals a desire to restrict the ambit of the Human Rights Act to a much greater degree than had been anticipated. The intention goes against the grain of the Strasbourg case law and is at odds with the political aspiration that the Human Rights Act should somehow or other introduce a broadly based culture of rights. It is not likely that the line can be successfully held in quite so conservative a position as that set out by their lordships especially when the analogy with Article 34 comes under critical scrutiny, as it surely will. In the meantime, we must gird ourselves in preparation for a plethora of cases on what is essentially a preliminary point of procedure, not an issue of substance.

The public/private distinction is especially important to the many bodies that operate for profit tasks that were once believed to be the exclusive preserve and responsibility of state organs: even if these are not 'public authorities' in the

---

[56] Ibid para [6] *per* Lord Nicholls.

[57] Ibid para [46] *per* Lord Hope. The most detailed exposition of the point is that of Lord Rodger, paras [158]–[165].

[58] Art 34 defines victim as any 'person, non-governmental organisation or group of individuals'.

[59] n 52 above, para [8] *per* Lord Nicholls.

[60] See p 160 n 76 above.

[61] n 52 above, paras [63]–[64] (Lord Hope); paras [87]–[90] (Lord Hobhouse); paras [169]–[171] (Lord Rodger). Lord Nicholls is a bit more liberal in his approach: see paras [11]–[12]. Lord Scott's different view is at paras [130]–[131].

formal sense, are they exercising functions of a public nature? This complex philosophical, but at the same time politically explosive, issue came before the courts in *R (Heather, Ward and Callin) v The Leonard Cheshire Foundation and the Attorney General*,[62] one of the earliest important cases under the Act, decided well before the Lords' ruling in the *Aston Cantlow* case. The claimants were three long-stay residents at a home run by the first defendant, a charitable foundation. Their places were largely paid for by their local council or by their local health authority, each exercising statutory powers available to them for the purpose of caring for people in the position of the claimants. The public authorities involved could have provided directly for their care but the law equally entitled them to farm the job out to a voluntary organization, which is what had happened here. In fact this is what most local authorities now choose to do. In September 2000, Leonard Cheshire decided to close the claimants' home in its then form and to reconstruct the place on different lines. The reorganization involved the relocation of certain residents into community-based units. The claimants challenged this decision, arguing that they had been promised a home for life where they presently were and that to move them now would be an infringement of their right to respect for their home as guaranteed by Article 8 of the European Convention. To this Leonard Cheshire responded with the un-attractive but tactically astute argument that as a non-governmental body it was beyond the reach of the Human Rights Act, and therefore free to ignore the Convention if it so desired.[63]

The judge to whom fell the duty of resolving this difficult issue at first instance, Stanley Burnton J, was aware that if the defendant was right, 'the increased privatisation of formerly governmental functions may involve the loss of judicial review of those functions and of the decisions made when exercising them'.[64] The judge first looked at the law prior to implementation of the Human Rights Act. This pointed strongly in the direction of a charity like the defendant, involved in the discharge of statutory duties on behalf of a public authority, not being amenable to traditional proceedings for ordinary judicial review.[65] Leonard Cheshire was not an agent of any public authority in the technical legal sense. There was 'not the statutory underpinning or statutory penetration' of its functions 'which would result in its being amenable to judicial

---

[62] [2001] EWHC 429 (Admin), [2002] EWCA Civ 366; [2002] 2 All ER 936 (CA). Only Heather and Callin pursued their appeals to the Court of Appeal. This is a subject that has already attracted a large amount of scholarship: see in particular E Palmer, 'Should Public Health be a Private Concern? Developing a Public Service Paradigm in English Law' (2002) 22 *OJLS* 663; P Craig, 'Contracting Out, the Human Rights Act and the Scope of Judicial Review' (2002) 118 *LQR* 551; M McDermont, 'The Elusive Nature of the "Public Function": *Poplar Housing and Regeneration Community Association Ltd v Donoghue*' (2003) 66 *MLR* 113.

[63] Cf *R (Madden) v Bury Metropolitan Borough Council* [2002] EWHC 1882 (Admin) and *R (Whitebread and Dudley) v East Sussex County Council* [2003] EWHC 1093 (Admin) where the homes which were in issue were run directly by the local authority concerned.

[64] n 62 above, para [20].

[65] Principally on account of *R (Goldsmith and Chatting) v Servite Houses and Wandsworth LBC* [2001] LGR 55.

review'.[66] Furthermore, its relationship between the authority and the charity 'was purely commercial', with the source of the latter's power being 'solely contractual' and therefore 'inconsistent with a public law jurisdiction'.[67] The presence of state funding did not in itself 'indicate that a body exercises public functions,'[68] and state regulation (which of course existed here) 'if anything points against the body regulated being a public authority'.[69] Were Leonard Cheshire amenable to judicial review, then 'proprietors of bed-and-breakfast homes who provide accommodation pursuant to arrangements with local authorities would be public authorities, as would contractors building roads for central government, or repairing roads for local government, or building homes for local authorities who are housing authorities.'[70]

Even if this version of the pre-existing law were true, the next question that arose was whether the Human Rights Act had made a difference. Counsel for the claimants argued that 'the Act had replaced the former complexity and uncertainty of the law by enacting a single test: that of function'.[71] Mr Justice Stanley Burnton accepted that s 6 'certainly appear[ed] to lay down a functional test'[72] but that if this were true, then 'the scope of judicial review and of the subjects of public law obligations ha[d] indeed been revolutionised by the Act'.[73] Anticipating the *Aston Cantlow* ruling, this was a step that the judge felt himself incapable of making. It was 'generally recognised that the object of the Convention was to grant to (or to confirm for) citizens the specified rights and freedoms as against government and governmental authorities', a point borne out by the construction of the document, in particular with its Article 1 reference to the obligations of 'High Contracting Parties', its assumption that only a governmental body could restrict many of the Convention rights, and its references to legitimate reasons for such restrictions of a sort which could only make sense to such bodies (the 'economic well-being of the country' in Article 8(2) for example).[74] In contrast to governmental bodies, a 'purely private body [was], within legal constraints, generally entitled to act in its own economic interests; it will often be compelled to act in those interests'.[75] The policy of privatization which meant 'in general . . . that functions formerly exercised by public authorities [were] now carried out by non-public entities, often for profit' clearly had 'inevitable consequences for the applicability of judicial review, which the courts are not free to avoid'.[76] The way to deal with the gap in judicial review that therefore resulted was by way of the development of private law, not by expanding the concept of the public authority or the notion of a public function.[77]

---

[66] *R (Heather, Ward and Callin) v Leonard Cheshire Homes*, n 62 above, para [46] quoting from *Servite*, n 65 above, with the remarks in which Burnton J 'so entirely agree[d]' that it was 'unnecessary for [him] to comment on them': ibid para [47].

[67] Ibid.   [68] Ibid para [48(i)].   [69] Ibid para [48(ii)].   [70] Ibid para [49].

[71] Ibid para [60].   [72] Ibid para [61].   [73] Ibid para [66].   [74] Ibid paras [70]–[71].

[75] Ibid para [72].

[76] Ibid para [104], citing (at para [105]) the 'instructive article' by Dawn Oliver, 'The Frontiers of the State: Public Authorities and Public Functions under the Human Rights Act' [2000] *PL* 476.

[77] Ibid para [106] again citing Oliver, ibid.

The reasoning of Mr Justice Stanley Burnton was largely followed in the Court of Appeal decision which later dismissed the claimants' appeal.[78] Like the judge at first instance, Lord Woolf and his colleagues (Laws and Dyson LJJ) appeared concerned that any wider analysis than that favoured at first instance might encompass within the Human Rights Act such bodies as 'a private company [carrying] out specialist services [for a hospital] such as analysing blood samples', or 'a small hotel [providing] bed and breakfast accommodation as a temporary measure, at the request of a housing authority that is under a duty to provide that accommodation', or a private school to which a local authority sent a child in order to discharge its statutory duties.[79] The court drew attention not only to the claimants' possible contractual remedies against Leonard Cheshire, but also to the fact that the various public authorities responsible for the claimants were still obliged to respect their Convention rights in all their dealings with them.[80] But the opportunity to have recourse to judicial review against the local or health authority does not mean much when the relevant contentious act that should attract the attention of the Convention and the s 6 duty is being performed by someone else.[81] The stimulation of the common law is also surely a poor substitute for proper human rights review. The Court of Appeal's suggestion that claimants like the ones before the court should 'require'[82] their local authorities to impose contractual duties on service providers guaranteeing respect for their Convention rights, seems rather unrealistic, to put it at its mildest. In contrast to the simplicity and speed of its public law alternative, the common law route is a pathway overgrown with ancient vegetation, difficult to traverse and carrying with it no guarantee that any suitable stopping point for an argument on the merits will ever be found.

Perhaps over time, the courts will evolve various imaginative devises to mitigate the effective gap in the law which the *Leonard Cheshire* case has partly exposed and partly created.[83] Certainly there will be many cases in which bodies that before the *Leonard Cheshire* case might have accepted they were exercising public functions will have a go at reclassifying themselves as private.[84] If the courts are not careful, the case law on the public/private distinction will become as tortuous and as procedurally constipated as the 1980s litigation that flowed

---

[78] n 62 above.
[79] Ibid paras [18] and [19]. All three examples came from the Court of Appeal decision in *Poplar Housing and Regeneration Community Association Ltd v Donoghue* [2001] EWCA Civ 595; [2002] QB 48 which anticipated some of the central issues in the *Leonard Cheshire* case.
[80] Ibid para [33].
[81] See *R (Haggerty) v St Helen's Council* [2003] EWHC 803 (Admin).
[82] *R (Heather, Ward and Callin) v Leonard Cheshire Homes*, n 62 above, para [34].
[83] Cf *Southwark London Borough Council v Long* [2002] EWCA Civ 403, [2002] LGR 530 where the local authority in the case was held liable for the action of its contractors. The standard of care in all kinds of care homes is an ongoing matter of concern: see '"Freedoms curbed" in care homes' *Guardian* 17 April 2003.
[84] Cf *R (Matthias Rath BV) v Advertising Standards Authority* [2001] HRLR 436.

from a similar attempt to develop a public/private divide in 1983.[85] From the perspective of this chapter, it is as a stimulus to collateral litigation that we can be most critical of the *Aston Cantlow* and *Leonard Cheshire* decisions. The Court of Appeal in the *Leonard Cheshire* case was right to point out that there are now sensible transfer arrangements in the civil procedure rules which mean that litigants wrongly commencing a case in public law can be redirected down the right procedural route without having their case defeated on this technicality alone.[86] This more liberal approach within the rules than pertained in the past is to be welcomed but it does nothing on its own to obviate the risk of the public/private argument taking over a case at a preliminary stage; indeed it might be thought to encourage it by removing one disincentive against claimants making broad assertions about the status of defendants in their statements of case. Perhaps there will be a need for case law on when the transfer rules should and should not be applied. Once a case is tempted down a procedural route, and away from the substantive straight and narrow, there is simply no end to the forks in the road that can then present themselves. As we have seen in the *Aston Cantlow* case the same result would have been achieved even if their Lordships had chosen to take an expansive view of s 6. Had the matter in the *Leonard Cheshire* case been dealt with on the substantive point, the charity could surely have pointed to many defensible reasons for acting in the way that it did. In neither case was there any reason to run scared of arguments based on Convention rights. This will often be the case—except of course in those situations where the infringement of rights is particularly egregious. But these are exactly the circumstances calling out for human rights oversight, something that, after the *Aston Cantlow* and *Leonard Cheshire* case, may not now be possible.

D. Noble lies and other deceits

I turn now to my final—and deepest—ambition for an analytically coherent approach to judicial interpretation of the Human Rights Act. In a recent House of Lords decision on causation in the tort of negligence, Lord Bingham cited Lord Wilberforce as having in an earlier case 'wisely deprecated resort to fictions' in the interpretation of the law.[87] The senior law lord thought it 'preferable, in the interests of transparency, that the courts' response to the

---

[85] Stimulated by *O'Reilly v Mackman* [1983] 2 AC 237. The cases have already begun: see *R(A) v Partnership in Care Limited* [2002] EWHC 529 (Admin), [2002] 1 WLR 2610 in which the decision of the managers of a private psychiatric hospital to change the focus of one of its wards was considered to be the exercise of a public function and so susceptible to judicial review, with the first instance ruling in the *Leonard Cheshire* case being distinguished on the facts; and *Hampshire County Council v Beer* [2003] EWCA Civ 1056 in which a private company managing a farmers' market for a local council was held to be involved in the exercise of a public function and to be properly classified as a public authority under s 6.

[86] *Leonard Cheshire*, n 62 above, paras [37]–[39].

[87] *Fairchild v Glenhaven Funeral Services Ltd and other cases* [2002] UKHL 22, [2002] 3 WLR 89, at para [35] citing Lord Wilberforce in *McGhee v National Coal Board* [1973] 1 WLR 1, 7.

special problem presented' by cases such as the one before him 'should be stated explicitly'.[88] The issue related to the burden of proof and the temptation that lay before Lord Bingham and his colleagues was to pretend by a trick of inference that the claimants had proved their case when in fact they had done nothing of the sort, and a new legal rule was in reality required if justice was to be done for them. In human rights law, as in law generally, it is sometimes the case that a solution to a particularly difficult issue will offer itself in the form of a convenient legal fiction. A pretence as to the true factual circumstances has the advantage of allowing a court to bridge the gap between what the law would appear to require and what, on the other hand, expedience or administrative necessity or even plain common sense would seem to demand. But such sleights of hand should be sparingly deployed lest they do disproportionate damage to the overall integrity of the law.

An example of a tempting fiction drawn from the human rights field is the notion of an assumed waiver of a right in a situation where the factual evidence for the breach of the right cannot be gainsaid, but where insistence on it carries a range of inconvenient societal costs. How far should this potentially malleable concept of waiver be stretched, and in what circumstances? Are wholly artificial waivers of rights, lies as to the true state of the facts, to be allowed? The European Court of Human Rights is clear that the answer to this last question is no. While a waiver of rights is possible,[89] the foregoing of one's rights is 'only effective if it is established in an unequivocal manner and is attended by the minimum safeguards commensurate with its importance'.[90] According to the Strasbourg case law, a waiver should be untainted by any evidence of coercion or other kind of unacceptable constraint on choice;[91] and it will not be enough to point to a contract with a party as evidence that a person has waived their rights.[92] The rights-holder must appreciate what he or she is doing when the (alleged) waiver is taking place.[93] All of this is surely very sensible. Of course an individual should be able consciously to forego his or her rights if he or she should choose to do so: the overriding commitment to individual freedom and human autonomy inherent in the concept of human rights demands that the subject not become coercive or dictatorial in the realization of its moral agenda. The exercise of one right will often render inevitable the waiver of other rights: in associating with others I forego some of my privacy rights; in participating in violent sport I waive aspects of my right to security of the person; and so on. Waiver in this sense is as vital to the concept of human rights as are the rights themselves.

---

[88] *Fairchild v Glenhaven Funeral Services Ltd and other cases* [2002] UKHL 22, [2002] 3 WLR 89, at para [35].

[89] See, among many authorities, *Pfeifer and Plankl v Austria* (1992) 14 EHRR 692.

[90] Clayton and Tomlinson, n 28 above, 333 where the authorities are gathered.

[91] *Deweer v Belgium* (1980) 2 EHRR 439. O de Schutter, 'Waiver of Rights and State Paternalism under the European Convention on Human Rights' (2000) 51 *NILQ* 481 is a detailed study.

[92] *Rommelfanger v Germany* (1989) 62 DR 151.

[93] *Bulut v Austria* (1996) 24 EHRR 84.

These issues of express and assumed waiver are now surfacing in the UK case law in the aftermath of implementation of the Human Rights Act. An early anxiety was as to the effect of the Act on Britain's thriving commercial arbitration business, a consensual procedure outside the ordinary law to which all the parties commit themselves, but so far the Strasbourg principles on the subject have not produced any great difficulty.[94] Similar issues have arisen in employment law.[95] In *R (V) v Metropolitan Police Commissioner; R (R) v Durham Constabulary*,[96] the final warning scheme put in place by the government to prevent offending and/or reoffending by young persons was found in breach of Article 6(1) and on the facts was not redeemed by any effective waiver in the form of a proper consent to the proceedings required under the scheme. In the Administrative Court's view, 'an effective waiver require[d] informed consent by the offender to the procedure being adopted'.[97] The 'appropriate practice' was 'to ensure that before a reprimand or final warning [was] administered, the offender and his or her parent, carer or other appropriate adult should be told of the consequences, and asked whether or not they consent[ed] to that course being taken'.[98]

An interesting example of what might be thought a rather opportunistic reliance upon a Convention right, and one which provoked an early discussion about waiver in the House of Lords, occurred in *R v Jones*.[99] The defendant had jumped bail prior to his trial, despite which, after a re-listing and an adjournment, the prosecution went ahead, with the trial judge having taken the view that the defendant had acted as he had with the intention of frustrating the criminal process against him. The defendant's legal team withdrew from the case and the trial in due course resulted in a conviction. When he was eventually caught, the defendant appealed, arguing that his Article 6 rights had been infringed by his trial in absentia (particularly in light of the absence of legal representation), and that therefore his conviction should be set aside. In terms of strict law, there was undoubtedly a serious point here, with the Strasbourg case law being unsurprisingly clear on the 'capital importance' of the attendance of a criminal defendant at his own trial.[100] On the other hand, common sense, administrative efficiency and the equitable principle of coming to court 'with clean hands' pointed in the opposite direction.

Lord Bingham found his solution to the conundrum in the law on waiver:

---

[94] See *Mousaka Inc v Golden Seagull Maritime Inc and another* [2002] 1 WLR 395; *BLCT (13096) v J Sainsbury plc* [2003] EWCA Civ 884. Cf *North Range Shipping Ltd v Seatrans Shipping Corporation* [2002] EWCA Civ 405, [2002] 1 WLR 2397. In *Department of Economic Policy and Development of the City of Moscow v Bankers Trust Co* [2003] EWHC 1377 (Comm), [2003] 1 WLR 2885, it was held that the presumption of open justice in Art. 6 was not directly applicable to arbitration claims.

[95] See G Morris, 'Fundamental Rights: Exclusion by Agreement' (2001) 30 *ILJ* 49.

[96] [2002] EWHC 2486 (Admin), [2003] 1 WLR 897.   [97] Ibid para [38] *per* Latham LJ.

[98] Ibid. For waiver of a right to the free assistance of an interpreter, see *R v Mihaly Unguari*, Court of Appeal, Criminal Division, 18 July 2003.

[99] [2002] UKHL 5, [2002] 2 WLR 524. See F Bennion, 'Consequences of an Overrule' [2001] *PL* 450.

[100] Ibid para [8] *per* Lord Bingham of Cornhill where the authorities are gathered.

While there is no direct evidence to show that the appellant knew what the consequences of his absconding would be, there is nothing to suggest a belief on his part that the trial would not go ahead in his absence or that, although absent, he would continue to be represented. His decision to abscond in flagrant breach of his bail conditions could reasonably be thought to show such complete indifference to what might happen in his absence as to support the finding of waiver.[101]

Lord Hutton and Lord Nolan agreed with this reasoning, with 'the critical question for the judge ... [being] whether the defendant ha[d] deliberately and consciously chosen to absent himself from the court' and this issue having been resolved against the defendant, his conduct 'could permissibly be described as a waiver of his rights of attendance and of legal representation at his trial, both at common law and under article 6' of the Convention.[102] Neither Lord Rodger of Earlsferry nor Lord Hoffmann was 'comfortable' with the application of waiver to these facts, however, principally because the concept required 'consciousness of the rights which have been waived' and there was nothing to show that the defendant *actually* knew of how events would unfold in his absence.[103] The right question was not whether the defendant 'waived the right to a fair trial but whether in all the circumstances [he] got one,' and because the process viewed overall had been fair the appeal could be dismissed, there having been no breach of Article 6 and therefore no need to fall back on the waiver escape route.[104] The reasoning of the majority is to be preferred here, the smaller lie being better than the larger one. It is more desirable to be honest about the fact that the trial was unfair, even though this involved being a little disingenuous about the defendant's 'decision' to 'give up' his right to a fair trial, than it is to assert—in the face of the facts and of legal principle—that everything had been entirely fair despite the absence of the defendant and his legal team. Given the common law's addiction to sideways argument by analogy, the latter ratio might soon have found itself turning up where it was not wanted, diluting the rights of defendants in far more problematic situations.

More difficult problems can arise where a breach of Article 6(1) is found some time after the event, either because the tribunal determining a case was not independent or impartial, or because a public hearing was not permitted, or for some other Article 6-related reason. In such circumstances it is sometimes hard to tell whether or not the right to a fair trial was waived by the party that allowed the case to proceed. Even in this area, the Strasbourg authorities are vigilant not to impute a false state of mind onto the applicant, being clear that to be effective in this kind of situation 'a waiver must be made in an unequivocal

---

[101] [2002] UKHL 5, [2002] 2 WLR 524, para [15].

[102] Ibid para [18] *per* Lord Nolan. See also the remarks of Lord Hutton at para [35].

[103] Ibid para [19] *per* Lord Hoffmann. The remarks of Lord Rodger to similar effect are at para [53].

[104] Ibid para [20] *per* Lord Hoffmann. Lord Rodger's conclusion is the same after an extensive review of the whole criminal process in the case before him: see paras [55]–[77]. For Strasbourg's ruling in the case, see *Jones v United Kingdom* (2003) 37 EHRR CD 269 (application inadmissible).

manner and must not run counter to any important public interest'.[105] Where the temptation to use waiver as a legal fiction is greatest of all is in those cases where a claimant asserts, like the defendant in the *Jones* case, that a procedure to which he or she has been subjected has in fact infringed his or her human rights, but where support for such an argument comes not from the party's own actions (as in the *Jones* case) but from some parallel and separate development in the law which has revealed *ex post facto* a human rights violation from which the party can now show he or she has suffered. This retrospective 'discovery' of a human rights violation is not opportunistic in quite the same way as was *Jones's* but it is bold nevertheless: why did the claimant not raise the point when he or she had the chance? Why wait for another litigant to do the work and then seek to avail of the fruits of that person's labour to escape a consequence to which the law has in your case already committed itself?

It is clear that successful reopening of cases in light of subsequent unrelated human rights litigation is capable of producing great administrative inconvenience. A commonplace difficulty in countries with written constitutions,[106] the point has already arisen in the context of the Human Rights Act, in the devolution/human rights decision of *Millar v Dickson*.[107] Each of the four appellants was the subject of criminal proceedings before a temporary sheriff in Scotland between May and November 1999. All were convicted. Then on 11 November 1999, in an entirely separate case, the High Court of Justiciary handed down its well-known ruling in *Starrs v Ruxton*[108] to the effect that temporary sheriffs were not an 'independent and impartial tribunal' within the meaning of Article 6(1) of the Convention. Relying on this case, the appellants promptly argued that their own trials were also fundamentally flawed by the same infringement of their rights and for that reason should be declared null and void. Needless to say they were not the only persons who had been convicted by temporary sheriffs in Scotland so there was a great deal riding on the case. The High Court rejected the submission, finding that the four persons before them had effectively waived their rights when they had not objected to being tried by a temporary sheriff.[109] On appeal to the Privy Council, this approach was unequivocally rejected. As Lord Bingham put it, 'it cannot meaningfully be said that a party has voluntarily elected not to claim a right or raise an objection if he is unaware that it is open to him to make the claim or raise the objection'.[110] His Lordship could not:

accept a declaratory theory of law, which depends upon a fiction, as apposite in the very practical field of waiver. That there is no waiver where a party relies on what is reasonably understood to be the law at the relevant time is not because such conduct is reasonable

---

[105] *Håkansson and Sturesson v Sweden* (1990) 13 EHRR 1, para [66].
[106] See for eg *Murphy v Attorney General* [1982] IR 241.
[107] [2001] UKPCD, [2002] 1 WLR 1615.
[108] 2000, JC 208.
[109] *Millar v Dickson* 2000, JC 648.
[110] *Millar v Dickson*, n 107 above, para [31].

(although it plainly is) but because the party lacks the knowledge necessary to make an informed choice.[111]

It was in Lord Bingham's opinion 'impossible to accept that the qualification of temporary sheriffs was generally known to be open to serious question' and he doubted 'very much if the outcome of *Starrs* [had been] widely foreseen'.[112] The Privy Council was determined that no 'derogation' from the principle of a fair trial in Article 6(1) was to be allowed 'even if the consequences of holding to it involve[d] the invalidation of convictions which from every other angle were safe and unimpeachable'.[113] This is a very robust restatement of the importance of honesty in the law, and since honesty produces clarity it is certainly to be applauded from the point of view of analytical coherence. The practical consequences of the decision were passed back to the High Court to unravel, so the Privy Council did not have to wrestle with the difficulties caused by its admirable intellectual purity. The impact of the general approach taken by the Privy Council here can be seen in the response of the authorities to the Strasbourg decision in Summer 2002 that punishments by prison governors which have involved extra detention have infringed the right to a fair trial of those subject to them: all those prisoners whose terms in prison had been lengthened in this way have been quickly released where the only reason for their having remained in jail was as a result of having to serve these extra 'terms'.[114]

E. Precedent in the European Court of Human Rights: truth or anarchy?

It is probably right that British judges should be as cautious as their European colleagues about the overuse of fictions, such as the implied waiver of rights, in the law. In a very profound sense, however, it would be true to say that the whole system of common law adjudication is itself constructed on the basis of a deception, namely that there is an unchanging body of law existing in some notional legal firmament which it is the job of judges to discover and apply in particular cases. It is only our over-familiarity with the common law that blinds us to the breathtaking claim that it makes for durability, intractability, and centuries-old consistency. The approach to adjudication in this country has for

---

[111] *Millar v Dickson*, n 107 above, [35].

[112] Ibid para [36]. Note too para [37]: 'The inescapable fact is that, until *Starrs*, no challenge was successfully made to the qualification of temporary sheriffs, despite their employment in greatly increased numbers over the years.'

[113] Ibid para [85] *per* Lord Clyde.

[114] *Ezeh and Connors v United Kingdom* (2002) 35 EHRR 691; [Grand Chamber] (2003) 15 BHRC 145. Another area where a response has been required by the authorities has been in relation to life tariff sentencing decisions by ministers: see *Stafford v United Kingdom* (2002) 35 EHRR 1121, on the reaction to which see (2002) 152 NLJ 901 and *R (Murray) v Parole Board* [2003] EWHC 360 (Admin). See further *R (Anderson) v Secretary of State for the Home Department* [2002] UKHL 46, [2003] 1 AC 837.

generations emphasized the importance of authority and the need to obey dictates from the past. This habit of submissiveness to precedent has spread from the true common law to the interpretation of statutes as well, with judges schooled in the common law tradition being imbued from the point of their elevation to the bench with a strong commitment to precedent in all areas of the law that come before them for analysis. True there has been some amelioration of the extreme rigour of the orthodox position in recent decades. In 1966, the House of Lords freed itself from having to follow ancient cases where they were as redundant to modern times as they were authoritative within the court hierarchy.[115] The courts have been more flexible than in the past,[116] and the more relaxed approach of the European Court of Justice has had some impact.[117] The Human Rights Act does its bit further to destabilize the ancient regime by its determination, articulated in s 3, that novel, human rights-consistent, interpretations of statutes are to be preferred even to those readings that have been 'right' for generations where such long-assumed rectitude cannot survive Convention scrutiny.[118] The section applies even where consistent and established authority points in the opposite (Convention-incompatible) direction. But as we have seen the Act goes further than this in subverting the assumptions of judicial reasoning in this country, by inviting into the jurisdiction (via the backdoor of s 2 which requires the material to be taken into account where relevant) a body of Strasbourg cases which emanate from a court sharing neither the Anglo-Saxon addiction to consistency with the past nor the common law's pretence that the law as declared by the judges is never capable of change.

The gulf between Strasbourg and British approaches to precedent can best be illustrated by considering the way the European Court of Human Rights has reached a position on an important moral question, namely the extent of the rights to be accorded to transsexuals. I have already touched on this topic from the perspective of judicial competence at the end of chapter six but I now need more closely to locate the legal issues in their factual matrix. The key decision for present purposes is *Goodwin v United Kingdom*.[119] The applicant was a post-operative male to female transsexual. From early childhood she had had a tendency to dress as a woman, and she had undergone aversion therapy in 1963–64. In the mid-1960s, she was diagnosed as a transsexual. Though she married a woman and they had four children, her conviction was that her 'brain sex' did not fit her body. From that time until 1984 she dressed as a man for work but as a woman in her free time. In January 1985, Ms Goodwin began treatment in earnest, attending appointments once every three months at a gender identity clinic, which visits included regular consultations with a psychiatrist as well as

---

[115] Practice Statement (Judicial Precedent) [1966] 1 WLR 1234.

[116] See eg *R v Shivpuri* [1987] AC 1 overruling *Anderton v Ryan* [1985] AC 560.

[117] On that court's methodology, see P Craig and G de Búrca, *EU Law. Text, Cases, and Materials* 3rd edn (Oxford: Oxford University Press, 2003), 96–102.

[118] For discussion of s 3 see generally chapter 3 above.

[119] (2002) 35 EHRR 447. See A Campbell and H Lardy, 'Transsexuals—the ECHR in Transition' (2003) 54 *NILQ* 209.

on occasion a psychologist. She was prescribed hormone therapy, began attending grooming classes and voice training. From this time on, she lived fully as a woman. In October 1986, she underwent surgery to shorten her vocal chords, and in 1990, she underwent gender re-assignment surgery at a national health service hospital. UK law however resolutely refused to accept her new status. In a case decided in 1971[120] it had been ruled that sex for marriage purposes was determined by the use of biological criteria and without regard to any surgical intervention. This decision was approved by the Court of Appeal in 1983[121] and given more general application, with the court in that case holding that a person born male had been correctly convicted under a statute penalizing men who live on the earnings of prostitution, notwithstanding the fact that the accused in the case had undergone gender reassignment therapy.

Fortified by these common law decisions, the authorities in charge of the registration of births refused as a matter of policy to accept that any error existed in the birth entry of a person who had undergone gender reassignment surgery, with the result that a transsexual continued to be recorded for social security, national insurance and employment purposes as being of the sex recorded at birth. The applicant suffered numerous indignities and difficulties as a result of the disconnection between her true and her legal gender. She lost her job allegedly for being a transsexual and claimed also to be suffering victimization at her new place of work, with the information on her legal gender having been too easily discoverable via her national insurance data. She had been informed that she would be ineligible for a state pension at the age of 60, the age of entitlement for women in the United Kingdom and that her pension contributions would have to be continued until the date at which she reached the age of 65, this being the age of entitlement for men. The applicant pointed to a number of instances where she had had to choose between revealing her birth certificate and foregoing certain advantages which were conditional upon her producing that certificate. In particular, she had not followed through a loan conditional upon life insurance, a re-mortgage offer and an entitlement to winter fuel allowance from the government. She had also had to continue paying the higher motor insurance premiums applicable to men.

At first glance the case seemed tailor-made for the application of the European Convention. The most obviously engaged right was the right to marry guaranteed by Article 12, with the applicant being explicitly disabled by law from marrying a person of what was now her opposite gender. Viewing the case from a wider angle, there would also seem to have been a series of unnecessary and disproportionate intrusions into a most private and intimate part of her life, namely her sexual identity, and this surely (both in principle and on the basis of dicta in other Strasbourg cases on sexuality)[122] also amounted to a breach of the

[120] *Corbett v Corbett* [1971] P 83.   [121] *R v Tan* [1983] QB 1053.
[122] Most recently in *Smith and Grady v United Kingdom* (1999) 29 EHRR 493; *Lustig-Prean and Beckett v United Kingdom* (1999) 29 EHRR 548.

right to respect for privacy guaranteed in Article 8 of the Convention. The European Court identified the privacy issue before it as being 'whether or not the respondent State ha[d] failed to comply with a positive obligation to ensure the right of the applicant, a post-operative male to female transsexual, to respect for her private life, in particular through the lack of legal recognition given to her gender re-assignment'.[123] In determining whether or not this positive obligation existed, the court considered that regard had to 'be had to the fair balance that ha[d] to be struck between the general interest of the community and the interests of the individual, the search for which balance [was] inherent in the whole of the Convention'.[124] There had been some movement in the UK on the issue, with anti-discrimination regulations specific to transsexuals having been promulgated in 1999, an interdepartmental working group having reported in April 2000, and a set of proposals on birth certification having been placed before Parliament early in 2002. But the law remained resolutely as it had always been, and indeed it had been recently restated in uncompromising terms by the English Court of Appeal where the majority judges had felt angry about the lack of parliamentary action but constrained nevertheless by the authority of the earlier case law—the mystical command structure of English law in other words—from taking any action themselves.[125]

Sympathetic though it was to the applicant's situation, the European Court had its own earlier case law to contend with. This had come down strongly against a number of applicants who had been in situations very similar to the one in which Ms Goodwin found herself.[126] Had the Strasbourg court taken a traditional, English-style approach to precedent, that would have been the end of the matter. But the influence of the past proved not so overwhelming:

The Court recalls that it has already examined complaints about the position of transsexuals in the United Kingdom. In those cases, it held that the refusal of the United Kingdom Government to alter the register of births or to issue birth certificates whose contents and nature differed from those of the original entries concerning the recorded gender of the individual could not be considered as an interference with the right to respect for private life. It also held that there was no positive obligation on the Government to alter their existing system for the registration of births by establishing a new system or type of documentation to provide proof of current civil status. Similarly, there was no duty on the Government to permit annotations to the existing register of births, or to keep any such annotation secret from third parties. It was found in those cases that the authorities had taken steps to minimise intrusive enquiries (for example, by allowing transsexuals to be issued with driving licences, passports and other types of documents in their new name and gender). Nor had it been shown that the failure to accord general legal recognition of

---

[123] *Goodwin v United Kingdom* n 119 above, para [71].

[124] Ibid para 72.

[125] *Bellinger v Bellinger* [2001] EWCA Civ 1140, [2002] Fam 150 but then later after the Strasbourg ruling in the *Goodwin* case [2003] UKHL 21, [2003] 2 AC 467. For a discussion of this case, see pp 140–141 above.

[126] See *Rees v United Kingdom* (1986) 9 EHRR 56; *Cossey v United Kingdom* (1990) 13 EHRR 622; *B v France* (1992) 16 EHRR 1; *Sheffield and Horsham v United Kingdom* (1998) 27 EHRR 163.

the change of gender had given rise in the applicants' own case histories to detriment of
sufficient seriousness to override the respondent State's margin of appreciation in this area.

While the Court is not formally bound to follow its previous judgments, it is in the
interests of legal certainty, foreseeability and equality before the law that it should not
depart, without good reason, from precedents laid down in previous cases. However, since
the Convention is first and foremost a system for the protection of human rights, the Court
must have regard to the changing conditions within the respondent State and within
Contracting States generally and respond, for example, to any evolving convergence as
to the standards to be achieved. It is of crucial importance that the Convention is
interpreted and applied in a manner which renders its rights practical and effective, not
theoretical and illusory. A failure by the Court to maintain a dynamic and evolutive
approach would indeed risk rendering it a bar to reform or improvement. In the present
context the Court has, on several occasions since 1986, signalled its consciousness of the
serious problems facing transsexuals and stressed the importance of keeping the need for
appropriate legal measures in this area under review.[127]

Having largely freed itself from the past, the court then felt able to go on 'to look
at the situation within and outside the Contracting State to assess "in the light of
present-day conditions" what [was] *now* the appropriate interpretation and
application of the Convention.'[128] After a close scrutiny of a large body of
comparative, medical and scientific data and international legal materials, the
court felt emboldened to detect an 'emerging consensus' within Europe and 'a
continuing international trend towards legal recognition' reflected in changes in
jurisdictions further afield.[129] A detailed assessment of the UK position confirmed the court's view, in which all the judges in the Grand Chamber joined,
that there were 'no significant factors of public interest to weigh against the
interest of this individual applicant in obtaining legal recognition of her gender
re-assignment,' and that therefore 'the fair balance that is inherent in the Convention now tilt[ed] decisively in favour of the applicant'.[130] It followed that
Article 8 had indeed been infringed, and the court went on for good measure to
find (also unanimously) that Article 12 had been violated as well.

This is a remarkable change of heart on the part of the court, with there being
much to applaud from the perspective of human dignity. Our interest in this
chapter lies in noticing how the Strasbourg court has managed to change its
perspective so radically and over such a short period of time. 'Legal certainty,
forseeability and equality before the law' need only a 'good reason' to be
subjugated to other interests, and the most obvious of these trumps is the
imperative of ensuring that enforcement of the Convention rights be rendered
'practical and effective, not theoretical and illusory' and that the court 'maintain
a dynamic and evolutive approach' without which it might itself become 'a bar
to reform or improvement'. This is a world away from the staid conservatism of

---

[127] *Goodwin v United Kingdom* n 119 above, paras [73]–[74] (citations omitted).
[128] Ibid para [75] (emphasis added).
[129] Ibid paras [81]–[84] with the extracts in the text being drawn from para [84].
[130] Ibid para [93].

the common law. But while it may certainly be true that the authority of the common law is based on a fundamentally deceitful claim about its own unchanging and immutable nature, is there not an argument for saying that, at least in the context of the operation of judge-made law in a democracy, this is not in some ways 'a noble lie'?[131] The common law method delivers a high degree of consistency, clarity, analytical coherence, discipline, and rigour to the law. These unyielding characteristics are to some degree then ameliorated by the subtleties of the ratio/obiter divide and the room that this leaves for a limited degree of growth. But under the common law system, radical change—when it is needed and how to bring it about—is largely a matter for the legislative rather than the judicial branch.

The effect of the *Goodwin* case on UK legal reasoning may not now be fully gauged in light of the undertaking by the government to legislate on the matter.[132] The issue cannot be long delayed, however. In contrast to the traditional approach of the British courts, the Strasbourg bench often resembles the select committee inquiry that it comes close to resembling in the *Goodwin* case, taking evidence from far and near, weighing up the various public interests in the case, eventually coming to a conclusion by a quasi-democratic show of the judges' hands. In the first case on the issue in 1986, the vote had been 12 to three against on Article 8 and a unanimous negative on Article 12.[133] In the next decision, the majorities against the applicant had shrunk to 10 to eight and 14 to four respectively.[134] The third British case, just four years before Goodwin, was 11 to nine against on Article 8 while the majority against the applicant on Article 12 had expanded to 18 to two.[135] Perhaps the decision would have gone the other way in the *Goodwin* case had the UK Parliament consciously voted down a proposal for change, rather than merely, through executive inertia, not had such a proposal put to it. Had there not been movement on the issue in other jurisdictions, we can be fairly sure that the Strasbourg court would not have been so confident as to put the issue to rest with its unanimous ruling in the *Goodwin* case. But what do such observations tell us about the nature of human rights? Is it not (supposedly) the job of the court to detect the breach of human rights in the abstract by a process of moral reasoning, and then to apply that insight to the facts before it, whatever the reaction of the domestic legislature or the position in the rest of Europe?

Certainly in abstract theory this might be what the court is required to do, but the inevitable contingency in the language of rights forces it to root around for other sources of inspiration as to what the law on human rights truly requires. Because these medical, psychological, or democratically-rooted sources are not

---

[131] See generally Plato, *The Republic* (any edition).
[132] Under proposals for a new civil partnership law. *A v Chief Constable of the West Yorkshire Police* [2002] EWCA Civ 1584, [2003] 1 All ER 255 contains an interesting though general discussion of the point. See the Lords decision in *Bellinger v Bellinger*, n 125 above.
[133] *Rees v United Kingdom*, n 126 above.
[134] *Cossey v United Kingdom*, n 126 above.
[135] *Sheffield and Horsham v United Kingdom*, n 126 above.

hierarchical in the way that the law is, they naturally and without embarrassment change over time. Relying upon them, the court's evaluation of what is a human right must therefore also change with them. Of course the outcomes of such a process can be pleasing when they lead to the rectification of error. But the result of this kind of judicial mimicry of the legislative branch is a much higher level of analytical incoherence in the law than a more disciplined approach to precedent would ever have allowed. And a further consequence is that a larger and brighter public spotlight is placed on the judicial branch than has in the past been thought normal in a representative democracy. Now, shorn of the myth of the unchangeability of the law, the judges must forsake their technician's overalls for a costume that is both more fitting to their new status as democratic society's moral guardians, and more agreeable to the public eye that will now be much more frequently upon them.

PART FOUR
CONCLUSION

9

Judging the Human Rights Act

A. Judicial self-consciousness

This book has been centrally concerned with the issue of where the Human Rights Act fits in the United Kingdom's legal and political culture, and the impact which the Act is having on the continuing evolution of that culture. The record reveals a paradoxical development in the thinking of proponents for and supporters of the Act. In the proselytizing era of the mid 1970s through to the mid 1990s, when enactment of a law like the Human Rights Act was but a distant liberal dream, those campaigning for such a measure naturally talked-up its potential and stressed its likely transformative effect. This strain of radical optimism persisted into the first couple of years of the new Labour Government during 1997–8, and indeed there is plenty of evidence of it in the parliamentary debates that accompanied the passage of the Human Rights Bill. Such language was of course inevitable; sponsors of any legislation rarely get far if they forbear from stressing the grandness and largeness of the scheme which they are seeking to persuade others to translate into law. With enactment of the Human Rights Act in November 1998, and in particular during the period prior to implementation in October 2000, however, a back-tracking in the rhetoric became apparent. The Act was now, it seemed, less sweeping than had been thought; it was to be introduced through rather than around the common law; practitioners and judges were to be on their guard against 'hopeless' cases and the taking of 'bad' human rights points; the courts were to be vigilant to ensure that they did not 'run riot'; there was no way that the Act was to be allowed to become a 'field day for crackpots . . . and a goldmine for lawyers' (in the words of one senior Scottish judge).[1] During the judicial training phase that, as we have seen, took place between enactment and implementation, there was a sense in which the judges were not only being trained in the Act but they were in turn learning how to tame it.

   In the years since implementation, the fault-line between these early radical claims and later efforts to apply a conservative gloss has been evident in the case law. There has been no bright linear line, however: the judges have not started off in a radical direction and then drifted towards conservatism, or vice versa. It is clear that since implementation, the majority of decisions have been conservative, rejecting human rights arguments outright or incorporating them with such

---

[1] The comments were by Lord McCluskey and appeared in a Sunday newspaper. They were drawn from a series of lectures he had given in 1986. For the consequences for Lord McCluskey of his journalistic intervention see *Hoekstra v Lord Advocate (No 2)* 2000, SCCR 367.

seamlessness into the pre-existing law that it has been hard to tell whether they have made any difference to the overall result. This book has been full of examples of such cases.[2] At the same time, popping up consistently since the Act came into force, there have been spectacularly radical decisions that have rewritten the law on sentencing,[3] on burden of proof,[4] on rape,[5] on free speech,[6] on our obligations towards asylum seekers,[7] and much else besides. These have not come just at a particular time in the Act's life or dealt only with one area in particular, but they have certainly at times amounted to interventions in public affairs that have been both brave and ambitious. So, has the Human Rights Act produced an activist or a passive response? Has the judicial performance been innovatory or cautious? Is the Act revolutionary, evolutionary or merely a restatement of the status quo in more contemporary language?

The argument of this book is that the interpretation of the Human Rights Act has been all of these things. Where one of the three principles discussed in chapters three to five has been engaged—respect for civil liberties, legality, and human dignity—what we have generally seen (with just a few exceptions of which I have been critical) has been an activist judiciary, willing to push back the barriers to creativity and achieve a decision that the judges have felt to be the right and just. In these cases there has been little talk of 'the margin of appreciation', the 'discretionary area of judgment', or deference; s 3 has been deployed if not quite with gusto then certainly without embarrassment about the abuse of power. In such cases, as Lord Justice Laws might put it, judicial tanks are on the right lawn,[8] or as I would say (echoing an analogy developed in chapter six), the judges are in the shallow end of the public policy pool, confident that they are not out of their depth.[9] These are the cases, many of them discussed in chapters three to five, that give the Human Rights Act a strong reputation for radicalism and judicial activism, and are the decisions whose outcomes have infuriated government ministers and state officials from time to time. It is worth noticing once more, however, that the principles that have energized the judges are hardly novel or foreign: the respect accorded to civil liberties echoes a central plank in Britain's unwritten constitution, and the principle of legality has long been a goal of both the common law and the nation's sovereign parliament, while the search to realize the dignity of the citizen has been perhaps the central characteristic of the democratic era. So the activism that I am suggesting we applaud here has deeper roots than might first appear, being conservative in motivation even if sometimes radical in effect.

---

[2] In particular in chapters six and seven.   [3] See above pp 76–77 and 158.
[4] See above pp 158–159.   [5] See above p 159.   [6] See above p 55–56.
[7] See above pp 98–99.   [8] See above p 144.
[9] See above pp 121–122. It follows that I do not entirely agree with the judgment of three well-known scholars that the Human Rights Act amounts so far to a 'perhaps disappointing story': D Bonner, H Fenwick and S Harris-Shurt, 'Judicial Approaches to the Human Rights Act' (2003) 59 *ICLQ* 549, 549. It may be true that 'in general the approach has been cautious and tentative rather than radical' (585) but this is often justified..

There is another, more passive side to judicial engagement with the Human Rights Act, and it is with this dimension to the record that we have been mainly concerned in the second half of this book. In chapters six and seven we explored the twin ideas of judicial restraint and judicial deference; what each of these terms connotes is a judicial branch that is mindful of its responsibilities, aware of where it fits in the scheme of government, whilst at the same time being always sensitive to the demands of its triangular partnership with Parliament and the executive. In chapter eight we saw a judicial branch trying in the main to avoid the intellectual confusion that can arise from poor deployment of its reasoning power or an over-slavish adherence to its system of precedent. Having reviewed the case law discussed in these last three chapters, we can say with confidence that the power that Parliament has given to the judges via the Human Rights Act has generally been exercised in an institutionally self-conscious way. Such awareness of place is conservative in the best sense, and it is a more positive and enabling quality that the phrases 'judicial restraint' and 'judicial deference' seem to suggest.[10] The notion of 'judicial self-consciousness' captures the essence of what those terms involve, a self-aware judiciary going about business that is confident is its own, without the whiff of quiescence that the phrases 'judicial restraint' and 'judicial deference' carry when used in isolation and out of constitutional context.

This book is an argument for judicial self-consciousness, for an affirmation of the necessity for independent adjudication and interpretation within a representative democracy. In short it is a programme for judges to do what judges do best. From the perspective of litigation under the Human Rights Act, this involves the robust, creative and, if necessary, fearless application of principle to particular sets of facts, with such litigation always being carefully set in constitutional context. In the absence of a written constitution, 'constitutional context' here essentially means a Human Rights Act the breadth and range of which is properly understood in light of an awareness of the proper judicial function, which in turn requires an appreciation of the idea of separation of powers. If third party interventions[11] and amicus briefs are necessary in any given case to produce an outcome that is both principled and constitutionally sensitive, then the judges should not be slow to avail of them, but the test of necessity should be a real one.[12] The courts should be wary of transforming themselves into mini versions of the executive or legislative branches: why give up what you are very

---

[10] This point about the inappositeness of the language of judicial restraint was made to powerful effect by Justice Albie Sachs at a public lecture at the Centre for the Study of Human Rights, London School of Economics, 27 February 2003.

[11] *Matthews v Ministry of Defence; the PTSD group action intervening* [2002] EWCA Civ 533; *Re Northern Ireland Human Rights Commission* [2002] UKHL 25, on which see L Blom-Cooper at [2002] *PL* 602. See a thoughtful essay on the topic by S Hannett, 'Third Party Interventions: In the Public Interest?' [2003] *PL* 128. A comparative perspective is offered by A Loux, 'Writing Wrongs: Third-party Intervention Post-Incorporation' in A Boyle, C Himsworth, A Loux and H MacQueen (eds), *Human Rights and Scots Law* (Oxford: Hart Publishing, 2002), ch 16.

[12] For a highly critical perspective see C Harlow, 'Public Law and Popular Justice' (2002) 65 *MLR* 1.

good at to embrace a new role as the pale imitator of others?[13] We saw at the end of the last chapter how the Strasbourg court has sometimes been unable to prevent itself from looking more like a quasi-legislative chamber than a full-blooded court and how this has not assisted in the preservation of its overall legitimacy as a judicial body. Once again the principles outlined in this book are of assistance, guiding judges in their assessment of when they need to seek outside help and when it is best to knuckle down in a more traditional (it might even be thought unimaginative) fashion.

B. Reform of the judiciary?

The tricky issue of judicial accountability is also one that can be helpfully addressed through the interpretive model of the Human Rights Act for which I have argued. There is no doubt that—as was to be expected—the Human Rights Act has unleashed a huge interest by the public in the institution of the judiciary, and given a large impetus to the arguments of those who have long campaigned for reform of the way senior judges are selected.[14] A number of leading judges have also become involved in debates about their future. [15] The government's dramatic proposals in summer 2003, involving a change in the way the judges are appointed and the establishment of a new Supreme Court, were surprising for the breadth of what was being proposed.[16] It would seem unarguable that—Human Rights Act or no Human Rights Act—efforts to improve the transparency of the process of appointment to the bench (already underway) need to continue, and to become if anything even more radical in their ambition. Should reform go further than is being currently proposed?

A supreme court of the sort proposed is likely to amount to nothing more than a repackaged appellate committee separated from the upper house of Parliament. As such it would fail to grapple with the increasing need for specialization thrown up by the passing of the Human Rights Act and the constitutional case law that it has engendered, a specialization—or higher level judicial self-consciousness—for which this book has been arguing. Different panels would in all probability continue to hear a variety of cases drawn from all sectors of the law. Much would still depend on the accident of personnel. As an alternative to a supreme court, serious consideration should be given to a constitutional court, in

---

[13] For a highly critical perspective see C Harlow, 'Public Law and Popular Justice' (2002) 65 *MLR* 1.

[14] Bar Council, *Working Party on Judicial Appointments and Silk* (Chairman: Sir Iain Glidewell) (March 2003). See also B Hale, 'Equality and the Judiciary: Why Should We Want More Women Judges?' [2001] *PL* 489.

[15] Lord Steyn, 'The Case for a Supreme Court' (2002) 118 *LQR* 382; Lord Cooke, 'The Law Lords: an Endangered Heritage' (2003) 119 *LQR* 49. For a lively perspective on prevailing orthodoxies, see T Legg, 'Judges for the New Century' [2001] *PL* 62.

[16] Department of Constitutional Affairs, *Constitutional Reform: A Supreme Court for the United Kingdom* (July, 2003); ibid, *Constitutional Reform: a New Way of Appointing Judges* (July, 2003); and *Constitutional Reform: the Future of Queen's Counsel* (July, 2003). See A Le Sueur, 'New Labour's Next (Surprisingly Quick) Steps in Constitutional Reform' [2003] *PL* 368.

which only cases of constitutional importance would be heard.[17] Such a court should, as does the American Supreme Court, sit *en banc* rather than in panels. It should be able to deal not only with important human rights cases but also with devolution issues and other matters of an important constitutional character. This would enable consistent principles to be developed and also allow the court to decide, in a more considered way than at present, what cases to hear.

Whether a supreme court or constitutional court model is adopted, the appointment of members of such a body should involve input from a democratically accountable body—Parliament. One of the most potent sources of current tension between the courts and the executive lies in the fact that the judges are not democratically accountable, yet as this book has made clear they undoubtedly enjoy a position of considerable—and growing—power over the government of the day. At the same time it is clear that the judicial function is different from the other branches of government and its senior officials should not be not required—even in the democratic age—to submit themselves to the uncertainties of electoral politics. While judges should most certainly not be elected, it would not be right for the higher level courts, and in particular the constitutional court suggested above, to be immune from all forms of democratic engagement. Britain's new constitutional litigation has enormous importance and needs properly to be explained to the general public. It is not enough to point to a judgment that will often be unreadably technical to all but the legal insider. A properly functioning constitutional or supreme court should not be fearful of explaining its judgments in the form of press releases and if necessary press conferences. Its leading judges should equally be uninhibited about reflecting with members of the legislature about the nature of its judicial role. With such a body in place, it would be possible to envisage a Human Rights Act that enjoyed an improved democratic legitimacy and stronger analytical coherence.

C. Civil liberties, the judiciary and the political process

The model of the Human Rights Act that has been presented in this book has been firmly and deeply rooted in a properly functioning system of representative democracy. But is the British system sufficiently democratic to warrant the trust I have placed in it? The version of civil liberties developed here has required not just a commitment to traditional freedoms such as expression and assembly but also the right to vote and the legislative supremacy of the body to which the voters send their representatives. The principle of legality as explained in chapter four is designed as a democracy-reinforcing element in our constitution rather than as the autonomous notion of the rule of law for which (as we have seen) many others argue. Even our principle of human dignity is conclusively located

---

[17] C Gearty and R Gordon, 'Why a Supreme Court does not go far enough with Reform' *The Times LAW SUPPLEMENT* 9 July 2002.

in the Human Rights Act rather than in any anterior principle of justice, equality or autonomy. We are hitching ourselves to the actually existing UK parliamentary system. There are many who would say that this trust is misplaced. These critics assert that British democracy is seriously malfunctioning. They refer to the executive's control of the House of Commons, the unrepresentative composition of the House of Lords, and the overweening power of the prime minister. They point to a risk that, by seeing the Human Rights Act primarily as a democracy-reinforcing document when the democracy that it is reinforcing is manifestly flawed, we are reducing the Act's energy. On this argument the Human Rights Act should instead be viewed as a moral Trojan horse, through which to smuggle into the British system commitments to justice, equality, fairness that otherwise remain submerged. Such a critique leads to a position close to that of Trevor Allan, which I discussed in chapter four, but which (unlike Allan's principled argument on the rule of law) is rooted in how bad Parliament is at doing its job rather than in how good the judges are at doing theirs.

But what is Parliament's job? The legislative branch in the United Kingdom, as in most representative democracies, is required to discharge two constitutional duties: the enactment of laws usually but not always at the invitation of the executive; and secondly the holding of the executive to account for the exercise of its power, both under legislation and generally, as under the prerogative for example.[18] In the British system, Parliament does the first of these jobs uncommonly well. The 'first-past-the-post' method of voting and the deeply entrenched party system at Westminster combine to ensure that the executive can usually get its way as far as the enactment of laws is concerned. Unlike systems with more defined separation of powers, there is a clear route by which election manifesto pledges can be quickly and effectively translated, via whipped votes, into law. It is in relation to the second task, the holding of the government to account, that it is fair to say that the British system has been found wanting. There is certainly some truth in the deep-rooted and frequently repeated criticism that Parliament has over many decades become the poodle of the executive, not only translating its every wish into law but then allowing itself to be shorn of its capacity for critical appraisal of the actions in which that body then engages.[19] However things are not nearly so bad as is sometimes believed, particularly by lawyers and by advocates of strong human rights measures (that is, those who give judges far greater and wider oversight of the legislative branch than does the Human Rights Act).[20]

Whilst it is true that none of the political controls that constrain the executive provide legal limits to its power, it is nevertheless the case that parliamentary questions to ministers, select committee hearings and reports, and opposition day

---

[18] See generally K D Ewing and C A Gearty, *The Struggle for Civil Liberties* (Oxford: Oxford University Press, 2000).

[19] K D Ewing and C A Gearty, *Freedom under Thatcher* (Oxford: Oxford University Press, 1990), ch 1 and the references cited therein.

[20] See for a stimulating analysis by a lawyer, A Tomkins, 'In Defence of the Political Constitution' (2002) 22 *OJLS* 157.

motions in the Commons impose inhibitions on executive power that are none the less real for failing to amount to effective (legal) vetoes on action. The requirement for the enactment of government proposals into law also frequently necessitates compromise that should not be wholly ignored simply because it is primarily on matters of detail rather than grand purpose. Where lawyers see the easy translation of executive will into law, government ministers see a path towards the achievement of their policy goals which is strewn about with obstacles, unnecessary diversions, and occasional booby-traps. The truth as far as the UK constitution is concerned lies somewhere between these extremes. Even though it did deliberately preserve parliamentary supremacy, the Human Rights Act was not legislated into a constitutional system in which there existed no political safeguards against the abuse of executive power. This is evident from the terms of the Act itself, from the way in which the executive went about introducing it, and from the response of the legislature to its arrival; human rights protection under the Act was clearly not designed to be merely a matter of occasional judicial scrutiny, dependant only on the goodwill of the judges exercised in isolation from the other supposedly malfunctioning and/or malevolent branches of government.

Thus, the large-scale training that preceded the Act's implementation, and to which we have already earlier referred,[21] presaged a determination on the part of the executive to 'mainstream' the commitment to human rights across all its departments. With the same intention in mind, s 19 of the Act set out to require active consideration in a quite formal way of the human rights implications of legislation that the executive intended to ask Parliament to enact. This provision more than any other has led to the infiltration of human rights considerations deep into Whitehall. For its part, Parliament quickly established a joint committee on human rights, composed of members from both houses, with a mandate to take a broad oversight role over the whole UK domestic human rights agenda.[22] Other parliamentary committees, such as the Commons' committee on home affairs have interested themselves in the subject from time to time. A human rights commission is also, at the time of writing, a very real possibility. This is not a system which wholly ignores human rights other than when they can be placed before a court in the course of litigation. Nor is it one in which the executive branch has an untrammelled capacity to ride roughshod over the values that underpin the Human Rights Act.[23]

In an earlier chapter of this book, we outlined the kind of important legislation conducive to the public good that Parliament occasionally—perhaps even frequently—manages to enact, sometimes exactly as the executive desires, more

---

[21] See further: J Croft, 'Whitehall and the Human Rights Act 1998' [2001] *EHRLR* 392.

[22] See its terms of reference, set out at H C Debs, 24 July 2000, col 382 (written answer).

[23] See generally the thoughtful piece by M Hunt, published before implementation of the Act, 'The Human Rights Act and Legal Culture: the Judiciary and the Legal Profession' (1999) 26 *JLS* 86, in which the challenge the Act poses for the whole legal culture is assessed in a most stimulating way.

often after intelligent and informed debate.[24] From time to time, this is true also for matters of great civil libertarian importance. Thus, controls on campaign funding which are likely to improve greatly the health of the political process have recently been achieved via parliamentary action,[25] as has reform of the House of Lords[26] and a revitalization of standards in public life.[27] This is true even when external events put the system under enormous strain. That Parliament is more robust than is commonly believed may be seen by considering its response to the catastrophic attacks on New York's World Trade Centre and the Pentagon in Washington on 11 September 2001.[28] The government's legislative proposals in the aftermath of 11 September were markedly improved from the human rights/civil libertarian perspective by the changes that were conceded as a result of a strong parliamentary engagement with the relevant issues of principles. Much of the Act in its final form may still be thought deplorable from a civil libertarian perspective, particularly those provisions which permit the detention of non-residents without charge;[29] which greatly expand state power in relation to terrorism[30] and access to communications data;[31] and which allow for the implementation of the third pillar of the European Union without effective democratic scrutiny. It is also right to decry the fact that the legislation, which is long and complex, was pushed through Parliament at alarming speed. Yet despite all this, important amendments on matters of substance were achieved. Proposals to introduce retrospective criminal legislation on bomb hoaxes were dropped even before the Bill was published after the idea had provoked a strong and very critical response. An expansion of the law to include incitement to religious hatred was omitted after a negative report on the proposal from the Home Affairs Committee of the House of Commons.[32] That body's critical appraisal of the government's plans also led to other beneficial changes such as the 'sunset' provision limiting the life of the internment power to

---

[24] See above ch 5.

[25] The Political Parties, Elections and Referendums Act 2000, on which see K D Ewing, 'Transparency, Accountability and Equality: The Political Parties, Elections and Referendums Act 2000' [2001] *PL* 542 and J Rowbottom, 'Political Donations and the Democratic Process: Rationales for Reform' [2002] *PL* 758.

[26] See G Phillipson, 'The Powers of a Reformed Second Chamber' [2003] *PL* 32.

[27] See Committee on Standards in Public Life, *Standards of Conduct in the House of Commons*, Eighth Report (Cm 5663, 2002). Some attempts at reform have perhaps not been so successful: see G Drewry, 'Whatever Happened to the Citizen's Charter?' [2002] *PL* 9.

[28] The points that follow are developed at greater length in C A Gearty, 'Civil Liberties and Human Rights' in P Leyland and N Bamforth (eds) *Public Law in a Multi-Layered Constitution* (Oxford: Hart Publishing, 2003) ch14.

[29] Anti-terrorism, Crime and Security Act 2001, part 4. There has been a vast range of critical commentary: see A Tomkins [2002] *PL* 205; J Black-Branch, 'Powers of Detention of Suspected International Terrorists under the United Kingdom Anti-Terrorism, Crime and Security Act 2001: Dismantling the Cornerstone of a Civil Society' (2002) 27 *European Law Review Human Rights Survey* 19; P A Thomas, 'September 11th and Good Governance' (2002) 53 *NILQ* 366; H Fenwick, 'The Anti-Terrorism, Crime and Security Act 2001: A Proportionate Response to 11th September?' (2002) 65 *MLR* 724. See generally C. A. Gearty, 'Reflections on Civil Liberties in an Age of Counter-Terrorism' (2003) 41 *Osgoode Hall Law Journal* 185.

[30] See in particular ss 117–120.   [31] Ibid, part 11.

[32] House of Commons Home Affairs Committee, First Report, The Anti-Terrorism, Crime and Security Bill 2001 (HC 351 of 2001–2002).

five years,[33] with its renewal on an annual basis also being required to be based on an annual review by an independent person.[34]

Following other critical reports from another parliamentary body, the Joint Committee on Human Rights, the government found itself having strongly to defend its assertion that there was 'a public emergency threatening the life of the nation' sufficiently grave to warrant the derogation from Article 5 of the European Convention that the Home Secretary had judged was necessary in order to be able lawfully to introduce its new detention powers.[35] As a result of legislative pressure, the Act in its final form provides for a committee of privy counsellors to conduct a review of the whole measure[36] and this body was established in April 2002.[37] Of course none of this is perfect, and a parliamentary body operating at the level of civil libertarian perfection would have done much more.[38] But in the context of the time, one of unparalleled anxiety and concern about the future, it was not as bad a performance as is widely believed, and certainly not one which justifies any claim that Parliament is simply and always the lapdog of the executive branch.

There is a somewhat depressing contrast here with the narrow rulings of the Special Immigration Appeals Commission and the Court of Appeal, upholding the detention without trial of British residents on the basis both that there is a public emergency threatening the life of the nation as asserted by the government, and that no unlawful discrimination is involved in exposing only foreign nationals to indefinite incarceration under the Act.[39] Not dissimilar in effect is *Secretary of State for the Home Department v Rehman*,[40] in which the House of Lords took a very deferential approach to the question of when it is appropriate to deport a person on the ground that it was for the public good in the interests of national security. The tone of these decisions recalls cases of a similarly restrictive nature legitimizing the exercise of state power in a way inimical to civil liberties during both world wars,[41] the Cold War,[42] and arising out of the conflict in

[33] See s 29 of the 2001 Act.

[34] Ibid s 28. The task has been assigned to Lord Carlile of Berriew who is also responsible for review of certain of the powers in the Terrorism Act 2000. Lord Carlile's first report was published on 12 February 2003 and is available on the Home Office web site.

[35] The Human Rights Act 1998 (Designated Derogation) Order 2001 (SI 3644). The two Joint Committee on Human Rights reports are at HL Paper 37, HC 372 and HL Paper 51, HC 420 respectively.

[36] Anti-Terrorism, Crime and Security Act 2001, s 122.

[37] Its members are Lord Newton of Braintree (chair), Chris Smith MP, Joyce Quinn MP, Sir Brian Mawhinney MP, Alan Beith MP, Terry Davis MP, Baroness Hayman, Lord Holme of Cheltenham, and the retired law lord Lord Browne-Wilkinson. Its report, published in December 2003, was highly critical of the provisions in Part 4 of the Act: Privy Counsellor Review Committee, *Anti-Terrorism, Crime and Security Act Review: Report*, HC Paper 100 (2003)

[38] But see further D Feldman, 'Parliamentary Scrutiny of Legislation and Human Rights' [2002] PL 323.

[39] *A and others v Secretary of State for the Home Department* Special Immigration Appeals Commission, 30 July 2002, [2002] EWCA Civ 1502, [2003] 2 WLR 564; and see further *Ajouaou, A, B, C, D v Secretary of State for the Home Department*, Special Immigration Appeals Commission, 29 October 2003.

[40] [2001] UKHL 47, [2002] 1 AC 153.

[41] *R (Zadig) v Halliday* [1917] AC 260; *Liversidge v Anderson* [1942] AC 204.

[42] *Chandler v DPP* [1964] AC 763.

Northern Ireland.[43] Just as we should not make too much of the weakness of the legislative branch as a control on executive power, so too should we be careful before we claim too much for the courts as the guardians of human rights. I have been aware of this not entirely seemly record as I have developed my theory of proper judicial activism in the course of this book, and I do not assume that courts are immune from external pressure, even in cases falling full-square within what I have argued here is their constitutional remit under the Human Rights Act.[44] Indeed, it is perfectly possible to argue that in the course of this book I have reposed altogether too much confidence not in the legislative but rather in the judicial branch. The record since October 2000 complements well the theory of adjudication developed here but—as the cases of *A* and *Rehman* demonstrate—a different narrative is possible. What the principles for which I have argued here have called for has been for the courts to be activist in their reinforcing of our democratic system; what these principles have not demanded has been that the judges be Herculean in their daily assessment of what is in our interests in the name of justice, equality and the like—these are matters that unequivocally belong to a democratic forum less dysfunctional than is often believed.[45]

D. Conclusion

This book is enthusiastic about the way in which the British constitutional order has embraced and engaged with the language of human rights. Displaying an intuitive talent for give and take that reflects centuries of slow growth and cautious radicalism, the UK constitution has now 'taken on' human rights, just as earlier it 'took on' democracy and social justice. To take something on is both to welcome and at the same time to confront it. It is this doubled-edged quality that makes the interaction between the pre-existing constitutional order and the Human Rights Act so fascinating. Neither side is wholly victorious, just as in previous generations of innovation neither the new nor the old could claim total success. The Human Rights Act both influences and is influenced by the ideology that precedes it, just as that ideology was in turn influenced by what went before. Ever the master of compromise, anxious to avoid extremism, and always on the look out for ways to make pragmatic progress in line with the spirit of the age, the UK constitution moves gracefully on. Its reconciliation of the demands of self-rule with the need to respect the human rights of those within its remit is just the latest example of its flexible genius. The judges' task is to bring this deep talent home to litigants—and therefore the wider public—every day of the week.

---

[43] *McEldowney v Forde* [1971] AC 632; *R (Brind) v Secretary of State for the Home Department* [1991] 1 AC 696.

[44] For the historical record, which does not excite confidence in the capacity of the judicial branch to perform the tasks for which this book has argued, see above p 40.

[45] 'I do not relish the role of Platonic guardian and I am pleased to live in a society that does not thrust it upon me': Lord Hoffmann, 'Human Rights and the House of Lords' (1999) 62 *MLR* 159, 161.

Select Bibliography

ADJEI, C. 1995. 'Human Rights Theory and the Bill of Rights Debate' (58) *Modern Law Review* 17.

ALLAN, T. R. S. 1998. 'Fairness, Equality, Rationality: Constitutional Theory and Judicial Review' in Forsyth, C. and Hare, I. (eds.), *The Golden Metwand and the Crooked Cord* (Oxford: Oxford University Press).

ALLAN, T. R. S. 2001. *Constitutional Justice. A Liberal Theory of the Rule of Law* (Oxford: Oxford University Press).

ALLAN, T. R. S. 1999. 'The Rule of Law as the Rule of Reason: Consent and Constitutionalism' (115) *Law Quarterly Review* 221.

ALLAN, T. R. S. 2003. 'Doctrine and Theory in Administrative Law: An Elusive Quest for the Limits of Jurisdiction' *Public Law* 429.

ALSTON, P. (ed.) 1999. *The EU and Human Rights* (Oxford: Oxford University Press).

ANDERSON, G. 1997. 'Review Article: Rights and the Art of Boundary Maintenance' (60) *Modern Law Review* 120.

ANDERSON, G. W. (ed.) 1999. *Rights and Democracy. Essays in UK-Canadian Constitutionalism* (London: Blackstone Press).

ARAI-TAKAHASHI, Y. 2002. *The Margin of Appreciation Doctrine and the Principle of Proportionality in the Jurisprudence of the ECHR* (Antwerp: Intersentia).

ARTHURS, H. W. 1979. 'Rethinking Administrative Law: A Slightly Dicey Business' (17) *Osgoode Hall Law Journal* 1.

ASHWORTH, A. 2002. *Human Rights, Serious Crime and Criminal Procedure* (London: Sweet and Maxwell).

BAMFORTH, N. 2001. 'The True Horizontal effect of the Human Rights Act 1998' (117) *Law Quarterly Review* 34.

BAR COUNCIL. 2003. *Working Party on Judicial Appointments and Silk* (Chairman: Sir Iain Glidewell).

BENNION, F. A. R. 1997. *Statutory Interpretation. A Code*, 3rd edn. (London: Butterworths).

BENNION, F. 2001. 'Consequences of an Overrule' *Public Law* 450.

BERNSTEIN, E. 1993. *The Preconditions of Socialism* (H. Tudor (ed.) (Cambridge: Cambridge University Press).

BEYLEVELD, D. and BROWNSWORD, R. 1998. 'Human Dignity, Human Rights, and Human Genetics' (61) *Modern Law Review* 661.

BEYLEVELD, D. and PATTISON, S. D. 2002. 'Horizontal Applicability and Direct Effect' (118) *Law Quarterly Review* 623.

BEYLEVELD, D., KIRKHAM, R. and TOWNEND, D. 2002. 'Which Presumption? A Critique of the House of Lords' Reasoning on Retrospectivity and the Human Rights Act' (22) *Legal Studies* 185.

BILLINGS, P. and PONTIN, B. 2001. 'Prerogative Powers and the Human Rights Act; Elevating the Status of Orders in Council' *Public Law* 21.

BINGHAM, T. 2000. *The Business of Judging. Selected Essays and Speeches* (Oxford: Oxford University Press).

BLACK-BRANCH, J. 2002. 'Powers of Detention of Suspected International Terrorists under the United Kingdom Anti-Terrorism, Crime and Security Act 2001: Dismantling the Cornerstone of a Civil Society' (27) *European Law Review Human Rights Survey* 19.

BLOM-COOPER, L. 2002. 'Third Party Intervention and Judicial Dissent' *Public Law* 602.

BOBBIO, N. 1996. *The Age of Rights* (Cambridge: Polity Press).

BOYLE, A., HIMSWORTH, C., LOUX, A., and MACQUEEN, H. (eds.). 2002. *Human Rights and Scots Law* (Oxford: Hart Publishing).

BUXTON, R. 2000. 'The Human Rights Act and Private Law' (116) *Law Quarterly Review* 48.

CAMPBELL, T. 1983. *The Left and Rights. A Conceptual Analysis of the Idea of Socialist Rights* (London: Routledge and Kegan Paul).

CAMPBELL, T. 1999. 'Human Rights: A Culture of Controversy' (26 *Journal of Legal Studies* 6.

CAMPBELL, T., EWING, K. D., and TOMKINS, A. (eds.) 2001. *Sceptical Essays on Human Rights* (Oxford: Oxford University Press).

CARLILE OF BERRIEW, LORD. 2003. 'Review of Part 4 Section 28 of the Anti-Terrorism, Crime and Security Act 2001' (Home Office).

CLAYTON, R. and TOMLINSON, H. *The Law of Human Rights* (Oxford: Oxford University Press, 2000).

COMMISSIONER FOR HUMAN RIGHTS. 2002. Opinion 1/2002 of the Commissioner for Human Rights, Mr Alvaro Gil-Robles on certain aspects of the United Kingdom 2001 derogation from article 5(1) of the European Convention on Human Rights (Comm DH (2002) 7. Strasbourg, 28 August 2002).

COMMITTEE ON STANDARDS IN PUBLIC LIFE. 2002. *Standards of Conduct in the House of Commons*, Eight Report (Cm 5663).

COOKE, LORD. 2003. 'The Law Lords: an Endangered Heritage' (119) *Law Quarterly Review* 49.

CRAIG, P. 1998. 'Ultra Vires and the Foundations of Judicial Review' (57) *Cambridge Law Journal* 63.

CRAIG, P. 2002. 'Contracting Out, the Human Rights Act and the Scope of Judicial Review' (118) *Law Quarterly Review* 551.

CRAIG, P. and DE BURCA, G. 2003. *EU Law. Text, Cases, and Materials*, 3rd edn. (Oxford: Oxford University Press).

CROFT, J. 2001. 'Whitehall and the Human Rights Act 1998' *European Human Rights Law Review* 392.

DE MERIEUX, M. 2001. 'Deriving Environmental Rights from the European Convention for the Protection of Human Rights and Fundamental Freedoms' (21) *Oxford Journal of Legal Studies* 521.

DEPARTMENT OF CONSTITUTIONAL AFFAIRS. 2003. *Constitutional Reform: A Supreme Court for the United Kingdom*.

DEPARTMENT OF CONSTITUTIONAL AFFAIRS. 2003. *Constitutional Reform: a New Way of Appointing Judges*.

DEPARTMENT OF CONSTITUTIONAL AFFAIRS. 2003. *Constitutional Reform: the Future of Queen's Counsel*.

DE SHUTTER, O. 2000. 'Waiver of Rights and State Paternalism under the European Convention on Human Rights' (51) *Northern Ireland Legal Quarterly* 481.

DICEY, A. V. 1885. *Lectures Introductory to a Study of the Law of the Constitution*, 2nd edn. (London: Macmillan).

DONNELLY, J. 1989. *Universal Human Rights in Theory and Practice* (Ithaca: Cornell University Press).

DOUZINAS, C. 2000. 'Human Rights and Postmodern Utopia' (11) *Law and Critique* 219.

DOUZINAS, C. 2000. *The End of Human Rights* (Oxford: Hart Publishing).

DREWRY, G. 2002. 'Whatever Happened to the Citizen's Charter?' *Public Law* 9.

DWORKIN, R. 1984. 'Rights as Trumps' in Waldron, J. (ed.), *Theories of Rights* (Oxford: Oxford University Press).

DWYER, C. 2001. 'Human Rights—Values for a Godless Age?' (146) *Law & Justice* 28.

EDWARDS, R. A. 2002. 'Judicial Deference under the Human Rights Act' (65) *Modern Law Review* 859.

EKINS, R. 2003. 'Judicial Supremacy and the Rule of Law' (119) *Law Quarterly Review* 127.

ELLIOTT, M. 2001. *The Constitutional Foundations of Judicial Review* (Oxford: Hart Publishing)

ELY JR, J. W. 1998. *The Guardian of Every Other Right. A Constitutional History of Property Rights*, 2nd edn. (New York: Oxford University Press).

EWING, K. D. 1999. 'The Human Rights Act and Parliamentary Democracy' (62) *Modern Law Review* 79.

EWING, K. D. 2000. 'The Politics of the British Constitution' *Public Law* 405.

EWING, K. D. 2001. 'Transparency, Accountability and Equality: The Political Parties, Elections and Referendums Act 2000' *Public Law* 542.

EWING, K. D. 2001. 'The Unbalanced Constitution' in Campbell, T., Ewing, K. D., and Tomkins, A. (eds.), *Sceptical Essays on Human Rights* (Oxford: Oxford University Press).

EWING, K. D. and GEARTY, C. A. 1990. *Freedom under Thatcher. Civil Liberties in Modern Britain* (Oxford: Clarendon Press).

EWING, K. D. and GEARTY, C. A. 1991. *Democracy or a Bill of Rights* (London: Society of Labour Lawyers).

EWING, K. D. and GEARTY, C. A. 2000. *The Struggle for Civil Liberties. Political Freedom and the Rule of Law in Britain, 1914–45* (Oxford: Oxford University Press).

EWING, K. D., GEARTY, C. A., and HEPPLE, B. A. (eds.). 1994. *Human Rights and Labour Law. Essays for Paul O'Higgins* (London: Mansell).

FEINBERG, J. 1980. *Rights, Justice, and the Bounds of Liberty. Essays in Social Philosophy* (New Jersey: Princeton University Press).

FELDMAN, D. 2002. *Civil liberties and Human Rights in England and Wales*, 2nd edn. (Oxford: Oxford University Press).

FELDMAN, D. 1999. 'Human Dignity as a Legal Value' *Public Law* 682.

FELDMAN, D. 2002. 'Parliamentary Scrutiny of Legislation and Human Rights' *Public Law* 323.

FENWICK, H. 2000. *Civil Rights: New Labour, Freedom and the Human Rights Act* (Harlow: Longman).

FENWICK, H. 2002. 'The Anti-Terrorism, Crime and Security Act 2001: A Proportionate Response to 11th September?' (65) *Modern Law Review* 724.

FILIBECK, G. 1994. *Human Rights in the Teaching of the Church: from John XXIII to John Paul II* (Vatican City: Libreria Editrice Vaticana).

FINNIS, J. *Natural Law and Natural Rights* (Oxford: Clarendon Press).

FORSYTH, C. F. (ed.) 2000. *Judicial Review and the Constitution* (Oxford: Hart Publishing).

FORSYTH, C. and HARE, I. (eds.). 1998. *The Golden Metwand and the Crooked Cord* (Oxford: Oxford University Press).

FOSTER, S. 2002. 'Prisoners' Rights, Freedom of Expression and the Human Rights Act' (7) *Journal of Civil Liberties* 53.

GARWOOD-GOWERS, A. 2002. 'Improving Protection Against Indirect Interference with the Use and Enjoyment of Home: Challenging the Legacy of Hunter v Canary Wharf using the European Convention on Human Rights and Human Rights Act 1998' (11) *Nottingham Law Journal* 1.

GEARTY, C. A. 1992. 'The Politics of Abortion' (19) *Journal of Legal Studies* 441.

GEARTY, C. A. (ed.). 1997. *European Civil Liberties and the European Convention on Human Rights. A Comparative Study* (The Hague: Martinus Nijhoff).

GEARTY, C. A. 1997. 'The United Kingdom' in Gearty, C. A. (ed.), *European Civil Liberties and the European Convention on Human Rights. A Comparative Study* (The Hague: Martinus Nijhoff).

GEARTY, C. A. 2000. 'Democracy and Human Rights in the European Court of Human Rights: A Critical Reappraisal' (51) *Northern Ireland Law Quarterly* 381.

GEARTY, C. A. 2001. 'Reflections on Human Rights and Civil Liberties in Light of the United Kingdom's Human Rights Act 1998' (35) *University of Richmond Law Review* 1.

GEARTY, C. A. 2001. 'Unravelling Osman' (64) *Modern Law Review* 159.

GEARTY, C. A. 2002. 'Reconciling Parliamentary Democracy and Human Rights' (118) *Law Quarterly Review* 248.

GEARTY, C. A. 2003. 'Reflections on Civil Liberties in an Age of Counter-Terrorism' (41) *Osgoode Hall Law Journal* 185.

GEARTY, C. A. 2003. 'Civil Liberties and Human Rights' in Leyland, P. and Bamforth, N. (eds.), *The Contemporary Constitution* (Oxford: Hart Publishing).

GEARTY, C. A. and GORDON, R. 2002. 'Why a Supreme Court Does Not Go Far Enough With Reform' (9 July) *The Times LAW SUPPLEMENT.*

GEARTY, C. A. and TOMKINS, A. (eds.) 1996. *Understanding Human Rights* (London: Mansell Publishing Ltd.).

GEDDIS, A. 2002. 'What Future for Political Advertising on the United Kingdom's Television Screens?' *Public Law* 615.

GEWIRTH, A. 1982. *Human Rights. Essays on Justification and Applications* (Chicago: University of Chicago Press).

GLENDON, M. A. 1991. *Rights Talk. The Impoverishment of Political Discourse* (New York: The Free Press).

GOLDSWORTHY, J. 1999. *The Sovereignty of Parliament* (Oxford: Clarendon Press).

GREEN, T. H. 1991. 'Liberal Legislation and Freedom of Contract' in Miller, D. (ed.), *Liberty* (Oxford: Oxford University Press).

GRETTON, G. L. 2002. 'The Protection of Property Rights' in Boyle, A., Himsworth, C., Loux, A., and Macqueen, H. (eds.), *Human Rights and Scots Law* (Oxford: Hart Publishing).

GRIFFITH, J. A. G. 1979. 'The Political Constitution' (42) *Modern Law Review* 1.

GRIFFITH, J. A. G. 1997. *The Politics of the Judiciary*, 5th edn. (London, Fontana Press).

HALE, B. 2001. 'Equality and the Judiciary: Why Should We Want More Women Judges?' *Public Law* 489.

HALPIN, A. 1997. *Rights and Law. Analysis and Theory* (Oxford: Hart Publishing).

HANNETT, S. 2003. 'Third Party Interventions: In the Public Interest?' *Public Law* 128

HARLOW, C. 2002. 'Public Law and Popular Justice' (65) *Modern Law Review* 1

HILSON, C. 2002. 'Judicial Review, Policies and the Fettering of Discretion' *Public Law* 111.

HOFFMANN, LORD. 1999. 'Human Rights and the House of Lords' (62) *Modern Law Review* 159.

HOHFIELD, W. N. 1923. *Fundamental Legal Conceptions as Applied in Judicial Reasoning* (Cook, W. W. (ed.)) (New Haven: Yale University Press).

HOLLAND, J. A. and WEBB, J. S. 1991. *Learning Legal Rules* (London: Blackstone Press Ltd).

HOUSE OF COMMONS SELECT COMMITTEE ON HOME AFFAIRS. 2001. 'The Anti-Terrorism, Crime and Security Bill 2001' First Report (HC 351).

HUNT, M. 1997. *Using Human Rights Law in English Courts* (Oxford: Hart Publishing).

HUNT, M. 1998. 'The "Horizontal Effect" of the Human Rights Act' *Public Law* 423.

HUNT, M. 1999. 'The Human Rights Act and Legal Culture: The Judiciary and the Legal Profession' (26) *Journal of Legal Studies* 86.

IRVINE OF LAIRG, LORD. 2003. 'The Impact of the Human Rights Act: Parliament, the Courts and the Executive' *Public Law* 308.

ISON, T. 1985. 'The Sovereignty of the Judiciary' (10) *Adelaide Law Review* 3.

JOINT COMMITTEE ON HUMAN RIGHTS. 2001. Making of Remedial Orders, 7th report (H.L. 58, H.C. 473 of Session 2001–2).

JOINT COMMITTEE ON HUMAN RIGHTS. 2001. 'Anti-Terrorism, Crime and Security Bill' (HL Paper 37, HC 372)

JOINT COMMITTEE ON HUMAN RIGHTS. 2001. 'Anti-Terrorism, Crime and Security Bill: Further Report (HL 51, HC 420).

JOWELL, J. 2000. 'Beyond the Rule of Law: Towards Constitutional Judicial Review' *Public Law* 671.

JOWELL, J. and COOPER, J. (eds.) 2001. *Understanding Human Rights Principles* (Oxford: Hart Publishing).

KLOTH, M. 2002. 'Immunities and the Right of Access to Court under the European Convention on Human Rights' (27) *European Law Review Human Rights Survey* 33.

KLUG, F. 2000. *Values for a Godless Age. The Story of the United Kingdom's New Bill of Rights* (London: Penguin Books Ltd.).

KLUG, F. 2003. 'Judicial Deference under the Human Rights Act' *European Human Rights Law Review* 125.

KOSKENNIEMI, M. 1999. 'The Effect of Rights on Political Culture' in Alston, P. (ed.), The EU and Human Rights (Oxford: Oxford University Press).

KRAMER, M.H., SIMMONDS, N.E., and STEINER, H. 1998. *A Debate over Rights. Philosophical Inquiries* (Oxford: Clarendon Press).

LAW COMMISSION. 2000. *Damages under the Human Rights Act 1998* (Cm 4853).

LARDY, H. 2002. 'Prison Disenfranchisement: Constitutional Rights and Wrongs' *Public Law* 524.

LASKI, H. 1930. *Liberty in the Modern State* (London: Faber and Faber).

LEGG, T. 2001. 'Judges for the New Century' *Public Law* 62.

LEIGH, I. 2002. 'Taking Rights Proportionately: Judicial Review, the Human Rights Act and Strasbourg' *Public Law* 265.

LEIGH I. 2002. 'Bias, Necessity and the Convention' *Public Law* 407.

LESTER OF HERNE HILL, LORD, 1998. 'The Art of the Possible—Interpreting Statutes under the Human Rights Act' *European Human Rights Law Review* 665.

LE SUEUR, A. 2003. 'New Labour's Next (Surprisingly Quick) Steps in Constitutional Reform' *Public Law* 368.

LEYLAND, P. 2003. 'The Human Rights Act and Local Government: Keeping the Courts at Bay' (54) *Northern Ireland Legal Quarterly* 136.

LEYLAND, P. and BAMFORTH, N. (eds.) 2003. *The Contemporary Constitution* (Oxford: Hart Publishing).

LIBERTY. 1991. *A People's Charter* (London: National Council for Civil Liberties).

LIVINGSTONE, S. 1994. 'The House of Lords and the Northern Ireland Conflict' (57) *Modern Law Review* 333.

LOUGHLIN, M. 1999. 'Rights Discourse and Public Law Thought in the United Kingdom' in Anderson, G. W. (ed.), *Rights and Democracy. Essays in UK-Canadian Constitutionalism* (London: Blackstone Press).

LOUGHLIN, M. 2001. 'Rights, Democracy, and Law' in Campbell, T., Ewing, K.D., and Tomkins, A. (eds.), *Sceptical Essays on Human Rights* (Oxford: Oxford University Press).

LOUX, A. 2002. 'Writing Wrongs: Third-party Intervention Post-Incorporation' in Boyle, A., Himsworth, C., Loux, A., and MacQueen, H. (eds.), *Human Rights and Scots Law* (Oxford: Hart Publishing).

LOVELAND, I. 2003. 'Does Homelessness Decision-making engage Article 6(1) of the European Convention on Human Rights?' *European Human Rights Law Review* 177.

MCDERMONT, M. 2003. 'The Elusive Nature of the "Public Function": *Poplar Housing and Regeneration Community Association Ltd v Donoghue*' (66) *Modern Law Review* 113.

MCDERMOTT, P. 2000. 'The Separation of Powers and the Doctrine of Non-Justiciability' (35) *Irish Jurist* 280.

MACINTYRE, A. 1985. *After Virtue: A Study in Moral Theory*, 2nd edn. (London: Duckworth).

MACKENZIE, R. 2003. 'Bringing Human Rights to the Prison Population' (48) *Journal of the Law Society of Scotland*, no. 1, p. 26.

MACPHERSON, C. B. 1962. *The Political Theory of Possessive Individualism* (Oxford: Oxford University Press).

MANDEL, M, 1994. *The Charter of Rights and the Legalisation of Politics in Canada*, 2nd edn. (Toronto: Thompson Educational Press).

MANDEL, M. 1998. 'A Brief History of the New Constitutionalism, or "How We Changed Everything So That Everything would Remain The Same"' (32) *Israel Law Review* 250.

MARSHALL, G. 2003. 'The Lynchpin of Parliamentary Intention: Lost, Stolen or Strained' *Public Law* 236.

MILLER, D. (ed.) 1991. *Liberty* (Oxford: Oxford University Press).

MOREHAM, N. 2001. '*Douglas and others v Hello! Ltd*—the Protection of Privacy in English Private Law' (64) *Modern Law Review* 767.

MORGAN, J. 2002. 'Questioning the "true effect" of the Human Rights Act' (22) *Legal Studies* 259.

MORRIS, G. 2001. 'Fundamental Rights: Exclusion by Agreement' (30) *Industrial Law Journal* 49.

MOWBRAY, A. 1999. 'The Role of the European Court of Human Rights in the Protection of Democracy' *Public Law* 703.

MUNRO, C. 2003. 'The Value of Commercial Speech' (62) *Cambridge Law Journal* 134.

NINO, C. S. 1991. *The Ethics of Human Rights* (Oxford: Clarendon Press).

OLIVER, D. 2000. 'The Frontiers of the State: Public Authorities and Public Functions under the Human Rights Act' *Public Law* 476.

PALMER, E. 2002. 'Should Public Health be a Private Concern? Developing a Public Service Paradigm in English Law' (22) *Oxford Journal of Legal Studies* 663.

PEDAIN, A. 2003. 'The Human Rights Dimension of the *Diane Pretty* case' (62) *Cambridge Law Journal* 181.

PERRY, M. J. 1998. *The Idea of Human Rights, Four Inquiries* (New York: Oxford University Press).

PHILLIPSON, G. 2003. 'The Powers of a Reformed Second Chamber' *Public Law* 32.

PHILLIPSON, G. 2003. '(Mis)-reading Section 3 of the Human Rights Act' (119) *LQR* 183.

PLANT, R. 2001. *Politics, Theology and History* (Cambridge: Cambridge University Press).

POOLE, T. 2002. 'Dogmatic Liberalism? T R S Allan and the Common Law Constitution' (65) *Modern Law Review* 463.

RAZ, J. 1984. 'Right-Based Moralities' in Waldron, J. (ed.), *Theories of Rights* (Oxford: Oxford University Press).

RAZ, J. 1994. *Ethics in the Public Domain. Essays in the Morality of Law and Politics* (Oxford: Clarendon Press).

RORTY, R. 1993. 'Human Rights, Rationality and Sentimentality' in Shute, S. and Hurley, S. (eds.), *On Human Rights* (New York: Basic Books).

ROSENBERG, J. 1994. *The Search for Justice* (London: Hodder and Stoughton).

ROWBOTTOM, J. 2002. 'Political Donations and the Democratic Process: Rationales for Reform' *Public Law* 758.

SANDEL, M. J. 1998. *Liberalism and the Limits of Justice*, 2nd edn. (Cambridge: Cambridge University Press).

SCOTT, A. 2003. '"A Monstrous and Unjustifiable Infringement?" Political Expression and the Broadcasting Ban on Advocacy Advertising' (66) *Modern Law Review* 224.

SEDLEY, S. 1999. *Freedom, Law and Justice* (London: Sweet and Maxwell).

SEDLEY, S. 2002. 'Learning Human Rights' in Butler, F. (ed.), *Human Rights Protection: Methods and Effectiveness* (London: Kluwer Law International).

SHUTE, S. and HURLEY, S. (eds.), 1993. *On Human Rights* (New York: Basic Books).

SIEGHART, P. 1986. *The Lawful Rights of Mankind* (Oxford: Oxford University Press).

SIMPSON, A. W. B. 2001. *Human Rights and the End of Empire. Britain and the Genesis of the European Convention* (Oxford: Oxford University Press).

SINGH, R. 1997. *The Future of Human Rights in the United Kingdom. Essays on Law and Practice* (Oxford: Hart Publishing).

SMYTH, M. 2000. *Business and the Human Rights Act 1998* (Bristol: Jordan Publishing).

SNIDERMAN, P. M., FLETCHER, J. F., RUSSELL, P. H., and TETLOCK, P. E. 1996. *The Clash of Rights. Liberty, Equality, and Legitimacy in Pluralist Democracy* (New Haven: Yale University Press).

SQUIRES, D. 2000. 'Judicial Review of the Prerogative after the Human Rights Act' (116) *Law Quarterly Review* 572.

STARMER, K. 1999. *European Human Rights Law. The Human Rights Act 1998 and the European Convention on Human Rights* (London: Legal Action Group).

STARMER, K. 2001. 'Positive Obligations Under the Convention' in Jowell, J. and Cooper, J. (eds.), *Understanding Human Rights Principles* (Oxford: Hart Publishing).

STEINER, H. 1998. 'Working Rights' in Kramer, M.H., Simmonds, N.E., and Steiner, H., *A Debate over Rights. Philosophical Inquiries* (Oxford: Clarendon Press).

STEYN, LORD. 2001. 'Perspectives of Corrective and Distributive Justice in Tort Law' John Maurice Kelly Memorial Lecture, 1 November 2001 published by the Law Faculty of UCD.

STEYN, LORD. 2002. 'The Case for a Supreme Court' (118) *Law Quarterly Review* 382.

STEYN, LORD. 2002. 'Democracy through Law', The 2002 Robin Cooke Lecture, 18 September 2002.

SYPNOWICH, C. 1990. *The Concept of Socialist Law* (Oxford: Clarendon Press).

TAGGART, M. 1998. 'Expropriation, Public Purpose and the Constitution' in Forsyth, C. and Hare, I. (eds), *The Golden Metawand and the Crooked Cord. Essays on Public Law in Honour of Sir William Wade QC* (Oxford: Oxford University Press).

TAYLOR, C. 1989. *Sources of the Self: The Making of the Modern Identity* (Cambridge, Mass: Harvard University Press).

THOMAS, P. A. 2002. 'September 11th and Good Governance' (53) *Northern Ireland Legal Quarterly* 366.

TOMKINS, A. 2002. 'Defining and Delimiting National Security' (118) *Law Quarterly Review* 200.

TOMKINS, A. 2002. 'In Defence of the Political Constitution' (22) *Oxford Journal of Legal Studies* 157.

TOMKINS, A. 2002 'Legislating Against Terror: The Anti-Terrorism, Crime and Security Act 2001 *Public Law* 205.

TUSHNET, M. 1996. 'Living with a Bill of Rights' in Gearty, C. and Tomkins, A. (eds.), *Understanding Human Rights* (London: Mansell Publishing Ltd.).

VOGT, G. S. and WADHAM, J. 2003. 'Deaths in Custody: Redress and Remedies' (London: The Civil Liberties Trust).

WADE, H. W. R. 2000. 'Horizons of Horizontality' (116) *Law Quarterly Review* 217.

WALDRON, J. (ed.) 1984. *Theories of Rights* (Oxford: Oxford University Press).

WALDRON, J. (ed.) 1987. *'Nonsense upon Stilts.' Bentham, Burke and Marx on the Rights of Man* (London: Methuen, 1987).

WALDRON, J. 1988. *The Right to Private Property* (Oxford: Clarendon Press).

WHITTY, N., MURPHY, T., and LIVINGSTONE, S. 2001. *Civil Liberties Law: The Human Rights Act Era* (London: Butterworths).

WILLIAMS, G. 1982. *Learning the Law*, 11th edn. (London: Stevens and Sons).

YOUNG, A. L. 2002. 'Remedial and Substantive Horizontality: the Common Law and *Douglas v Hello! Ltd*' *Public Law* 232.

Index

.

18690812R00147

Printed in Great Britain
by Amazon